D0497728

Body Movement
and
Interpersonal Communication

Body Movement
and
Interpersonal Communication

Peter Bull
University of York

JOHN WILEY & SONS
Chichester · New York · Brisbane · Toronto · Singapore

Library of Congress Cataloging in Publication Data:

Bull, Peter.
  Body movement and interpersonal communication.

  Bibliography: p.
  Includes index.
  1. Nonverbal communication (Psychology)   2. Movement,
Psychology of.   I. Title.
BF637.C45B84   1983   153.6   82–23767

ISBN 0 471 90069 9

British Library Cataloguing in Publication Data:

Bull, Peter
  Body movement and interpersonal communication.
  1. Nonverbal communication (Psychology)
  I. Title
  303.2'22   BF637.C45

ISBN 0 471 90069 9

Photosetting by Thomson Press (India) Limited, New Delhi
and printed by Page Brothers, Norwich

Contents

Acknowledgements ix

Preface xi

Chapter 1. **Concepts and methods in non-verbal communication research** 1

CONCEPTS OF NON-VERBAL COMMUNICATION 1

METHODOLOGY. 10

1. The context of measurement 11

(i) *The ethological approach* 11

(ii) *The structural approach* 11

(iii) *The sociological approach* 12

(iv) *The psychological approach* 12

2. Measurement of bodily cues 14

(i) *Facial expression* 16

(ii) *Gaze* 16

(iii) *Pupil size* 18

(iv) *Posture and gesture* 19

(v) *Interpersonal distance* 21

SUMMARY 23

Chapter 2. **Emotion** 24

THE INNATE HYPOTHESIS OF EMOTIONAL EXPRESSION 24

THE FUNCTIONS OF EMOTIONAL EXPRESSION 36

1. As adaptive responses 36

2. Regulation of emotion 37

3. The experience of emotion 38

THE GENERALITY OF THE INNATE HYPOTHESIS OF EMOTIONAL EXPRESSION 40

1. The number of innate facial expressions of emotion . . 41

2. Other bodily cues and the innate hypothesis of emotional
expression 43

(i) *Blushing* 43

(ii) *Pupil size* 43

(iii) *Gaze* 43

(iv) *Posture and gesture* 46

(v) *Interpersonal distance* 50
(vi) Other bodily cues and the innate hypothesis of emotional
expression: summary 51
3. The innate hypothesis and the decoding of emotional expression 51
OTHER SOURCES OF INFORMATION ABOUT EMOTION 53
1. Speech content 54
2. Vocal cues 54
3. Situational context 55
SUMMARY 56

Chapter 3. **Body movement and speech** 58
EMBLEMS 61
ILLUSTRATORS 63
REGULATORS 68
1. Greetings 68
2. Turn-taking 69
3. Partings 75
SUMMARY 76

Chapter 4. **Individual differences** 77
STUDIES OF ENCODING 77
1. Culture 77
2. Personality 79
(i) The Duncan and Fiske study 80
(ii) Single-trait approaches 82
(a) Extraversion/introversion 82
(b) Field dependence/independence 83
(c) Affiliation 84
(d) Dominance 85
(iii) Global personality differences 85
(a) Internalizers and externalizers 86
(b) Self-monitoring 86
(iv) Personality differences in encoding: summary . . . 87
3. Psychopathology 87
(i) Anxiety 87
(ii) Depression 88
(iii) Schizophrenia 89
(iv) Autism 91
(v) Psychopathy 92
(vi) Psychopathological differences in encoding: summary . 94
4. Sex 94
(i) Gaze 95
(ii) Facial expression 96
(iii) Posture and gesture 96

(iv) Interpersonal distance 99
(v) Sex differences in encoding: summary 99
STUDIES OF DECODING 100
1. Age 101
2. Culture 102
3. Personality 103
4. Psychopathology 105
5. Sex 108
EXPLANATIONS OF SEX DIFFERENCES IN NON-VERBAL CUES . . . 108
(i) Empathy 109
(ii) Social roles 109
(iii) Differences in power 110
(iv) Practice effects 111
(v) Accommodation 111
(vi) Explanations of sex differences in non-verbal cues: summary 112
SUMMARY 113

Chapter 5. **Specific contexts** 115
RELATIONSHIPS 115
1. Dimensions of interpersonal relationships 120
(i) Affiliation 120
(ii) Dominance 128
2. Role relationships 136
(i) Mother–infant relationships 136
(ii) Marital relationships 139
SITUATIONS 140
1. Psychotherapy 140
2. Education 143
3. Interviews 147
4. Helping 150
5. Deception 152
6. The psychological experiment 156
MEDIUM OF COMMUNICATION 157
SUMMARY 164

Chapter 6. **Body movement and social skills training** . . . 166

Chapter 7. **Conclusions** 177

REFERENCES 180

INDEX 198

Acknowledgements

I would like to thank Derek Rutter and Ann Gore for their helpful and instructive comments on earlier drafts of the manuscript on which this book is based. I would also like to thank Tony Barton for preparing the drawings.

Peter Bull

Preface

The main purpose of this book is to consider the social significance of body movement according to a definition put forward by Wiener *et al.* (1972), that there should be a shared signal system with both systematic encoding and appropriate decoding for a non-verbal behaviour to be regarded as communicative. One important implication of this definition is that the social significance of non-verbal behaviour may not necessarily lie in communication: there may be systematic encoding without appropriate decoding, which would suggest that non-verbal behaviour constitutes a useful but neglected source of information about others, or there may be decoding without systematic encoding, according to which people erroneously attribute significance to non-verbal behaviour which it does not in fact possess; only in the case where there is systematic encoding and appropriate decoding is the social significance of body movement regarded as communicative. In this book, research on body movement is reviewed in the context of this encoding/decoding distinction, not by discussing the significance of each body part in turn, but by considering what is the type of information conveyed by bodily cues. To this end, body movement is discussed in relation to emotion, speech and individual differences; it is also argued that body movement needs to be understood within the specific contexts of interpersonal relationships, situations and the medium of communication employed; finally, methods of changing people's use and awareness of body movement are discussed on the basis of the preceding theoretical discussion. Thus the purpose of the book is to consider the social significance of body movement in the context of the encoding/decoding distinction through a discussion of the type of information it conveys, in short, to consider what is the relationship between body movement and interpersonal communication.

Chapter 1

Concepts and Methods in Non-verbal Communication Research

CONCEPTS OF NON-VERBAL COMMUNICATION

In defining the non-verbal element of non-verbal communication, two useful distinctions have been drawn by Laver and Hutcheson (1972) between the verbal and non-verbal, and between the vocal and non-vocal. Vocal behaviour consists of all the actions involved in producing speech, whereas non-vocal behaviour refers to communicative activities other than speech, and therefore includes such features as facial and bodily movements. The verbal elements in conversation are taken to mean the actual words used (distinct from all vocal considerations of how they might be pronounced), while non-verbal behaviour refers to all vocal and non-vocal behaviour which is not verbal in the sense defined above.

The term 'non-verbal' then is a definition by exclusion. If the verbal elements in conversation are taken to mean only the actual words used, then the term 'non-verbal' can refer to non-verbal vocal features such as tone of voice, stress and intonation. It can also refer to facial movement, gaze, pupil size, body movement and interpersonal distance. It can refer as well to communication through touch, through smell and through various kinds of artefacts, such as masks, clothes or formalized communication systems such as semaphore; in fact the number of features which can be included under artefacts is virtually limitless.

However, in this review it is intended to focus discussion on one aspect of non-verbal communication—that of human bodily movement. The reasons for this are both practical and conceptual. The sheer range of phenomena embraced by the term 'non-verbal communication' is so vast that to do justice to the subject some degree of specialization is necessary. For example, non-verbal vocal behaviour covers such a wide range of phenomena (such as intonation, emphasis, speech rate, accent and loudness), that it certainly merits a separate

1

treatment in its own right. Hence in this review studies of non-verbal vocal behaviour are discussed only when they enhance our understanding of the significance of body movement through direct comparisons between body movement and non-verbal vocal behaviour as distinctive sources of information. At the same time, the features which can be included under the term 'body movement' do form a separate and distinctive form of communication. The term refers in effect to communication through visible forms of body movement—through movements of the facial muscles, the eyes, the pupils and the limbs, and movements of the body in relation to other people. Such movements can be seen as constituting one distinctive type of non-verbal communication, and will subsequently be referred to in this review as 'bodily cues'; the term 'non-verbal cues' will be used in a wider sense to include non-visual as well as visual forms of non-verbal communication.

The notion of communication to be employed is based on the definition of Wiener *et al.* (1972). They have argued that to use the term 'non-verbal communication', there should be non-verbal behaviours with shared meanings which constitute a code through which messages are conveyed by an encoder and responded to systematically and appropriately by a decoder. According to this definition, the issue of whether a person intends to communicate is considered unimportant because of the difficulty of deciding what constitutes intentional behaviour; once it is accepted that a person may be confused about his intentions, may lie about them or may be simply unaware of what they are, then there is no necessary basis in the behaviours themselves for deciding whether they should be considered intentional. Wiener *et al.* are less explicit with regard to the relationship between awareness and communication, but the position taken by the present author is that awareness is irrelevant as to what behaviour is regarded as communicative; provided it can be shown that an encoder transmits a message through non-verbal behaviours which are accurately decoded by another person, then it is not important whether either encoder or decoder can identify the specific non-verbal cues through which the message was transmitted. Indeed, it can be argued that a significant proportion of non-verbal communication takes this form; people may be left with the feeling that someone was upset, or that one person did or did not like another person, without being able to say precisely why they formed that particular impression.

Research on how the pupils of the eyes respond to emotion provides a useful example of what this concept of communication means in practice. Hess and Polt (1960) aroused considerable interest by reporting an experiment in which subjects viewed a series of pictures while their eyes were recorded on film. The pupil size of the subjects viewing the pictures was compared with the size when viewing control pictures which had been matched for luminance, and Hess and Polt claimed that the pupils of the subjects dilated when viewing pictures of particular interest. Hence the pupils of women dilated when they viewed a picture of a nude male and a picture of a mother and a baby, while the pupils of men dilated when they viewed a picture of a nude female. Hess (1965) describes another experiment in which a series of pictures were shown to 20

Figure 1. Photographs of a woman with dilated and constricted pupils. (Reprinted by permission from E. H. Hess (1965), Attitude and pupil size. *Scientific American*, **212** (4), 46–54)

young men, which included two photographs of an attractive young woman. In one case the pupils of the young woman had been touched up to be extra large, in another case to be extra small (see Figure 1). The average pupillary response to the picture with large pupils was more than twice as strong as to the picture with small pupils; but most men said the pictures were identical, and none noticed that one had larger pupils than the other. Hess interpreted these findings as showing that the men found the woman with dilated pupils as more attractive, presumably because they felt she was more attracted to them. In what appears to have been a subsequent replication of this experiment, Hess (1975a) again reports that none of his male subjects noticed the difference in pupil size in the two photos of the woman, but when asked to describe her, they said that the woman with large pupils was 'soft', 'more feminine' or 'pretty', while the same woman with small pupils was described as being 'hard', 'selfish' or 'cold'.

All these experiments can be used to illustrate the application of Wiener *et al.*'s definition of non-verbal communication. The fact that male subjects responded differently to the pictures of the same woman with dilated and constricted pupils illustrates how non-verbal communication can take place without awareness of which particular non-verbal cue is responsible for transmitting a particular message, or for creating a particular impression. At the same time, findings on pupil size are also relevant to the issue of intentionality and communication. Pupil size is governed by the autonomic nervous system, so that although it is possible through the administration of drugs (e.g. atropine) to enlarge the pupils artificially, it is not possible to dilate or constrict them through direct voluntary control. Hence, if we accept Hess's claims that the pupils dilate when we are attracted to someone, and that other people perceive dilated pupils as conveying attraction, then it can be argued that according to Wiener *et al.*'s definition pupil dilation constitutes a means of non-verbally communicating attraction, even though it is not a voluntary response and can convey its meaning without the decoder being aware that he is responding to the dilated pupil.

One difficulty with this definition is that as soon as we cease to regard awareness and intentionality as integral to communication, then it can become difficult to establish what is actually communicated by a particular behaviour. In the case, for example, of a hitch-hiker who stands at the road-side with his thumb outstretched, it is well known in contemporary Western society that he is attempting to obtain a lift from passing cars. He uses the signal quite intentionally, and with full awareness of its meaning; similarly, the drivers of passing cars are well aware of its meaning, and will respond as they see fit. In this case, the outstretched thumb is clearly recognized as a well-established form of non-verbal communication.

But once we abandon the criteria of awareness and intentionality as checks on the meaning of a particular communication, can we be sure that we have interpreted its meaning correctly? Can we be sure, for example, that pupil dilation does non-verbally communicate attraction? Hess's argument is that the pupils dilate in response to stimuli we find attractive, and actually constrict in response to stimuli we find unattractive (the aversion–constriction hypothesis). If this were true, it would make pupil size a unique response, in that instead of simply indicating differences in degree of arousal like other psychophysiological variables (e.g. heart rate or respiration rate), it actually indicates whether the nature of the affect is positive or negative. But this view of pupil size is in fact explicitly rejected by many other research workers (e.g. Janisse, 1977), and hence needs to be evaluated in the light of the available evidence. The ensuing discussion of the controversy surrounding the significance of pupil dilation is intended as an illustrative example of the problems of establishing what actually is communicated by a particular non-verbal behaviour.

The main criticism of Hess's work stems from his reliance on the use of pictures in his research. The problem with this technique is that the pupils respond to light, dilating to lower levels of illumination and constricting to higher levels of illumination; hence it is important in pictorial experiments where pupil size is investigated as an emotional response to control both for the overall level of illumination and for the relative differences in light stemming from different parts of the picture. As Janisse and Peavler (1974) point out, if a study was carried out using a picture of a white male, wearing only dark trousers, the pupil would be larger if the subject looked at the trousers rather than if he looked at the face. If two subjects (one male, one female) looked at different parts of the picture, they would have different pupillary responses which might be interpreted quite spuriously as indicating an emotionally toned sex difference in response to this picture.

Hess has in fact employed two techniques for controlling for the effects of light in his research. One technique involves making special control slides which can be compared with the experimental pictures under investigation, where the control and experimental slides are matched for overall brightness and the brightness contrast of the pictures is reduced by a special photographic technique. Woodmansee (1970) used a set of pictures especially prepared in Hess's laboratory and still found an average constriction of 2 per cent when a subject's gaze shifted from a dark to a brighter area of the picture. Since the hypothesized emotionally arousing effects on pupil diameter are usually less than 5 per cent, this could represent a serious source of artefact in these experiments.

A second technique which Hess has employed (Hess, 1965) involves using only the general room lighting to illuminate the rear-projection screen of the apparatus; hence when the stimulus slide comes on, every part of the screen is at least somewhat brighter than it had been during the control period. According to this approach, if the eye responds only to light intensity, then the pupil should constrict; if it dilates, as Hess claims it does, then this can be interpreted as an emotional response to the particular picture displayed. The difficulty with this technique is that it cannot be used to investigate pupil constriction, which forms a major part of Hess's interpretation of the emotional response of the pupil.

The fact that other pictorial studies on pupil size have failed to replicate Hess's findings lends support to criticisms of this research technique. For example, Woodmansee (1970) carried out a pair of studies with American female students known to differ in racial attitudes to Negroes (from their responses to a questionnaire), and found that the pupils of both the group with positive attitudes and the group with negative attitudes dilated in response to pictures depicting Negroes in a variety of situations. In that same paper, Woodmansee reports another study in which he showed American female students a picture taken shortly after another female student had been brutally murdered in a music practice room; the photograph showed the murder scene with blood on the floor and the outline of the girl's body where it lay. This particular study was carried out just two weeks after the murder had actually occurred, and the pupils of the subject dilated in response to this photograph even when they said it repelled and disgusted them. Woodmansee's results would seem to be in direct contradiction to those obtained by Hess, unless one assumes that the students with attitudes hostile to Negroes were secretly attracted to them, or that the students who saw the photograph of the murder scene were secretely excited by it.

Studies of pupil size have also been carried out using non-pictorial stimuli, which typically involve measuring the pupil size of subjects listening to pleasant or unpleasant words; a number of such studies are reviewed by Janisse (1977). For example, in an experiment by White and Maltzman (1978), American male students listened to three 120-second passages from the same novel; one segment was intended to be neutral, one erotic and one an unpleasant description of a lynching mutilation. The authors found an immediate dilation at the beginning of each passage, with erotic and mutilation passages maintaining pupil dilation for about 60 seconds. No evidence was found in support of the aversion–constriction hypothesis, and this has also been the case with other studies which have made use of non-pictorial stimuli (Janisse, 1977). Hence the hypothesis that the pupils convey information about whether a person finds a stimulus pleasant or unpleasant can scarcely be said to have been firmly established. But the pupil certainly does respond to emotional stimuli, and the research findings can most parsimoniously be explained by the hypothesis that the pupils simply dilate in response to increased emotional arousal (Janisse, 1977). Loewenfeld (1966) in fact argues that all psychological and sensory stimuli (with the exception of light) dilate the pupil, and none of them constrict it.

If the pupil simply conveys information about the degree of emotional arousal, regardless of whether it is pleasant or unpleasant, does this mean that Hess's subjects, who saw a woman with constricted pupils as less pleasant than a woman with dilated pupils (Hess, 1975a), were misled about the information that the pupil conveys? Hess of course argues that the dilated pupil is perceived as conveying a positive message, and Janisse (1977) concurs with this conclusion, maintaining that in the studies he has reviewed, dilated pupils are consistently perceived as conveying positive attributes of friendliness, youthfulness and attractiveness.

There are, however, several criticisms which can be made of this conclusion. One problem is that dilated pupils are not always perceived more favourably. Kirkland and Smith (1978) set out to replicate Hess's (1975a) finding that women show a preference for infants with dilated pupils. Four photographs of the same infant face were mounted on to separate display cards; with the exception of the infant's pupils, each photograph was identical (see Figure 2).

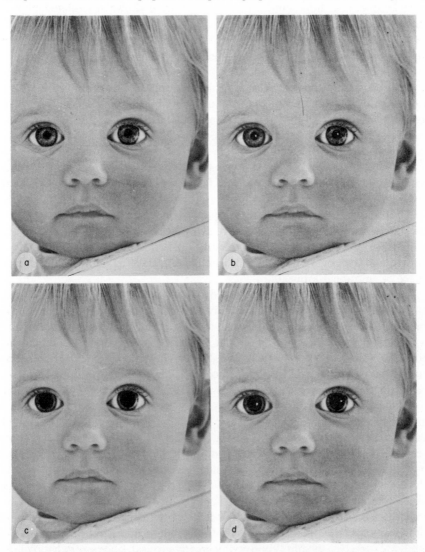

Figure 2. Infant faces with modified pupils used for "attractiveness" selections, where a = constricted, non-highlighted; b = constricted, highlighted; c = dilated, non-highlighted; d = dilated, highlighted. (Reproduced by permission from Kirkland, J. and Smith, J. (1978) Preferences for infant pictures with modified eye-pupils. *Journal of Biological Psychology*, **20**, 33–34)

The pupils were retouched to provide two levels of highlighting (presence or absence) and two levels of pupil size (constricted or dilated). The photographs were presented in pairs to unaccompanied female shoppers in a supermarket car-park, who were asked to say which baby was the more attractive, and to give the reasons for their choice. The results were statistically highly significant, with subjects showing the greatest preference for the baby with highlighted, constricted pupils; no significant preferences were shown for dilated pupils, whether highlighted or not. The subjects certainly seemed aware of the different appearance of the pupils, the majority of them (64 per cent) mentioning the eyes when giving reasons for their preferences.

A second problem is that in decoding studies of pupil size, an adequate range of facial expressions has never been properly sampled. For example, in Hess's (1975a) study, subjects saw the woman with dilated pupils as having more positive attributes than the same woman with constricted pupils, but this does not necessarily mean that dilated pupils are always perceived as conveying a positive message. In the context of the particular facial expression shown in that picture, it may well be the case that the dilated pupils make the woman look more attractive; but with another facial expression, say of anger, dilated pupils might make the woman look more angry, and hence she might be perceived more negatively with dilated pupils. Hence a decoding study of pupil size should be performed in which a range of facial expressions of emotion are sampled, in order to test whether dilated pupils are perceived as conveying a positive message, or whether they are simply perceived as indicating a greater degree of emotional arousal.

Hess (1975b) does in fact cite one study which can be interpreted as showing that dilated pupils are decoded as conveying information about intensity of emotional arousal, rather than positive or negative affect. He describes a study by Shrout (Hess, 1975b, pp. 216–217) in which he gave six copies of a schematic face to subjects who knew nothing about research on pupil size. The schematic face contained only the outline of the face, the nose, the eyes without pupils and the hairline. Subjects were asked to draw in the missing parts on the faces that would make them appropriately express six different moods—very happy, very tired, displeased, complacent, bored and very angry and threatening. The results showed that subjects sketched in significantly larger pupils for the very happy face than for the displeased, bored and very tired faces. But the results also showed that the very angry and threatening face was portrayed with large pupils which were second in size only to those for the very happy face; in other respects this face resembled the displeased face, since for both faces subjects drew in frowns and darkened brows. Thus the results from this study are consistent not with Hess's aversion–constriction hypothesis, but with the notion that dilated pupils are perceived as simply conveying greater arousal, since a very happy face and a very angry and threatening face would be expected to be construed as more aroused than displeased, bored and very tired faces.

What then can we say about pupil size as a form of non-verbal communication? The evidence reviewed above does not seem to be consistent with Hess's notion that the pupil conveys information about positive and negative emotional states, but rather with the hypothesis that it simply encodes information about arousal which Shrout's study would suggest is decoded appropriately. Nevertheless, Hess's work has been useful in showing how pupil size can transmit messages to observers without them being aware of the cue which is responsible for those messages. At the same time, as a response of the autonomic nervous system it is not under direct voluntary control, and hence can be used to illustrate the notion that communication can take place without any intention to communicate.

The controversy about what pupil size actually does convey illustrates some of the problems of applying Wiener *et al.*'s definition of communication. The fact that we may be mistaken either about encoding or decoding can be used to illustrate another point about non-verbal cues—that their significance may not necessarily lie in communication. Communication requires both encoding and decoding, but encoding may take place without decoding, while decoding may also be inaccurate. The implications of these distinctions allow three different kinds of status for non-verbal cues.

Firstly, if an emotion, for example, is encoded by a particular non-verbal cue, but is not decoded by other people, then it suggests that non-verbal cues may be a valuable source of information which is generally neglected. This kind of approach has been particularly associated with some psychoanalysts, who have maintained that bodily cues can provide valuable guides to psychodynamics. Deutsch (1947, 1949, 1952), for example, set out to record all the postures of patients undergoing psychoanalysis, together with a transcript of what the patient actually said. He gives numerous examples of how different postures accompanied different free associations; for example, he describes how one female patient held her hands under her neck when fearful of being punished for masturbation, lifted her right hand and held her left hand protectively over her head when she was angry with men, and lifted both arms when she was angry with both parents (Deutsch, 1947). Deutsch argues that an awareness of postural expression is of great value in psychoanalysis both for the analyst in providing him with clues to psychodynamics, and for the patient in helping him to become aware of his own repressed feelings through the analyst's interpretation of the particular postures adopted. According to this view, non-verbal cues are significant not because they constitute a generalized system of communication, but as a source of valuable information which only a skilled perceiver can learn to understand through careful observation.

A second possibility is that non-verbal cues are commonly perceived as conveying a meaning which they do not in fact possess (decoding errors); in this case their social significance would be quite different. They might in fact be of considerable social significance, but in the sense that they lead people to make erroneous attributions about others, and possibly to act upon those mistakes. It is commonly assumed, for example, that non-verbal cues tell us a great deal about personality, but empirical research (reviewed in Chapter 4, pp. 79–87) has provided little support for this belief; this may be an example of a decoding error. A problem of particular importance here is the difficulty of establishing exactly what is encoded by a specific non-verbal cue, as has already been illustrated in the research reviewed on pupil size. In fact many studies of non-verbal cues have relied upon decoding designs alone, and there is a real danger that in the absence of satisfactory encoding studies, the evidence obtained only from decoding may be quite misleading.

The third possibility is of course that non-verbal cues may be both encoded and decoded appropriately, and that in this case their social significance lies in their role as a means of communication. The importance of the preceding discussion is that the social significance of non-verbal cues does not necessarily lie in communication, and hence the importance of the encoding/decoding distinction always needs to be considered in evaluating research on non-verbal cues. In the subsequent discussion, the term 'non-verbal cues' will be used where the term 'cue' is intended to indicate that the behaviour may be informative but not necessarily communicative; the term 'communication' will only be used where it is considered that systematic and appropriate encoding and decoding of that particular behaviour has been demonstrated.

The purpose of the book as a whole is to discuss the social significance of bodily cues in relation to the encoding/decoding distinction: to consider whether bodily cues encode information without appropriate decoding, or whether bodily cues are inappropriately decoded in the absence of systematic encoding, or whether bodily cues are both encoded and decoded appropriately; in short, to consider what is the relationship between body movement and interpersonal communication. The approach taken is not to discuss each body part in turn, but to consider what is the type of information conveyed by bodily cues. To this end, body movement is discussed in relation to emotion, speech and individual differences; it is also argued that body movement needs to be understood within the specific contexts of interpersonal relationships, situations and the medium of communication employed; finally, methods of changing people's use and awareness of body movement are discussed. But before beginning this theoretical discussion, the methods used to measure body movement are reviewed in the remaining part of this chapter.

METHODOLOGY

A discussion of the methodologies employed in research on bodily cues can be approached from two main viewpoints. Firstly, there is the question of the context in which bodily cues should be observed. For example, should observations be obtained through carefully controlled laboratory experimentation or through field studies? Secondly, there is the question simply of how bodily cues should be measured. If, for example, facial expression is being studied, a coding system is required which will provide the main units of measurement as well as a system of categories for describing the units. Clearly, these two questions are not independent of one another, since the measurements obtained from field studies may not be as precise as those obtained from laboratory studies, although of course the proponents of field studies would argue that their particular approach has compensating advantages in that behaviour can be observed in its natural context.

1. The Context of Measurement

Von Cranach and Vine (1973) have argued that four distinctive approaches to the study of non-verbal communication can be distinguished, and refer to these approaches respectively as ethological, structural, sociological and external variable (psychological); each of these approaches differ with respect to the methodology they recommend.

(i) The Ethological Approach

Ethology developed initially as a branch of zoology, but in recent years the techniques of ethology have been applied to human behaviour (e.g. Grant, 1969; Blurton Jones, 1971; Eibl-Eibesfeldt, 1972, 1973a, 1973b). There are a number of distinctive features which characterize the ethological approach. Special emphasis is laid on observational, natural history techniques as the starting-point for the generation of hypotheses. Ethologists have also worked on the assumption that human behaviours depend to a considerable extent on phylogenetically inherited, adaptive predispositions, and they typically try to interpret behaviour in this framework. Consequently, they seek to study behaviour in its natural environment, and the typical research methods employed are naturalistic observation and field experiment; where films or tapes are made, ethologists have developed a number of techniques for concealed filming in order not to upset the natural flow of behaviour.

(ii) The Structural Approach

The structural approach is best exemplified by the work of Birdwhistell (e.g. 1971), Scheflen (e.g. 1966, 1968) and Duncan (e.g. Duncan, 1972; Duncan and Fiske, 1977). According to Scheflen (1968), many aspects of social interaction are programmed; that is, they occur in specific sequences and those sequences can be hierarchically ordered. Such behaviours do have meanings, but their meanings can be best understood only in the context in which behaviour occurs. Scheflen (1968, pp. 47–48) quotes with approval Bateson's dictum that 'Meaning is relative; the less ambiguity about the contexts of a unit, the more meaning can be ascribed to it.' Scheflen (1966) has criticized those psychological studies which rely simply on frequency counts of isolated units of behaviour. According to Scheflen, non-verbal cues are linked together through a system of rules. The task of the researcher is to describe those rules not through the isolation of single variables but through a structural analysis where the significance of particular aspects of behaviour can be understood in their total context. The methodological approach which Scheflen recommends is a natural history one, where the investigator through repeated viewing of a tape learns which of the non-verbal cues are ordered in sequential arrangements.

However, there is in fact no reason why statistical analysis should not be applied to the study of structure. Scheflen (1966) explicitly rejects the use of statistical analysis because he claims that the nature of a sequential rule is such that the various elements will appear together in the appropriate order on each occasion. But such a rule is in fact an inference from observed behaviour, and just as people sometimes breach the rules of grammar when they are talking, so there may well be breaches of the rules which govern the sequential ordering of non-verbal cues. In fact in more recent structural approaches (e.g. Duncan and Fiske, 1977), statistical analysis is an accepted part of the research procedure, although the emphasis remains very firmly on the sequential ordering of non-verbal cues in the overall communicative structure.

(iii) The Sociological Approach

Closely related to the structural approach is the sociological approach, whose most well-known exponent is Goffman. Goffman (1956) has proposed an analysis of social interaction in terms of theatre, according to which people set out to project certain impressions of themselves through appropriate performance. According to Goffman, to present a performance is to sustain the relevant standards of behaviour, often without awareness or intention to be dishonest; in presenting such a performance, non-verbal cues may be of considerable significance. How others perceive the performance will depend on the framework in which they structure events (Goffman, 1975). Thus exactly the same behaviours can be reinterpreted in different ways according to the frame in which they are perceived; a 'couple' kissing can also be a 'man' greeting his 'wife' or 'John' being careful with 'Mary's' make-up, depending upon how the relationship between the two people is construed. In his emphasis on social context, Goffman's approach is very similar to that of the structuralists. But whereas structuralists maintain that the significance of behaviour cannot be understood without reference to its sequential and hierarchical ordering, Goffman argues that its significance cannot be appreciated without an understanding of the roles and relationships of the performers.

(iv) The Psychological Approach

Duncan (1969) has argued that the structural approach can be distinguished from what he calls the external variable approach. This is so named because of its basic strategy of attempting to relate aspects of non-verbal behaviour to features external to the communicative context, for example, by investigating whether particular non-verbal behaviours are associated with particular personality traits. This typifies, according to Duncan, the psychological approach to the study of non-verbal cues, and he criticizes it for a failure to take adequate account of the structural organization of non-verbal behaviour. However, there is no reason why psychological studies should necessarily take the external variable form; as was argued above (pp. 11–12, there is no reason why psychological techniques of statistical analysis should not be used to investigate sequential relationships between non-verbal behaviours, and this approach, for example, has been used particularly in studies of mother–infant interaction (see pp. 136–139).

What in fact is more central to the psychological approach is the use of laboratory experimentation and statistical analysis. Exponents of the other approaches criticize laboratory studies because they claim that the results so obtained may fail to correspond to behaviour occurring outside the laboratory, while experimental social psychologists defend this approach because of the advantages of experimental control in testing hypotheses more rigorously, a feature which is usually lacking in field studies.

The use of experimental techniques in the study of non-verbal cues can be conveniently divided into encoding and decoding designs. The study of decoding presents fewer methodological problems than the study of encoding, and probably as a consequence many psychologists have concentrated on a decoding approach. Typically, subjects are presented with a range of behaviours which they are asked to judge on a number of rating scales. If, for example, the experimenter is interested in how the expression of one particular emotion is decoded, he will nevertheless provide his subjects with a number of different rating scales to avoid 'cuing' them to the particular emotion in which he is interested. The major issue which arises concerns the way in which the behaviours to be rated should be presented. In many studies, drawings or photographs have been used, but this approach has been criticized because only static positions can be depicted in this way, thus giving very impoverished information about bodily cues. This problem can be avoided through the use of videotape or film, which also has the advantage that decoding can be investigated in different channels of communication. For example, subjects can be asked to rate a tape from the vision alone, from the sound alone, and from the vision and sound together, to investigate the relative influence of these different sources of information. One problem which arises with this approach is whether the judgements so obtained correspond to the judgements people make of others when they are actually conversing with them. One way of avoiding this problem is to use a confederate of the experimenter who is asked to behave in a prearranged fashion when conversing with an experimental subject, to investigate how the subject perceives the prearranged behaviours. This approach has also been criticized both because the experimenter may not know which actions the confederate should control, and because the confederate may not necessarily be able to exert adequate control over his own behaviour (Duncan and Fiske, 1977). The alternative recommended by Duncan and Fiske is to study behaviour in naturally occurring situations, but this of course means that the experimenter cannot directly manipulate the behaviours he may wish to investigate.

The study of encoding presents greater problems for the experimental social psychologist particularly if he wishes to study the encoding of emotions and attitudes, since he needs some kind of technique for arousing the emotions or attitudes he wishes to investigate. Early studies of encoding used role-play techniques, where subjects were asked to adopt, for example, the postures they would employ when they like someone (Mehrabian, 1969). The problem with this approach is of course that people may simply not know what non-verbal cues they use when they like someone, or the behaviours they use may represent what they think they would do rather than what they do in a given situation. One way of avoiding these problems is to use film or tape to arouse particular emotions or attitudes. Subjects can be asked to rate the films or tape in terms of a number of emotion categories, and their ratings used to analyse the behaviours displayed while watching the tapes (Bull, 1978a). The advantages of this technique are both that it is possible to arouse different emotions and attitudes in this way, and that the results so obtained are not dependent on the subject's awareness of their own non-verbal encoding.

However, the problem still arises of how experimental social psychologists can study the encoding of non-verbal behaviour in ordinary conversation, again with particular reference to the investigation of emotions and attitudes. Nevertheless, there have been a number of studies in which this has been managed quite successfully. For example, Exline and Winters (1965) arranged for subjects to have separate conversations with two different people, and then asked them which person they liked better; the purpose of this experiment was to study the patterns of gaze associated with affiliation. Edelmann and Hampson (1979) arranged a structured interview of 15 questions concerning a picture which the subject had selected prior to the interview as the one which he least liked from a collection of pictures. In the eighth question, the interviewer revealed that he himself had painted the picture (he had in fact painted all the pictures in the original collection); the purpose of this experimental design was to study embarrassment. After the interview was over, each subject was shown a videotape of the interview and asked to rate his response to the eighth question on a list of 19 emotion categories which included embarrassment, to check that the experimental manipulation had been successful. Edelmann and Hampson were then able to investigate the encoding of embarrassment by comparing the behaviour of the group who reported themselves as embarrassed in response to the critical eighth question with the behaviour of those who did not report themselves as embarrassed.

It is argued that through techniques such as these, non-verbal cues can be effectively studied through laboratory experimentation, and the approach taken in this review is primarily psychological, although studies carried out from a sociological, structural or ethological viewpoint are also reviewed where appropriate.

2. Measurement of Bodily Cues

Most contemporary studies of bodily cues have used either film or videotape as the main technique of observation. Studies have also been carried out where an observer takes a 'live' record of behaviour, often concealed from the subjects behind a one-way screen, which permits the observer to see without being seen. But this approach has a number of real disadvantages in comparison with recording on videotape or film. If the observer misses any behaviours, there is no way of going back to rectify the omission. Moreover, a number of bodily cues (especially facial expressions) are simply too rapid to be noted by an observer without the aid of repeated viewing of a particular behavioural sequence, or sometimes without the use of slow-motion replay facilities. Another advantage of film or tape is that the duration of a particular behaviour can be timed much more precisely from frame numbers superimposed on the recording. Frame numbering is useful both as a method of referencing particular sequences of behaviour through the unique number given to each frame, and as a method of measuring the duration of any given behaviour in real time; it is certainly for more accurate than timing movements with a stop-watch.

Whether to use film or videotape depends upon the nature of the investigation being carried out. Video recording has the advantage of immediate playback, whereas film has to be developed; videotapes are also cheaper to buy, and can be used on more than one occasion. Film gives a much better resolution of the image, and so is particularly well suited for behavioural sequences requiring very detailed analysis; it also provides a much more precise and flexible technique for slow-motion analysis, which is still superior to any of the slow-motion videotape-recorders currently available on the market (Kendon, 1978).

But irrespective of the relative merits of film or videotape, the main disadvantage of all visual methods of analysing bodily cues is that they rely on a human observer to code the behaviour accurately into different behavioural categories. It is customary to check an observer's scoring by carrying out a reliability study in which his coding of behaviour is correlated with that of an independent observer; adequate reliability has been demonstrated for all the main scoring systems described below, except where explicit mention is made to the contrary. Nevertheless, the procedure of coding behaviour from film or tape is still exceedingly time-consuming and fatiguing, and it would clearly be desirable if fully automated systems of recording behaviour were available. Unfortunately, where such systems do exist, they usually raise different kinds of problems. For example, electromyographic techniques have been used as a way of recording changes in facial expressions (e.g. Schwartz *et al.*, 1976a, b), but this necessitates placing electrodes on particular facial muscles, which of course fundamentally changes the social situation in which the measurements are taken. A non-obtrusive technique for measuring hand gestures was employed by Sainsbury and Woods (1977), using an ultrasonic system developed by Haines (1974). This system measured the ultrasound waves created in the air by hand gestures, so that the measurements could be made quite unobtrusively. The problem here is that although such a record provides an indication of the frequency of hand gestures, it tells us nothing about their visual appearance, which is essential if we are to discuss visual communication.

Hence at present the main technique for measuring bodily cues is to make a behavioural record through tape or film, and to analyse that record through some kind of coding system. What follows is a brief review of the main techniques of coding which have been developed to categorize different kinds of body movement.

(i) Facial Expression

A number of systems have been developed for the coding of facial expression; Ekman (1979a) has identified 14 such systems (including his own). Ekman and Friesen (1978) have developed what they call the Facial Action Coding System (FACS), which is distinguished from other scoring procedures in a number of important respects. The aim of FACS is to describe visible facial movements in terms of their underlying anatomical basis; the manual provides a description of the muscular changes which are responsible for producing particular facial expressions. The coder's task is to describe a facial expression in terms of what are called action units, since in some cases several muscles may be responsible for one particular facial movement, while in other cases the same muscle may be responsible for more than one facial movement.

There are two main advantages to this system. The first is that it is essentially descriptive; it does not attempt to assert what particular facial expressions mean. This distinguishes it from a number of other scoring procedures; for example, Grant (1969) talks about the 'aggressive frown', while Blurton Jones (1971) describes the 'lower lip pout', thus confounding description of the movement with inference concerning its meaning. The advantage of separating description from inference, as Ekman and Friesen have done is that inferences about the meanings of particular expressions can be tested independently from the procedures employed to describe those expressions.

A second advantage of the system is its comprehensiveness. Ekman and Friesen's main aim was to develop a system which would be comprehensive, and to do this they rejected a purely inductive approach, whereby categories are developed on a purely *ad hoc* basis to describe instances of movement as they are observed; by concentrating on the anatomical basis of facial movement, they claim it is possible to describe any facial expression in terms of the system. Ekman (1979a) mantains that all the facial movements described by other investigators can be described in terms of his own scoring procedure, as well as many more facial movements which have been neglected by other investigators; in fact Ekman and Friesen's system is widely accepted as the main technique available for coding facial expression.

(ii) Gaze

Gaze is usually recorded by observers who are each asked to monitor the gaze of a particular subject; each observer presses the key of an event recorder when his subject looks at another subject, and releases the key when the subject averts his gaze. The keys are connected to pen recorders or more elaborate equipment through which the data can be wholly or partially analysed (Argyle and Cook, 1976). Gaze is most commonly measured in terms either of the duration or frequency of looks one person gives to another, or in terms of the frequency and duration of mutual gaze.

The major issue in the measurement of gaze has been whether an observer can in fact be certain that one person is looking into the eyes of another. One procedure for assessing the validity of measurements of gaze has been to arrange for a confederate of the experimenter to gaze continually at a subject while in conversation with him, and to press a concealed button whenever he considered the subject was looking into his eyes (e.g. Rutter, Morley and Graham, 1972). This record can then be used as a criterion against which to compare the judgements of an observer as to whether mutual gaze has occurred. Another procedure (e.g. Rimé and McCusker, 1976) has been to arrange for one subject to look continually at another subject, while the other subject is given instructions when to look into his partner's eyes and when to look away. According to this procedure, the instructions are then used as the criterion against which to compare the judgements of an observer as to whether mutual gaze has occurred.

The results of such studies do indicate that it is possible for an observer to make valid judgements about mutual gaze. At the same time, research has also indicated that judgements can be affected by certain kinds of systematic bias. In particular, Stephenson and Rutter (1970) have argued that judgements of mutual gaze become more inaccurate as the distance between the conversational partners is increased. This argument is derived from the fact that with increasing distance the angle between a subject's gaze towards and away from the other subject becomes progressively finer, and hence the judgement of mutual gaze becomes more difficult. To test this hypothesis, Stephenson and Rutter arranged for conversations to take place between pairs of subjects (British male and female students) at three different distances (2 feet, 6 feet and 10 feet). One subject was instructed to gaze continually into the eyes of the other, and to record when he was being looked in the eye by pressing the button of a concealed event recorder. The second subject was instructed to gaze for the first minute into the other subject's eyes, for the second minute at his ears, and for the third minute at his shoulders; he was given these instructions by a light signal which was not visible to the first subject. Observers judged the amount of mutual gaze which occurred from behind a one-way screen, and the results showed that the observers did erroneously judge more mutual gaze as occurring at greater distances, especially for the shoulder-gaze condition. On the basis of these findings, Stephenson and Rutter argue that a camera with a zoom lens should be used in preference to observers behind a one-way screen, so that a close-up image of the subject's face can be recorded irrespective of distance; this procedure was subsequently introduced in an experiment by Stephenson, Rutter and Dore (1973).

Of course the problem with the Stephenson and Rutter study, as Argyle (1970) pointed out, is that people do not necessarily look at one another's ears or shoulders during conversation. Argyle argued from his own observations that people either look at one another's eyes or look away. Nevertheless, Stephenson and Rutter's study raised two important issues concerning the measurement of mutual gaze, pertaining both to the effects of distance on judged eye contact, and to whether these effects can be remedied through the use of a zoom-lens camera.

Rimé and McCusker (1976) carried out a study which provides answers to both these questions. They set out to investigate the validity of a number of different measures of eye contact under different conditions. On each experimental session, five subjects (male and female students) were individually assigned to the roles of gaze sender, gaze receiver, direct-sight observer (an observer who was in the same room as the subjects), television observer (an observer who saw a close-up of the gaze sender's face) or one-way mirror observer. The gaze sender had to look into the gaze receiver's eyes each time he received a pre-recorded signal through earphones; when not looking into the receiver's eyes, the gaze sender could look in any other direction he liked. The gaze receiver had to look continuously at the gaze sender, and record whenever the gaze sender looked into his eyes, as did the three observers. The conversations took place at two distances (6 feet and 9 feet). The results showed that the gaze receiver, the television observer and the direct-sight observer showed equivalent accuracy (as judged by agreement with the programmed signals), which was significantly better than that of the one-way screen observer. The results also showed that, at the greater distance, all observers except only the television observer recorded longer periods of eye contact, although there was no difference in the programmed instructions. Thus the results supported both the hypothesis that errors increase as the distance between the conversational partners increases, and the belief that this source of bias can be corrected through the use of a close-up television picture focused on each subject's face.

(iii) Pupil Size

There are two main techniques for the measurement of pupil size. The first technique involves simply filming the eye of the subject. The film is then projected on to a flat surface, where it has to be analysed frame by frame; the surface is often calibrated, so that the measurement of pupil size can be established if the degree of magnification is known. But Janisse (1977) points out that there are a number of difficulties with this procedure. One problem is simply the amount of work it entails. Janisse mentions that he measured 20,000 frames for his doctoral dissertation, and has spoken to students who have made over 100,000 measurements for a single study. Since Henke and Globerson (1979) report that experienced raters measure only 300 to 600 frames per hour, the amount of work involved using this procedure is quite prodigious. A second problem is inter-scorer reliability, which can vary quite considerably. Janisse, for example, reports inter-observer correlations of 0.56, 0.86, and 0.88 for three studies (Janisse, 1977). This variability can sometimes be due to poor picture resolution, since even a small head movement by the subject can put the eye out of focus for the camera and so affect the definition of the pupil. A refinement of this technique has been developed by Henke and Globerson (1979), based on a type of microscope eyepiece which is especially designed to measure the diameters of small round features. In such eyepieces, the separation of two overlapping images of the feature to be measured is adjustable, and can be read from a scale when the circular images have been displaced to a point where they touch but do not intersect one another. Henke and Globerson report that inter-observer reliability using this technique is very high (0.983), as is the comparison between this technique and the conventional approach (0.94); they also report that it is possible to score 1000 frames per hour when using this procedure.

The other main technique for measuring pupil size involves the use of some kind of electronic scanning device. The apparatus usually measures scan lines as a function of light either emitted or reflected by the iris or the pupil and the cornea. The size of the pupil is then estimated through a system of calibration, and a continuous immediate measure of pupil size can be obtained. One problem with this technique is that until recently the devices have been of questionable accuracy, but Janisse (1977) reports that television pupillometers have now been developed which are both reliable and accurate, providing as many measurements as 60 per second. Some machines also have the capacity to monitor the point of focus of the subject, thus providing data both on pupil size and on eye movements. Nevertheless, the problem still remains that such equipment is relatively expensive and immobile, and is therefore suitable only for laboratory experiments (Henke and Globerson, 1979). Clearly, then, choice of the best technique for measuring pupil size depends on the context in which the measurements are to be made.

(iv) Posture and Gesture

There is no accepted procedure at present for coding posture and gesture. Friesen, Ekman and Wallblatt (1980) describe a relatively simple system for classifying hand movements, which distinguishes between what are called emblems, illustrators and manipulators. Emblems are symbolic hand gestures with a verbal meaning known to the members of a particular social group. Illustrators are hand movements which follow the rhythm and content of speech, and typically do not involve contact with an object or part of the body. Manipulators can be divided into those movements which satisfy self or bodily needs (self-manipulators), and those movements in which some instrumental task is performed (object-manipulators). The system also records which hand is involved in the activity, and which part of the body is manipulated. The main problem with these distinctions is that the observer is asked to make an inference concerning the function of a particular aspect of behaviour, whereas as Ekman and Friesen have pointed out in their work on facial movement it is better to separate the description of a movement from inferences concerning its meaning or function. While it is certainly clear that some hand movements involve touching the body, that others involve touching objects, and others neither, it would be much simpler to refer to these movements as 'body-contact', 'object-contact' and 'non-contact' movements, rather than ask the observer to make any judgements about their hypothesized social or psychological functions. A more fundamental problem with this system of categories is that no attempt is made to describe the visual appearance of particular movements, a feature which is important if we are to discuss visual communication.

Mehrabian (1968a) has described a slightly more elaborate procedure for coding bodily posture. For example, he proposes that relaxation of the legs can be coded on a 4-point scale ranging from a symmetrical stance of the legs with insteps touching to an asymmetrical stance of the legs with both feet resting flat on the floor. The main problem with Mehrabian's system is that it is highly selective and omits many common forms of bodily posture.

Much more elaborate systems have been proposed by Birdwhistell (1971) and Frey (Frey and von Cranach, 1973). Birdwhistell's system has a very detailed range of categories, but it is not clear how these categories were derived nor how they should be applied in practice. For example, it is not clear whether the categories refer to movements or positions or both. Nor is it clear whether the categories are intended to be independent of one another, or whether one behavioural unit can be described in terms of more than one category. Finally, no reliability data are reported for the system, so it is not clear how successfully it has been applied in practice.

Frey (Frey and von Cranach, 1973) is much more explicit with regard to these questions. He describes a system whereby the positions of the body are scored at different time intervals. The positions of the head and trunk are defined in relation to three main axes, dissecting the body front to back, side to side and top to bottom. Hand positions are classified according to whether 11 spatial areas (e.g. head, hand or desk) are touched by the hands. Foot positions are classified according to whether four parts of the foot (heels, toes, inner and outer edge) are touching one of five areas (floor, chair, thigh, lower part of leg or foot). Movements are scored by assessing the position of the body at different time intervals, so that the system is essentially static, characterizing all body movement in terms of a series of positions. The main difficulty with this approach is that it destroys the natural structure of body movement. For example, in Frey's system it would not be possible to describe a head nod as a single behavioural unit; instead it would have to be described in terms of three positions (head upright, head dropped, head upright), and hence the basic unity of the movement is lost.

The author has recently devised a system which attempts to avoid these kinds of problems by taking as its basic unit of analysis the single movement act (Bull, 1981). Hence the system is dynamic, not static; it describes gestures as a series of movement acts rather than as a series of positions. A basic distinction is made between those movements which involve contact with an object or part of the body, and those movements which do not involve any such contact. Body-contact and object-contact acts are described in terms of the way the contact is made (e.g. touching, grasping, scratching) and the object or part of the body with which the contact is made. Non-contact movements are described in terms of the various movements which are possible from each of the major joints of the body (neck, spine, hips, knees, ankles, toes, shoulder girdle, shoulders, elbows, wrists and fingers). For example, the forearm can bend, straighten, rotate inwards and rotate outwards. The head can lower, raise, nod (lower and raise), tilt to one side, rock (tilt from side to side), turn, shake (turn from side to side) and rotate. Some of these movements can occur in combination; for example, a person can turn his head away from another person while nodding it at the same time, or lower his head while shaking it. In a number of respects, this system aims to implement the same principles adopted by Ekman and Friesen in their Facial Action Coding System. It aims to be descriptive rather than inferential; it employs the single movement act ('action unit') as its basic unit, and aims to provide descriptive categories based on the range of movements which are possible from each of the joints of the body.

(v) Interpersonal Distance

In the early formulations of interpersonal distance (e.g. Sommer, 1969), the term 'personal space' was used to refer to a spatial zone which serves comfortably to separate one person from another. This personal space 'bubble' (as it became known) was commonly measured by an experimenter approaching the subject from a number of different directions, the subject being instructed to tell the experimenter to stop when he had reached a point which was uncomfortably close. A number of other procedures have been devised to measure personal space, using, for example, questionnaires, dolls, silhouettes, figure drawings and videotape simulations. A questionnaire procedure was devised by Duke and Nowicki (1972) (the Comfortable Interpersonal Distance Scale), in which a schematic representation is shown of a 'round' room with eight doors. Subjects are asked to imagine themselves to be in the centre of the room, to imagine that a person described by the experimenter is approaching from one of the doors and to indicate what would be a comfortable interpersonal distance. Duke and Wilson (1973) have also developed a version of this procedure for use with children which employs small wooden and plastic dolls. Pedersen (1973a) has developed a technique using pairs of movable profiles, which the subject is asked to adjust to one of the figures which is intended to represent himself in each pair to an appropriate and comfortable distance. Rawls, Trego and McGaffey (1968) have developed a technique using figure drawings of five views of a man facing in different directions; subjects are asked to imagine each figure is a representation of them and to draw a circle around the figure showing how far they would like people to stay away during ordinary social situations. Walkey and Gilmour (1979) have developed a videotaped simulation technique, in which a videotape is presented of an actor walking towards and stopping near another actor from five different directions at one of seven different distances. Subjects are asked to imagine they are the person being approached, and to rate how comfortable they would find each interpersonal distance.

A number of studies have been carried out comparing these different techniques with direct observations of behaviour. For example, Veitch, Getsinger and Arkkelin (1976) report a number of validation studies using the Comfortable Interpersonal Distance Scale in which the results showed correlations of between 0.52 and 0.76 between the questionnaire responses and direct behavioural observations. Walkey and Gilmour (1979) compared their own videotaped simulation procedure with the Comfortable Interpersonal Distance Scale, the Pedersen Personal Space Measure, the Rawls, Trego and McGaffey personal space measure, and a direct behavioural observation, in which a confederate approached the subject from a number of different directions (the subjects were male European students). Walkey and Gilmour reported the highest correlation between their own videotaped simulation technique and the direct observation of behaviour (0.83); the other correlations with direct behavioural observation were 0.55 for the Rawls, Trego and McGaffey measure, 0.48 for the Comfortable Interpersonal Distance Scale and 0.46 for the Pedersen Personal Space Measure.

The comparatively low correlations found between most of these techniques and direct behavioural observations raise considerable doubts about the value of these techniques as alternatives to direct behavioural observation. Jones and Aiello (1979) have in fact argued that administering a whole battery of tests (as in the Walkey and Gilmour study) means that such consistency as exists may have been overestimated, since by making personal space the clear focus of the study, subjects may produce more consistent results than they might otherwise. In their own study, Jones and Aiello (1979) compared a direct measure of interaction distance taken unobtrusively by asking American high school students to work in pairs on a discussion task with a measure either of the distance at which they felt comfortable when a confederate approached them, or a task in which they were asked to place silhouettes on a board to represent the distance they would adopt with their partner in the previous exercise, as well as with a number of other figures. Jones and Aiello found the correlations between the different measures were mainly around zero, suggesting not only that simulated measures may fail to correspond to preferred distances when approached by a confederate, but also that the technique of asking subjects to state their preferred distance when approached by a confederate may bear little resemblance to the distances they actually do adopt in a naturally occurring interaction. Patterson (1975) has criticized the whole notion of personal space on the grounds that there is too much variability in interpersonal distance to support the concept of a consistent comfortable distance as an attribute of personality. Patterson suggests that instead we should use the term 'interpersonal distance', which can be considered in terms of the physical distance between people and their angle of orientation towards one another. The lack of correspondence between unobtrusive and self-report measures of behaviour (whether behavioural or non-behavioural) would also suggest that reports of the interpersonal distances people say they adopt cannot be relied upon as measures of the interpersonal distances they actually do adopt. A number of unobtrusive measures have in fact been commonly used in studies of interpersonal distance. For example, an approach employed in field studies has been to take observations from an area covered by a tiled surface, where the size of the tiles can be used as a way of calculating interaction distance (e.g. Dean, Willis and Hewitt, 1975). One laboratory technique involves asking, say, a couple of subjects to fetch chairs from the side of the room and to sit down and discuss a controversial issue (e.g. Pedersen, 1973b). The distance and angle of the chairs in relation to one another can then be measured without having to make subjects aware that this is the purpose of the investigation. It is maintained that in the light of the above discussion, non-obtrusive techniques such as these are the most appropriate way of measuring interpersonal distance.

SUMMARY

To use the term 'non-verbal communication', it has been argued that there should be non-verbal behaviours with shared meanings which constitute a code through which messages are conveyed by an encoder and responded to systematically and appropriately by a decoder. The purpose of the book as a whole is to discuss the social significance of bodily cues in relating to this encoding/decoding distinction: to consider whether bodily cues encode information without appropriate decoding, or whether bodily cues are decoded inappropriately, or whether bodily cues are both encoded and decoded appropriately. The methods used in non-verbal communication research can be seen to be derived from four distinctive theoretical approaches, namely, ethological, structural, sociological and psychological; techniques have also been discussed for measuring facial expression, gaze, pupil size, posture and gesture and interpersonal distance.

Chapter 2

Emotion

THE INNATE HYPOTHESIS OF EMOTIONAL EXPRESSION

In Chapter 1, the ethological, structural, sociological and psychological approaches to the study of non-verbal communication were discussed. It must be emphasized, however, that the differences between these approaches are more than just methodological. One of the prime areas of conflict centres around the extent to which non-verbal cues are learned or inherited. In the structural and sociological approaches, all non-verbal cues are seen as the product of learning, and the study of situational context, interpersonal relationships and culture become the prime focus of investigation. Ethologists have attempted to explain behaviour in terms of its evolutionary background, proposing interpretations in terms of phylogenetically inherited predispositions. Psychologists in recent years have adopted a mixed approach, based on the view that certain facial expressions are universal and inherited, while most non-verbal cues are learned and specific to particular cultures. Nowhere is the conflict between these different approaches more apparent than in the study of emotional expression, and the issue of whether such expressions should be considered innate or learned forms the central theme of this chapter.

The belief that emotions are expressed in the same way in different cultures, and that emotional expressions are innate can be traced to the work of Charles Darwin (1872). Darwin argued that if the emotions are expressed in the same way in different cultures, then these expressions are probably inherited, whereas if they differ between cultures, then they are probably learned. Darwin sent a list of 16 questions to observers working in different countries, and from the results he obtained, he argued that there are certain expressions of emotion which are both universal and innate.

The most explicit rejection of this view has come from Birdwhistell (1971). Birdwhistell described how he was initially influenced by Darwin's views, but came to recognize not only how the incidence of, say, smiling varied between different social groups, but also how its meaning might vary between those groups. Hence he observed that middle-class individuals from Ohio, Indiana and Illinois smiled more often (as counted on the street) than people with a

24

comparable background from Massachusetts, New Hampshire and Maine. He also observed that whereas in one part of the United States an unsmiling individual might be asked whether he was 'angry about something', in another region a smiling individual might be asked 'What's so funny?'; whereas in one context a smile might indicate good manners and friendliness, in another context it might indicate just the reverse. Hence Birdwhistell reached the conclusion that 'charts of smile frequency were not going to be very reliable as maps for the location of happy Americans'. Birdwhistell came to reject the view that smiles directly express underlying physiological states, arguing instead that meaning can only be understood within a particular social context.

Ekman (e.g. 1972, 1973) has discussed these issues at length and presented evidence to support Darwin's claim that certain expressions of emotion are universal. Ekman, Friesen and Ellsworth (1972) reviewed a number of decoding studies in literate cultures in which it was shown that observers label certain facial expressions in the same way irrespective of culture. In spite of this evidence, it could still be argued that the encoding of facial expressions of emotion is culturally variable, but that the common interpretation given to them by these different cultures is attributable to learning, for example, through exposure to the same mass media presentations. To test this hypothesis, Ekman and Friesen (1971) carried out a study with an isolated, non-literate tribe in New Guinea, who had had virtually no contact with Western society. The method used was to show the subjects three pictures of facial expressions hypothesized to be associated with different emotions while telling the subject a story through an interpreter; the subject was asked to choose which picture he considered most appropriate for the story. The six emotions studied were those which had been found by more then one investigator to be discriminable within any one literate culture (happiness, sadness, anger, disgust, fear, surprise). The photographs used to show the facial behaviour for each of the six emotions had been judged by more than 70 per cent of the observers in studies of more than one literate culture as showing that emotion. The results showed that the New Guinea subjects could successfullly discriminate all six emotions, with the exception only of fear and surprise; since these are somewhat similar expressions it is perhaps not surprising that they were confused (see pp. 29–31).

Ekman has argued that this study strongly supports the hypothesis that there are universals of emotional expression which are decoded in the same way irrespective of culture. At the same time he acknowledges (Ekman, 1973) that the demonstration of universals in decoding does not prove that inheritance determines the form and appearance of facial expressions, it simply increases the probability that this explanation is valid. The only hypothesis necessary to account for universality in facial expressions is that whatever is responsible for common facial expressions is constant for all mankind; thus common inheritance is one such factor, but learning experiences common to all mankind could equally well be another.

Eibl-Eibesfeldt (1973a) has argued that the best test of the innate hypothesis comes from the study of people who are deprived of the opportunity to learn the basic expressive behaviour patterns. This is to a great extent the case with individuals born deaf and blind, who are unable either to see or to hear the expressive behaviours of others. Eibl-Eibesfeldt has filmed six children, three girls and two boys deaf and blind from birth, and one boy deaf and blind from the age of 18 months. He found that these children all showed many of the expressive behaviours of normal children. Thus all the children smiled, usually during social play or when being patted or tickled. Raising the eyebrows in surprise occurred for one child when sniffing at an object, for another when tasting a piece of salted apple. One little girl would frown quite clearly when she was repeatedly offered a disliked object, or when people persisted in unwelcome attempts at social contact.

Although Eibl-Eibesfeldt's presentation of his observations is rather informal, his findings do strongly suggest that visual and auditory communication is unnecessary for the development of expressive behaviours. But Eibl-Eibesfeldt goes on to argue that his observations create difficulties for all explanations couched in terms of learning. He hypothesizes that children might learn the expressions by touching the face, but claims to have observed the same basic facial expressions with thalidomide children who have no arms. He discusses the possibility that learning might take place through some kind of behaviour shaping, with children who smile receiving social rewards for doing so, but argues that this is unlikely since smiling can be observed in highly retarded children born deaf and blind who have to be taught even how to guide a spoon to their mouths. He also argues that it would be difficult to see how the expression of anger could be acquired through behaviour shaping, since this expression is considered socially undesirable and would never be rewarded at all.

However, neither of these arguments carry much conviction. One might imagine that guiding a spoon could be an exceedingly difficult task for a retarded child without sight and hearing; it certainly does not rule out the possibility that children learn to smile through some kind of behaviour shaping, if, for example, they find that smiling prolongs the duration of social play. Similarly, it is quite easy to see how anger expressions might be reinforced, if a child finds that such expressions lead to the cessation of a behaviour the child finds undesirable. Hence Eibl-Eibesfeldt's observations would seem to rule out only the possibility of learning expressive behaviours through auditory and visual communication, not the possibility of learning as such.

Studies of infants who have not been born handicapped have shown that the facial musculature is fully formed and functional at birth. Oster and Ekman (1977), using Ekman and Friesen's FACS, have shown that all but one of the discrete facial muscle actions visible in the adult can be identified in new-born infants, both full-term and premature. Evidence for organization and temporal patterning in expressive movements such as smiling, brow knitting and pouting has also been found. Neonatal smiles are called endogenous or spontaneous because they occur in the absence of known external stimulation, most commonly during sleep (Sroufe and Waters, 1976); they occur primarily during rapid eye movement sleep and seem to reflect periodic fluctuations in central nervous system activity (Ekman and Oster, 1979). Steiner (1974) has described facial expressions in neonates resembling the adult expression of disgust; he describes how the infants in response to sour tastes pursed their lips, and in response to bitter tastes created an arch-like mouth opening with the mouth angles depressed and the central part of the upper lip elevated. All this developmental evidence suggests that infants are born with the capacity both to fire individual muscles in the same way as an adult, and to organize those muscles in terms of particular facial expressions. But this does not prove the association of particular facial expressions with particular emotions is innate; although Steiner, for example, has described facial expressions of disgust in neonates in response to unpleasant tastes, this does not explain how the facial expression of disgust may be produced in response to a wide range of unpleasant situations. As Birdwhistell (1971) has observed, smiling can be called a universal gesture if we are speaking at the articulatory level of description; but this does not mean that it is innately associated with the emotion of happiness, nor that it has a universal meaning.

Thus, although the evidence is consistent with the hypothesis that certain facial expressions of emotion are innate, it is by no means conclusive. Nevertheless Ekman (1972) has put forward what he calls a neuro-cultural model of emotional expression in which he attempts to reconcile what he assumes to be the innate and learned aspects of emotional expression. From the existence of cultural universals in facial expression, he assumes the existence of at least six fundamental emotions with innate expressions. He also argues that it is possible to modify these innate expressions by the learning of what he calls display rules; display rules refer to norms governing the expression of emotion in different social contexts. Ekman distinguishes four ways in which an emotional expression can be modified—through weakening its intensity (attenuation), through exaggerating its intensity (amplification), through hiding emotion by adopting a neutral face (concealment) and through showing a different expression from the emotion which is being experienced (substitution). Ekman (1977) also distinguishes between what he calls cultural display rules and personal display rules, which may sometimes conflict with one another. For example, a woman might have the personal display rule never to show feelings of distress which, depending upon her culture, could put her in conflict in situations (e.g. a funeral) where expressions of distress might be expected of her.

An experiment carried out by Ekman on cross-cultural differences illustrates the use of the model quite neatly. Ekman, Friesen and Malmstrom (1970) (reported in Ekman, Friesen and Ellsworth, 1972, pp. 163–166) showed two films to Japanese and American subjects. One film was intended to be stressful, the other to be neutral; subjects watched the film alone, and were videotaped while doing so without their knowledge. Both groups of subjects differed in their response to the neutral and stress films, while the frequencies of expressions associated with the six fundamental emotions correlated positively between groups at a statistically significant level. After the stress film, a member of each subject's own culture entered the room and conducted an interview about the experience. Japanese subjects appeared to engage in concealment by showing happy faces when interviewed by Japanese interviewers, whereas the Americans typically did not conceal signs of negative feelings when they talked to an American interviewer. The results of this experiment are certainly consistent with informal accounts of Japanese culture where there is said to be a taboo governing the expression of negative emotions in public. At the same time, it suggests that the innate facial expressions of emotion may have been displayed when the subjects watched the films alone, but that the cultural differences occurred when the subjects were in the presence of another member of their own culture and observed the appropriate display rules.

A cross-cultural study of decoding by Shimoda, Argyle and Bitti (1978) also supports the interactionist model proposed by Ekman. Shimoda, Argyle and Bitti criticized the majority of cross-cultural studies of decoding for a failure to vary the culture of the encoder as well as that of the decoder. They asked English, Italian and Japanese students to pose expressions in front of a camera for eight emotions (surprised, depressed, sad, disgusted, friendly, happy, anxious, angry, afraid) and for four interpersonal attitudes (superior, submissive, friendly and hostile); each encoder acted out each expression while counting 1 to 15 in his own language. On the basis of the quality of the recordings, two males from each of the three cultural groups were selected, and other students from each nationality were then asked to judge which emotion was being posed. Results showed that for the judgements of emotion, observers were able to recognize emotions from other cultures at a level significantly above what would be excepted by chance, with the exception only of Italians judging Japanese expressions. The results also showed that the Japanese expressed emotions and attitudes significantly less clearly than the other two cultures, since the subjects from all three cultures (including the Japanese) did significantly worse when judging Japanese expressions. When the different emotions and attitudes were compared with one another, it was found that the Japanese expressed happiness and friendliness more clearly than any other emotions or attitudes. Thus the results of this study supported both the hypothesis that there are culturally universal patterns of facial expression (which can be decoded at a level significantly above chance by members of other cultures), and that there are cultural display rules which result in the Japanese expressing most emotions and attitudes less clearly than the English and Italians.

Ekman and Friesen (1975) have also described in detail the particular facial expressions they believe are associated with each of the six fundamental emotions. These descriptions stem both from their own observations and from the observations of others (e.g. Darwin, 1872; Huber, 1931; Plutchik, 1962; Tomkins, 1962, 1963). They have been systematized in what Ekman and Friesen call a facial atlas, which depicts photographically each of the facial expressions of emotion which they consider to be universal (Ekman and Friesen, in preparation). To test the validity of the descriptions in this atlas, Ekman and

Friesen (1975) describe four studies which they have carried out. For example, in the study referred to earlier comparing the expressions of Japanese and American subjects (Ekman, Friesen and Malmstrom, 1970; reported in Ekman, Friesen and Ellsworth, 1972, pp. 163–166) they found that the facial atlas could successfully discriminate between which films the subjects had been watching (stressful or pleasant), regardless of whether the subjects were American or Japanese.

Of course this experiment does not show whether the atlas correctly depicts the facial appearance of each of the six emotional expressions; it only demonstrates the validity of the atlas in distinguishing between pleasant and unpleasant emotions. However, psychophysiological research on emotion has shown that there are markedly different patterns of heart-rate acceleration and deceleration with the emotions of surprise and disgust. If the atlas is correct in discriminating between facial expressions of surprise and disgust, then there should be different patterns of heart rate associated with each facial expression; heart-rate measures obtained from the study of American and Japanese subjects showed that was in fact the case.

Evidence that the other emotions (happiness, sadness, anger, fear) are encoded as Ekman and Friesen maintain comes from a study of posed emotions. Dental and nursing students were asked to pose each of the six emotions, and from the atlas it was possible to predict successfully which emotion the students had been attempting to portray. This was corroborated by a decoding study which showed that the atlas could successfully predict the emotions perceived by three observers (who were technicians). Ekman and Friesen also mention that the Swedish anatomist Hjortsjö (1970), working independently, has produced descriptions of emotional expressions which are virtually identical to those outlined in their own facial atlas. Thus, taking their four experiments together, and in conjunction with the independent descriptions of the same expressions by Hjortsjö, they argue that they have reasonable evidence for arguing that the atlas contains a valid description of the facial expressions which encode six fundamental emotions.

In making these descriptions, Ekman and Friesen distinguish three main areas of the face which are capable of independent movement: the eyebrows and forehead; the eyes, eyelids and root of the nose; and the lower face (cheeks, mouth, most of the nose and chin). There follows a description of the facial expression they consider to be associated with each emotion, together with illustrative line drawings based on the descriptions and photographs provided by Ekman and Friesen (1975). Thus in surprise, for example, they argue that there is a distinctive expression associated with each of the three main areas of the face. The eyebrows are raised so that they are curved and high, stretching the skin below the brow and creating horizontal wrinkles across the forehead. The eyes are opened wide by raising the upper lid, and drawing down the lower lid, revealing the sclera (white of the eye) above the iris, and often below as well. The jaw drops open, parting the lips and the teeth, but there is no tension or stretching of the mouth (see Figure 3).

In fear (see Figure 4), the eyebrows are also raised as in surprise, but in

30

Figure 3. Surprise (Based on a photograph in P. Ekman and W. V. Friesen (1975), *Unmasking the Face*, Englewood Cliffs, New Jersey: Prentice-Hall. Reproduced by permission)

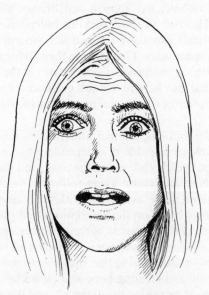

Figure 4. Fear. (Based on a photograph in P. Ekman and W. V. Friesen (1975), *Unmasking the Face*, Englewood Cliffs, New Jersey: Prentice-Hall. Reproduced by permission)

Figure 5. Disgust. (Based on a photograph in P. Ekman and W. V. Friesen (1975), *Unmasking the Face*, Englewood Cliffs, New Jersey: Prentice-Hall. Reproduced by permission)

addition they are drawn together so that the inner corners of the brow are closer together than in surprise, giving a more straightened appearance to the outer corners of the eyebrow; there are usually horizontal wrinkles across the forehead, but typically they do not run across the entire forehead as in surprise. In both fear and surprise the upper lid is raised, exposing the sclera, but in fear the lower eyelid is typically tense and raised. As in surprise, the mouth is open, but the lips are not relaxed as in surprise; they may be either slightly tensed and drawn back, or stretched and drawn back. Although fear and surprise differ in a number of important ways, there are also some important similarities, so that it is perhaps not surprising that these should be the two emotions which were not successfully discriminated in Ekman and Friesen's (1971) study in New Guinea.

Disgust (see Figure 5), Ekman and Friesen maintain, is displayed primarily in the lower face and the lower eyelids. The upper lip is raised, while the lower lip is also raised and pushed up to the upper lip, or is lowered and slightly protruding. The nose is wrinkled, and the cheeks are raised. Lines show below the lower eyelids, and the lids are pushed up but not tense. Ekman and Friesen also maintain that the eyebrows are lowered in disgust, thus lowering the eyelids, but Ekman (1979b) has subsequently withdrawn this observation.

Anger (see Figure 6) is manifested in all three main areas of the face, and Ekman and Friesen maintain that the expression will be ambiguous unless it is displayed in all three areas. In anger, the eyebrows are lowered and drawn

32

Figure 6. Anger. (Based on photographs in P. Ekman and W. V. Friesen (1975), *Unmasking the Face*, Englewood Cliffs, New Jersey: Prentice-Hall. Reproduced by permission)

Figure 7. Happiness. (Based on a photograph in P. Ekman and W. V. Friesen
(1975), *Unmasking the Face*, Englewood
Cliffs, New Jersey: Prentice-Hall. Reproduced by permission)

together, and vertical lines may appear between the eyebrows. Both eyelids are
tense; the upper eyelids may be lowered by the actions of the eyebrows, while
the lower lids may be raised. The eyes have a hard stare and may have a bulging
appearance. The nostrils may be dilated, but this is not essential to the anger
facial expression, and may also occur in sadness. The lips take one of two basic
positions; they are either pressed firmly together, with the corners straight or
down, or open, tensed in a squarish shape as if shouting.

Happiness (see Figure 7), Ekman and Friesen maintain is displayed primarily
in the lower face and lower eyelids. The corners of the lips are drawn back and
up, and the mouth may be parted with the teeth exposed. Wrinkles running
from the nose to the outer edge beyond the lip corners (the naso-labial folds)
occur partly as a result of pulling the corners of the lips back and up; the
cheeks also become raised when there is a pronounced smile or grin. Wrinkling
occurs below the lower eyelids, which may be raised but not tense. 'Crow's-feet'
wrinkling is also sometimes formed at the outer corners of the eyes. The more
extreme the smile or grin, the more pronounced will be the naso-labial folds,
the raising of the cheeks, the crow's feet and the lines under the eyes. With a
wide-mouth grin, the cheeks may be lifted far enough actually to narrow the eyes.

In sadness (see Figure 8), there is a distinctive appearance in each of the
three facial areas. The inner corners of the eyebrows are raised and may be
drawn together, resulting in the skin below the eyebrows forming the shape of

34

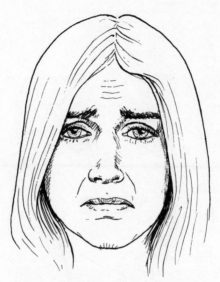

Figure 8. Sadness. (Based on a photograph in P. Ekman and W. V. Friesen
(1975), *Unmasking* the Face, Englewood
Cliffs, New Jersey: Prentice-Hall. Reproduced by permission)

a triangle; the lower eyelids may also appear raised. The corners of the lips
are drawn down, or the lips appear to tremble.

There has recently been some controversy with regard to whether emotions
are expressed more intensely on the left than on the right side of the face.
Sackeim and Gur (1978) and Sackeim, Gur and Saucy (1978) tested this
hypothesis by preparing special photographs from those presented by Ekman
and Friesen (1975). The photographs were split down the middle and re-
photographed using a mirror image of each half of the face, so that left-side
and right-side composite faces were constructed (see Figure 9). In all, 70
photographs of 14 encoders were selected to depict the six fundamental emotions
described by Ekman and Friesen with the inclusion also of a neutral facial
expression; the faces were presented to American male and female students in
the originals and in left- and right-side composites. The students rated the
photographs for the emotions depicted and for the intensity of emotional
expression. The results showed that left-side composite photographs were judged
as significantly more intense for all the emotions except happiness; there were
no significant interactions with the sex of the encoder.

Ekman (1980) has criticised these findings on the grounds that most of the
photographs used were of deliberate facial movements; in the only case where
the original photographs were of spontaneous facial expressions (that of
happiness), no significant effect for asymmetry was found. Ekman, Hager and
Friesen (1981) carried out a study in which children were asked to imitate
actions shown to them on a television screen; their imitations of smiles were

35

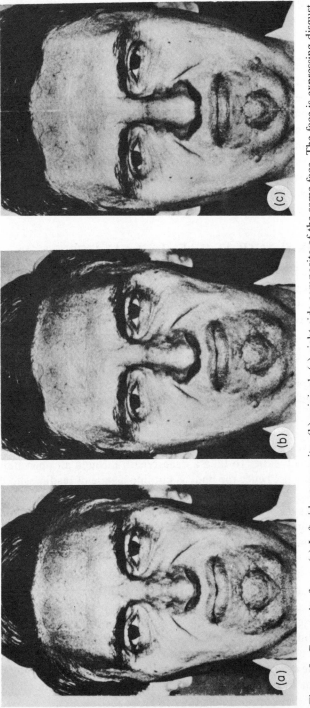

Figure 9. Composite faces. (a) Left-side composite; (b) original; (c) right-side composite of the same face. The face is expressing disgust. (Reprinted by permission from H. A. Sackeim, R. C. Gur and M. C. Saucy (1978) Emotions are expressed more intensely on the left side of the face. *Science*, **202**, 434–436. Copyright 1983 by the American Association for the Advancement of Science)

compared to spontaneous smiles they showed in reaction to jokes by the experimenter, and it was found that when scored with FACS, significantly more of the deliberate smiles were asymmetrical. In a second study reported in that same paper, the spontaneous smiles of adult females watching films were scored for asymmetry using FACS, and only 4 per cent of 110 smiles were found to be asymmetrical. Sackeim and Gur (1980) replied to these criticisms by pointing out that they never maintained that asymmetry was a feature of spontaneous facial expressions, stating instead (Sackeim, Gur and Saucy, 1978, p. 435) that, 'Whether or not the same asymmetry in intensity of expression would be obtained with more spontaneously occurring emotional expressions is a matter for future investigation'. Nevertheless, the discrepancy in asymmetry between deliberate and spontaneous expressions is in itself interesting, and suggests the intriguing possibility that asymmetry may be an important cue indicating whether an emotional expression is deliberate or spontaneous.

THE FUNCTIONS OF EMOTIONAL EXPRESSION

If we accept the hypothesis that certain facial expressions of emotion are innate, what functions would such cues serve? It is of course possible that they could have evolved purely as a means of communication, but in fact three other types of explanation have been proposed, which are reviewed below.

1. As Adaptive Responses

One type of explanation is that facial expressions evolved as part of the actions necessary for life, and this view can be traced directly to the work of Darwin (1872). Thus in surprise, for example, Darwin suggested that the eyebrows are raised because it is the quickest way of facilitating sight (rather than by just widening the eyelids, which he maintained takes longer), and that the jaw drops because it is much easier to take a deep breath through an open mouth than through the nostrils; hence the body is put into a state of readiness to deal with the unexpected. Ekman (1979b) is sceptical about the hypothesis that eyebrow raising facilitates the speed of the upper eyelid action, but does acknowledge that eyebrow raising increases the visual field and so facilitates visual scanning. Darwin also argued that in fear, the eyes and mouth are similarly opened wide to put the body in a state of readiness to deal with the object of fear. It is not clear, however, what function is served by the tense, raised lower eyelids, or the tense, stretched-back mouth which Ekman and Friesen describe, unless the facial expression of fear is seen as a kind of compromise between the need to put the body into a state of readiness and the need to protect the body from the object of fear (by shielding the mouth and eyes).

The movements of the lips in disgust are naturally related to expelling offensive matter from the mouth; wrinkling the nose, raising the cheeks, raising the lower eyelids, and the lines which occur below the lower eyelids can all be seen as by-products of these lip movements.

In anger, Ekman and Friesen describe how the eyebrows are lowered and drawn together, vertical lines may appear between the eyebrows, and the eyelids may be narrowed and tense. Darwin proposed a whole range of explanations for the act of frowning, only two of which Ekman (1979b) considers valid, namely, that frowning reduces the amount of light coming into the eyes and also may help to protect the eyeballs from the effects of blows. In anger the nostrils may also be dilated, which Darwin interpreted as facilitating breathing, since anger increases the rate of respiration. Of the two basic mouth positions associated with anger, Darwin interpreted the baring of the teeth as a vestigial remnant of preparing to bite and attack. Pressing the lips together Ekman (1972) considers to be part of an adaptive sequence in which the tight pressure of the lips helps to force air back towards the lungs to prevent rupture of the capillaries during exertion.

In sadness, Darwin argues that the raising of the inner corners of the eyebrows and the depressed corners of the mouth are movements which occur preparatory to crying, and he quotes a number of observers who reported seeing these particular movements just before a person burst into tears. The drawing up of the inner corners of the eyelids described by Ekman and Friesen would be a consequence of raising the inner corners of the eyebrows.

Happiness seems to present the greatest problem for explanations of facial expressions in terms of their adaptive value. The naso-labial folds, raising the cheeks, wrinkles below the lower eyelids and crow's feet wrinkling at the outer corners of the eyes can all be seen as a consequence of the intensity of smiling, but it is the function of smiling itself which is the difficulty. Darwin argued that laughter preceded smiling in human phylogeny, the smile being a subdued version of the laugh. Van Hooff (1972) has argued from comparative studies with non-human primates that laughter and smiling have a different phylogenetic development, drawing attention to the similarity on the one hand between smiling and what he calls the silent bared-teeth display in non-human primates, and on the other hand between laughter and what he calls the relaxed open-mouth display in non-human primates. But neither of these explanations delineate what is the adaptive function of smiling. Contemporary attachment theorists (e.g. Bowlby, 1958, 1969) have argued that smiling and crying evolved essentially as forms of communication, crying to secure the proximity of the caretaker, and smiling to retain that proximity. This would suggest that whereas the facial expressions of surprise, fear, disgust and anger have evolved as part of the actions necessary for life, the facial expressions of happiness and sadness have evolved primarily as a system of communication.

2. Regulation of Emotion

A second view of the functions of emotional expression is concerned with the regulation of emotion. Darwin maintained that the free expression of emotion ('by outward signs') intensifies it, while suppression of emotional expression weakens or 'softens' it. Subsequently, the opposite view has become prevalent, based on the belief that expression reduces the strength of emotion. The most famous exponent of this view is Freud (1946/1921) who maintained that verbal, bodily and physiological responses are alternative channels for releasing emotional energy; if one channel is blocked, the response through the others should increase in intensity. Consistent with this view, a number of studies have found significant negative correlations between overt facial expressions of emotion and physiological responsiveness. Typically, such studies have involved exposing an encoder to an emotionally arousing event while a decoder judges from his expression what event he is observing; the sender's heart rate or skin conductance are both continuously monitored during the stimulus presentation (e.g. Lanzetta and Kleck, 1970; Buck et al., 1972). The results of these studies consistently indicate that decoders are most accurate with the least physiologically aroused encoders, and least accurate with the most physiologically aroused encoders. One problem with these designs is that the assessment of overt expression is dependent on the measure of decoding accuracy, and on the assumption that this reflects expressiveness. More recently, however, studies have included direct observations of the amount of facial expressiveness, and have still found significant negative correlations with physiological arousal (Buck, 1977; Notarius and Levenson, 1979). A second problem, as Tourangeau and Ellsworth (1979) have pointed out, is that all studies to date have used between-subject rather than within-subject comparisons. Thus what has been demonstrated is that a highly physiologically aroused person will show little facial expressiveness; what still needs to be demonstrated is that a person in an emotionally arousing situation will show less physiological arousal after overt facial expression than before, if the drive-reduction hypothesis of facial expression is valid. Nevertheless, the evidence at present is at least consistent with the view that facial expression reduces the intensity of emotion; it provides no support for Darwin's view that facial expression increases the intensity of emotion.

3. The Experience of Emotion

In contrast to the regulatory view of the facial expression of emotion, there is the belief that facial expressions influence or even determine the experience of emotion. This specific hypothesis was originally proposed by Tomkins (1962), and subsequently elaborated by Gelhorn (1964) and Izard (1971, 1977). In the strongest version of this hypothesis, facial responses play the same critical role in the experience of emotion as that played by visceral changes in the old James–Lange theory of emotion (James, 1890; Lange, 1885). In the James–Lange theory, the experience of emotion is, for example, the experience of rapid breathing or a pounding heart; in Tomkins' view, the experience of emotion stems from proprioceptive feedback from movements of the facial musculature. The James–Lange theory of emotion was discredited by Cannon (1927), who showed in animal experiments that total separation of the viscera does not alter emotional behaviour. He also maintained that the viscera are too slow and insensitive to be a source of emotional feeling, that the same visceral changes occur in different emotional and non-emotional states and that artificial induction of the visceral changes typical of emotions does not produce emotional experience. But most of these arguments are not relevant to the hypothesis that facial expression is responsible for the experience of emotion. Unlike the viscera, facial responses are extremely rapid; they are also sufficiently differentiated to allow for the experience of different emotions, and of course experiments in which the viscera are separated from the central nervous system are not relevant to a discussion of the role of facial expression in emotional experience. Izard (1977) has in fact argued that changes in the facial musculature are responsible for the experience of distinctive emotions, but may be less critical in sustaining emotion; in this context visceral changes may be more important for the experience of emotional intensity.

Attempts to test the hypothesized role of facial expression in emotional experience have relied essentially on experiments in which subjects are asked voluntarily to adopt particular facial expressions. Laird (1974) asked American students to tense and relax various patterns of muscles into a smile and a frown, telling them that this was in order to record facial muscle activity. They were shown a series of pictures, and asked to rate their responses on a number of measures of emotion. Significant effects of the manipulated facial expressions were found on self-reports of aggression, elation and surgency; judgements of the pictures were also affected, cartoons being rated as funnier when viewed in the smiling condition. But Tourangeau and Ellsworth (1979) carried out a similar study which failed to replicate Laird's findings. They arranged for American students to watch films intended to evoke fear, sadness or no emotion. Subjects were instructed to hold their facial muscles in the positions characteristic of sadness, fear or what was described as an 'effortful but non-emotional grimace'; in the fourth condition, subjects received no specific facial instructions. Subjects were led to believe that the experiment concerned subliminal perception, and that the facial positions were necessary to prevent physiological recording artefacts. The films produced powerful effects on reported emotions, but the correlations between the manipulations of facial expression and reported emotions were negligible.

Tourangeau and Ellsworth's experiment has in fact been heavily criticized by other researchers. Tomkins (1981) and Izard (1981) criticize the experiment on the grounds that asking a person to hold a particular facial expression for two minutes does not necessarily correspond to naturally occurring facial expressions, which may take place in milliseconds. Hager and Ekman (1981) criticize the experiment on the grounds that it is not even valid in its own terms. For example, to create a fear expression the authors instructed the subjects to pull the corners of the mouth down and back; Hager and Ekman maintain that pulling the lips down is characteristic of sad expressions, and that these instructions would have had the effect of contracting the triangularis muscle rather than the risorius, which they maintain is appropriate for fear. Hager and Ekman also maintain that Tourangeau and Ellsworth's instructions could not have prevented subjects contracting other facial muscles which might have influenced their emotional experience.

Ellsworth and Tourangeau (1981) have replied to their critics by insisting that their subjects did produce the appropriate facial expressions; for example, they mention that if they left the word 'down' out of the fear instructions, then subjects tended to lift the corners of their mouths into a smile. Ellsworth and Tourangeau maintain that their subjects were given continuous feedback from the experimenter until the expressions were correct. They also maintain that their experiment does provide a test of the effect of voluntary facial expressions on emotional experience, and suggests a major qualification of the hypothesized functions of facial expression in emotional experience.

This claim is, however, highly debatable and is explicitly rejected by Tomkins (1981) and Izard (1981). Izard (1977), for example, maintained that a lack of correspondence between visible facial expressions and a person's emotional experience would not necessarily refute the hypothesis. He cites a study by Schwartz *et al.* (1973), who asked female subjects to visualize emotion-arousing situations while the activity of their facial muscles was recorded through an electromyograph from miniature electrodes placed on the frontalis, depressor, anguli oris and masseter muscles. The imagery they were asked to produce was for sadness, happiness and anger, and they were also asked to think about a typical day as an emotionally neutral control condition. Schwartz *et al.* found that muscular activity typically preceded any observable facial movements, and that the electromyograph reliably discriminated between all four conditions even when no facial movements were observable. Hence, if subjects are asked voluntarily to assume certain facial expressions, and those expressions show no influence on reported emotion, this does not disprove the hypothesis that facial expression is responsible for emotional experience; it may simply be the case that the subjects' experience of emotion is influenced by other changes in the facial musculature which are not visible. Consequently the hypothesis that facial expression is responsible for the experience of emotion can neither be said to have been proved or disproved; a more powerful test of the hypothesis requires an experimental design which is not dependent upon the use of voluntary facial expressions.

THE GENERALITY OF THE INNATE HYPOTHESIS OF EMOTIONAL EXPRESSION

It has thus been hypothesized that six facial expressions of emotion are innate, and four hypotheses for the evolution of such innate expressions have been discussed, although the evidence in respect of these hypotheses can scarcely be said to be definitive. A second issue in respect of the innate hypothesis of emotional expression concerns its generality, and this can be examined in three main ways, namely, whether the innate hypothesis should be confined to the six emotions discussed by Ekman, whether it should be confined to facial expressions alone and whether it should be restricted to encoding or can be extended to include the decoding of emotional expressions.

1. The Number of Innate Facial Expressions of Emotion

Ekman has hypothesized that there are six fundamental emotions which are associated with innate facial expressions of emotion (happiness, sadness, fear, disgust, anger and surprise). Other researchers have argued that more emotions should be added to this list. Interest and shame have been included by Tomkins (1962) and Izard and Tomkins (1966), and Izard has subsequently added contempt (Izard, 1971) and guilt (Izard, 1977).

Izard (1971) described a series of cross-cultural studies which have led to the inclusion of these additional emotions. He presented photographs to male and female university students from America, Japan and six European countries, asking them to choose an appropriate emotion label from a list of eight emotions which Izard at that time considered to be fundamental (interest–excitement, enjoyment–joy, disgust–contempt, anger–rage, shame–humiliation, surprise–startle, distress–anguish and fear–terror). (He also presented this task to African students, but since they did not receive the task in their own native language, they are excluded from this discussion.) The photographs selected were those which had achieved at least 70 per cent agreement between judgements of emotion category and the emotions the photographs were intended to depict in a pilot study with American students. Izard's results showed an average agreement across all cultures of 78 per cent between choice of emotion category and the emotions the photographs were intended to depict, whereas of course only $12\frac{1}{2}$ per cent agreement would be expected by chance.

Izard describes what he considers to be the facial expressions associated with interest–excitement and shame–humiliation. In interest, he maintains that the eyebrows may be raised, the lips parted and the jaw slightly dropped. The students showed a high level of agreement in judging the photographs intended to convey interest–excitement, the different groups ranging from 66 to 84.5 per cent agreement in their choice of this emotion category for these photographs. In shame, Izard maintains that the eyebrows are lowered, producing vertical wrinkles on the forehead, while the upper and lower eyelids may also be lowered. The lips may be drawn in, the corners of the mouth depressed; the lower lip may either protrude slightly, or be tucked between the teeth. Izard reports levels of agreement in judging the photographs intended to convey shame ranging mostly between 70 per cent and 77.2 per cent between the different groups in their choice of this emotion category, with the exception only of the English students (59.5 per cent) and the Japanese (41.2 per cent).

The results from Izard's pilot studies also suggested that disgust and contempt could be discriminated as separate emotions, so Izard modified the original picture series to include photographs selected to represent disgust–revulsion and contempt–scorn as separate categories. He showed this revised series to

42

male and female students from America, Turkey, India and Japan. The results from these new categories showed wide disparities in judgements, ranging from 86 per cent to 21 per cent agreement between cultures in their choice of the disgust–revulsion category for the photographs intended to convey that emotion, and ranging from 92 per cent to 7 per cent agreement between cultures in their choice of the contempt–scorn category for the photographs intended to depict that emotion. Izard has taken these findings as evidence to suggest that disgust and contempt may be considered as separate fundamental emotions. In contempt, he maintains that one eyebrow may be raised slightly higher than the other, and the eyes may be narrowed by lowering the upper eyelids and raising the lower eyelids. The corners of the mouth may be depressed, the lower lip raised (slightly protruding) and one side of the upper lip may be raised in a sneer. The cheeks are drawn down by the movement of the mouth, and the nostrils may be flared outward. More recently, Izard (1977) has argued that guilt should be included as a tenth fundamental emotion. However, he appears to have no cross-cultural data on associated facial expressions to support this, commenting only that in guilt a person's face may take on a heavy look.

In the absence of a detailed description of the facial expression of guilt and supporting cross-cultural evidence, there seems to be no real reason why this should be considered as a fundamental emotion. The evidence Izard (1971) presents for supporting a distinction between disgust and contempt is not very convincing, in view of the wide disparities in agreement in judging these emotions in his revised version of the original picture series. The evidence for interest and shame as two additional emotions is rather more convincing in view of the higher levels of agreement achieved in Izard's cross-cultural data, but Ekman

Figure 10. The Izard photographs of shame (left) and interest (right). (Reprinted by permission from C. E. Izard (1971), *The Face of Emotion.* New York: Appleton-Century-Crofts)

and Oster (1979) have criticized these findings, arguing that subjects' perceptions may have been affected by the head positions in these photographs rather than by the facial expressions. Certainly in the photographs reproduced by Izard (1971) (see Figure 10), shame is depicted with the head turned away from the camera, and interest with the head tilted to one side, which Hass (1970) from some informal cross-cultural observations has argued is associated with interest. In the light of these criticisms, it appears that the six facial expressions described by Ekman and Friesen (1975) are those which are most firmly based on the evidence available.

2. Other Bodily Cues and the Innate Hypothesis of Emotional Expression

(i) Blushing

The strongest argument for considering shame as an innate fundamental emotion comes in fact not from studies of the facial musculature but from the phenomenon of blushing. Blushing is apparently caused by an autonomic nervous system reaction which results in inhibition of the normal tonic and contracting activities of the face, allowing these vessels to increase with blood; the increased blood flow results in the flushed red appearance of the face (Izard, 1977). Although most commonly occurring in the face. Darwin (1872) observed that blushing may occur in other parts of the body as well. Darwin maintained that blushing occurs as a result of the emotion of shame, that it does not occur in non-humans and that it is innate.

(ii) Pupil Size

Pupil size is also an autonomic response, and in Chapter 1 it was argued that pupil size encodes information about degree of emotional arousal, regardless of whether the affect is positive or negative; hence dilated pupils might encode information about happiness, but they might also encode information about fear or anger. Some evidence was reviewed in Chapter 1 suggesting that dilated pupils are also decoded as conveying information about degree of emotional arousal. If dilated pupils communicate information only about intensity of emotional arousal, they are clearly subsidiary to facial expression, which appears to convey information about different categories of emotion.

(iii) Gaze

Research on the encoding of emotion through gaze has been relatively scanty. There have been no systematic cross-cultural studies of the kind carried out on facial expression to suggest that there are universal patterns of gaze associated with particular emotions. Nevertheless, Darwin's view that facial expressions of emotion evolved as part of the actions necessary for life does imply that certain patterns of gaze might innately encode particular emotions. For example, the notion that in surprise the eyebrows are raised to facilitate visual scanning suggests that the person gazes at the object of surprise. Similarly, since disgust is an emotion of rejection, one might expect people instinctively to avert their gaze from the object of disgust. In anger, one might expect people to gaze at the object of their rage. It is less clear, however, what patterns of gaze might be expected for the other basic emotions. Raising the eyebrows in fear to facilitate visual scanning might lead the person to gaze at the source of fear or to seek for means of escape. Since Darwin saw the facial expressions of happiness and sadness as partial expressions of laughing and crying it is not clear what gaze patterns might be expected for these emotions.

Of the experimental studies of gaze and emotion which have been carried out, one reasonably well-established finding is an association between sadness and gaze aversion. Fromme and Schmidt (1972) asked male American students to role play different emotions to a male experimenter, and found greatly reduced interpersonal gaze for sorrow in comparison to fear, anger and a neutral condition. Exline *et al.* (1968) asked American female schizophrenic patients and members of psychiatric staff to tell an interviewer of experiences which had made them sad, happy and angry. A silent film of their performance was shown to American students, who were asked to judge which story was being told; there were no significant differences in the way that patients and staff were judged, but stories with a higher proportion of downcast glances were judged significantly more successfully by the students as conveying sorrow. Thus, evidence from both encoding and decoding studies does suggest for an American sample that reduced gaze communicates sadness.

In the Fromme and Schmidt study, no significant differences in the encoding of gaze were found between the fear, anger and neutral conditions, which all had about twice the proportion of interpersonal gaze associated with sadness. This is rather surprising in view of a decoding study carried out by Cook and Smith (1975). They arranged for confederates of the experimenter to talk to British students, and to vary their gaze according to three conditions—normal, continuous or averted gaze. Each subject was asked to give a free description of the confederate they met in the interview, and it was found that confederates with averted gaze were perceived as more fearful than those with continuous gaze. Nevertheless, in another encoding study carried out by Hobson *et al.* (1973), no association was found between anxiety and reduced gaze duration. In one experiment, Hobson *et al.* arranged for British students each to talk to a confederate for two two-minute sessions; between each session, subjects were given feedback, and told they were doing either very badly, or very well or given neutral feedback. The negative feedback condition was intended to arouse anxiety, and these subjects were in fact significantly more anxious after the break as indicated by their responses to a questionnaire; they also made significantly more speech errors (commonly accepted as indicative of anxiety), but did not show shorter gaze duration than the other two groups. In a second experiment, Hobson *et al.* arranged for British students with high and low scores on the Taylor Manifest Anxiety Scale each to converse with a confederat of the experimenter, but found no significant differences in gaze duration between the two groups. It is of course always possible that better or differently designed encoding studies might show a relationship between gaze aversion and fear or anxiety; but in the light of the present evidence it would appear that Cook and Smith's finding that British students perceive averted gaze as conveying fearfulness may be an example of a decoding error.

Kimble and Olszewski (1980) carried out an experiment in which American female students were asked to learn three scripts (intended to convey liking, anger or to be neutral) and to repeat the scripts from memory to a camera; half were asked to recite the message with weak emotion, the other half with strong emotion. Results showed a significant effect for intensity, with longer gaze duration in the high-intensity condition, irrespective of the nature of the emotion.

Of the four emotions considered to be fundamental by Izard in addition to those discussed by Ekman and Friesen, three, Izard (1977) maintains, are accompanied by distinctive patterns of gaze. Interest, Izard affirms, is accompanied by gaze towards the person or object of interest, and he cites some informal cross-cultural observations of Hass (1970) in support of this. Shame and guilt, Izard maintains, are accompanied by averted gaze, but he gives no evidence in support of these observations.

It can thus be seen that emotion and gaze has not been as intensively investigated as emotion and facial expression. Although Darwin's explanation of the facial expressions of emotion would suggest that there may be distinctive patterns of gaze innately associated with different emotions, there is no direct evidence in support of this hypothesis. Even if such patterns of gaze were associated with each emotion, they could do no more than communicate the intensity of emotion, the category of emotion still being conveyed by facial expression. The way intensity might be conveyed would depend on the particular emotion; from the evidence reviewed above, one might expect a sad face to look sadder with downcast gaze, but an angry face to look angrier with direct gaze. But just as the interaction of pupil size with facial expression in the judgement of emotion has never been systematically investigated, the same is also true of facial expression and gaze. Nevertheless, the one decoding study in which the relative importance of facial expression and gaze was investigated did produce results broadly consistent with the argument outlined above. Graham and Argyle (1975a) arranged for British students to rate on 20 rating scales experimental confederates who had been asked to pose all four possible combinations of two facial expressions (frowning or smiling) and two gaze patterns (10 per cent or 90 per cent looking). The facial expressions primarily affected rating scales which were interpreted in terms of an evaluative/liking dimension (e.g. smiling was perceived as significantly more agreeable, warm and friendly). Gaze affected rating scales which were interpreted in terms of a dimension of potency; 90 per cent gaze was perceived as significantly more strong, aggressive and dominant. Only 2 out of the 20 scales were significantly

acial expression and gaze, and these were ratings of sociability
.h high gaze and smiling were perceived as more sociable and
.ham and Argyle argue that these findings are broadly consistent
.hat facial expression conveys information about the nature of
about its intensity.

(iv) Posture and Gesture

Just as gaze and pupil size have been hypothesized to convey information primarily about intensity of emotion, so too has bodily posture (Ekman, 1965). Ekman in fact carried out three studies on data which were obtained from structured interviews with a neutral phase, a stress phase in which the interviewer attacked and criticized the interviewee's choice of occupation, competence and motivation, and finally a catharsis phase in which the interviewer explained the purpose of the experiment and apologized for his earlier hostility.

In the first study, Ekman (1964) had still photographs taken of different phases of the interview, which were shown in pairs to American students together with short written speech extracts from the stress and catharsis phases; the students' task was to pick the photograph which matched the sample of speech. Ekman found that the students reached a significantly greater level of accuracy when shown pictures of the face alone than when shown pictures of the body alone.

Ekman (1965) then carried out another experiment comparing judgements from the face and the body. In this study, three separate groups of American students each viewed one version of the stimulus material—the face, the body or the whole person. All the photographs were rated on Schlosberg's (1954) dimensions of emotion for pleasantness/unpleasantness and sleep/tension. Ekman hypothesized that the face carries information primarily about what emotion is being experienced, the body carries information about its intensity. Thus he predicted that there would be higher agreement amongst judges on ratings of pleasantness/unpleasantness when the face was judged, but higher agreement on ratings of sleep/tension when the body was judged; this prediction was confirmed. Ekman also correlated judgements of the face and body with judgements of the whole person, and found significant positive correlations between judgements of the face and the whole person on ratings of pleasantness/unpleasantness and sleep/tension, whereas there were significant positive correlations between ratings of the body and the whole person only on judgements of sleep/tension. Thus these results suggested both that people appear to make their judgements of emotion more on the basis of the face than the body, and that the face is perceived as carrying information primarily about what emotion is being experienced, whereas the body is perceived as conveying information about the intensity of emotion.

Finally, Ekman and Friesen (1967) hypothesized that judges who view the face alone will show more agreement than judges who view the body alone when attempting to identify the nature of the emotion. The photographs were rated by American students in terms of surprise, happiness, fear, anger, disgust and contempt, and as predicted, subjects reached more agreement on the face than on the body. In that same study, Ekman and Friesen presented a reformulation of Ekman's position regarding the relative importance of the face and the body. They suggested that stationary facial expressions and postures are more likely to convey gross affect (such as liking), whereas movements of the face and body are more likely to convey specific emotions. In support of this view they found that body acts could be ascribed emotion categories more easily than could body positions.

Hence it can be seen that Ekman is making a number of statements about the relationship between the face and the body in the decoding of emotion. His research suggests that people make greater use of the face than the body in judgements of emotion, that their judgements are more accurate when made from the face and that they can reach greater agreement in judging the face. Ekman and Friesen also hypothesize that whereas stationary facial expressions and postures are more likely to convey gross affect, movements of the face and the body are more likely to convey specific emotions.

The assertion that judgements are more accurate when made from the face was for the most part supported by a study carried out by Graham, Bitti and Argyle (1975). In this study, English, northern Italian and southern Italian students were asked to role play certain emotions, and their performances were videotaped. Other groups of students from the same cultures were asked to identify these posed emotional expressions from videotapes of the face only, the body only or the whole person. Results showed that judgements from the face alone were significantly more accurate than judgements from the body alone for specific emotions and for the emotion dimension of pleasantness/ unpleasantness, while there were no significant differences between judgements of the face alone and judgements of the whole person (accuracy was scored in terms of the emotion the encoder intended to portray). However, significant interactions did show a number of exceptions to these findings. Judgements of anger were more accurate for the English when made from the body than from the face; judgements of fear were more accurate for the southern Italians when made from the body than from the face; judgements of sadness for the English were more accurate when made from the whole person than from either the face or the body alone.

Nevertheless, the problem with this whole approach is that the particular facial expressions and bodily positions may have varied considerably in their degree of informativeness; subjects may simply have paid more attention to whichever feature is carrying the most information. The main difficulty here is the relative scarcity of information on either the encoding or decoding of emotion through bodily posture or gesture. Darwin was primarily concerned with the facial expression of emotion, although he did make reference to lowering the head in sadness and trembling in fear. Izard (1977) has claimed that particular head positions are associated with different emotions. Interest, he maintains, is accompanied by an orientation of the head towards the focus of interest,

Figure 11. Posture of interest

contempt by lifting the head up and shame by dropping the head or turning it away. Bull (1978a, 1978b) has carried out some experimental studies on the encoding of emotion through posture, in which subjects were asked to listen to recorded talks and to rate those talks according to a number of emotion and attitude categories. While listening to the talks, subjects were videotaped without their knowledge, and their ratings of the tape-recordings were used to analyse the postures displayed on the videotape. In one study, Bull (1978a) found that during items judged as sad, British female students lowered their heads for a significantly longer period of time than during items judged as amusing. In another study, Bull (1978b) found that British male and female students leaned forward during items judged as interesting, and leaned forward and drew back their legs when talking to the experimenter afterwards about these extracts (see Figure 11). Listening to extracts judged to be boring was associated with lowering the head, tilting it to one side, turning the head away from the television monitor, supporting the head on one hand, leaning back and stretching out the legs (see Figure 12). A decoding study using line drawings showed that another group of British students judged these postural cues as conveying interest or boredom, suggesting that a postural code exists for the non-verbal communication of interest and boredom during listening.

Thus, in spite of Ekman's (1965) early formulation that posture may communicate information primarily about intensity of emotion, it does seem possible that specific postures may be associated with particular emotions. Ekman and Friesen (1967) subsequently reformulated this position by suggesting that whereas static facial and bodily positions may convey gross affect, facial or bodily movements may convey specific emotions. But this distinction is rather unconvincing, since static facial or bodily positions are usually only

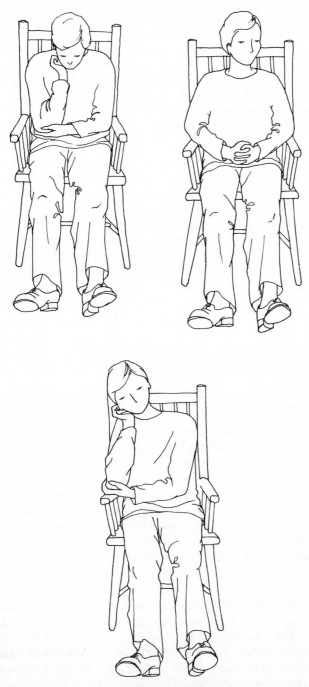

Figure 12. Postures of boredom

observed in pictures or photographs; face-to-face interaction is characterized by movement, positions being merely the products of particular movements.

Consequently, in the light of the present evidence, it is impossible to say what is the role of posture and gesture in relation to emotion. Certainly there is no evidence at present for cross-cultural universals such as have been demonstrated for facial expression. Where cross-cultural studies have been carried out, they have been focused not on the expression of emotion but simply on the incidence, for example, of different postures in different cultures. Hewes (1955, 1957) used photographs, paintings and the occasional descriptive statement to investigate posture in different cultures. He noted, for example, that chair-sitting, although widespread, is not universal amongst mankind, and that many cultures use either the cross-legged position or what he calls the deep squat, where the person sits with the soles of the feet flat and the buttocks either on the floor or the ground, or just above it. Such differences in seated posture are bound to affect the postures or gestures which may be associated with particular emotions, and suggest that they may be the product of learning. For example, drawing back the legs in interest and stretching them out in boredom which Bull (1978b) found in a British study would simply not be possible in cultures where chair-sitting is not employed. Movements of other parts of the body should be more independent of seating positions, but there is no need to assume that such cues are innate. For example, Darwin interpreted the head hanging in sorrow as being due to a slowing down in the circulation of the blood; equally it might simply reflect social convention.

(v) Interpersonal Distance

There have been comparatively few investigations of interpersonal distance and emotion. Fromme and Schmidt (1972), in the study referred to earlier in which American male students were asked to role play fear, anger and sorrow, as well as a neutral condition, also included measures of interpersonal distance. They found that the students adopted significantly greater distances for fear than for the other conditions, and a significantly greater distance for sorrow than for anger; there was no significant difference between the anger and the neutral condition. But O'Neal et al. (1979, 1980) did find a significant effect of anger on personal space. In one experiment (O'Neal et al., 1979), American male students were angered by hearing an insulting evaluation of them by a confederate made in response to a question by the experimenter, and in another experiment (O'Neal et al., 1980), they were angered by the experimenter scolding them for arriving late. The personal space preferences of the subjects were investigated by the experimenter approaching each subject from a number of different directions, the subject being asked to say when he felt the experimenter was uncomfortably close; when compared with other groups of control subjects, the angered subjects rated themselves as significantly more angry and showed significantly greater interpersonal distance preferences. These studies do suggest (not surprisingly) that interpersonal distance is related to emotion, but there has been no systematic investigation of how these distance preferences may be related to culture or situational context.

(vi) Other Bodily Cues and the Innate Hypothesis of Emotional Expression: Summary

The generality of the innate hypothesis of emotional expression has been discussed in relation to other bodily cues besides facial expression. It has been proposed that the phenomenon of blushing suggests the possible existence of a seventh fundamental emotion of shame, that pupil size and gaze convey information about intensity of emotion rather than category of emotion, and that the evidence on posture and gesture is insufficient to establish whether it conveys information about intensity or category of emotion. There is at present no real evidence to suggest that the innate hypothesis be extended to gaze, posture, gesture or interpersonal distance; it would appear that facial expression is the prime source of bodily information for at least six distinctive categories of emotion.

3. The Innate Hypothesis and the Decoding of Emotional Expression

The third issue with respect to the generality of the innate hypothesis concerns whether there is any evidence to suggest that the decoding of emotional expressions is innate. Darwin (1872) commented on this possibility, but noted how difficult it was to present evidence that the recognition of emotion is innate. Clearly, the linking of appropriate labels to particular emotional expressions is learned, and this view is supported by studies which show improvements in labelling of emotions with age. The earliest such study was carried out by Gates (1923), who investigated the ability of children (aged 3 to 14 years) to identify the facial expressions depicted on six photographs. Gates' results indicated that adults could recognize the six facial expressions with 84 per cent to 100 per cent accuracy, whereas the results with children indicated a developmental trend—laughter and pain being recognized earlier than surprise and scorn.

In Gates' study, the children had to produce the appropriate verbal label, so the task is heavily dependent on their verbal skills. An alternative technique (derived from Dashiell, 1927) is for children to select an appropriate picture for a story narrated by the experimenter. Ekman and Friesen (1971) used this technique in their study in New Guinea, and included two age groups (aged 6 to 7 and 14 to 15) in their study. They found no difference between the two groups, and members of both groups were able to select the appropriate photograph at a level significantly above chance, thus suggesting that the recognition of emotional expressions occurs at a fairly young age. Camras (1980) investigated young children's understanding of facial expressions observed to occur between children in conflict over a toy. American children, between 62 and 80 months in age, were told a story about two children fighting over a toy which one wanted to keep very much. They were shown six target expressions, which in a previous study (Camras, 1977) had been associated with greater reluctance on the part of a child to give up a toy (lowered eyebrows, oblique eyebrows (inner corners raised), nose wrinkle, both lips thrust forward and two instances of lips pressed together). They were also shown 10 non-target expressions, which in the previous study had been associated neither with greater reluctance on the part of one child to give up the toy nor with hesitation by the other child in renewing attempts to take it. When asked to select an expression for the child in the story, the children chose the target expressions significantly more often than the non-target expressions. In a second study, Camras found with another group of American children (between 60 and 79 months in age) that they were able to link the target expressions to stories intended to convey particular emotions; hence lowered brows were chosen to a significant degree for a story intended to convey anger, nose wrinkle was chosen for a story intended to convey disgust, and oblique brows for a story intended to convey sadness. Thus Camras's findings support Ekman and Friesen's conclusion that the recognition of emotional expressions occurs at a fairly younge age. Izard (1971) employed both emotion-recognition and emotion-labelling tasks with American and French children. In the emotion-recognition task, children were shown three pictures at a time, and were asked to indicate which person they thought, for example, was sad; in the emotion-labelling task, they were asked to judge how the person in the photograph was feeling, but they had to produce their own emotion labels in answer to the question. Izard's results confirmed that children can recognize emotions far sooner than they can produce the appropriate label.

Nevertheless, it is still possible that the capacity to recognize emotional expressions is innate, even if attaching the correct label is learned. Two main techniques have been used for investigating the perception of emotional expressions by young infants. One approach derives from Fantz's (e.g. 1964) technique of measuring the duration of visual fixation, the assumption being that if infants look significantly longer at one visual display rather than another, then they must be capable of discriminating between them. Using this technique, Young-Browne, Rosenfeld and Horowitz (1977) investigated whether infants (three months of age) could discriminate between sad, happy and surprise facial expressions (based on the descriptions in Ekman and Friesen, 1975). The infants were shown one facial expression until they had habituated to it, and then shown another photograph; discrimination was measured by increases in looking time following the presentation of a new expression, and significant differences in fixation times strongly suggested that the infants could discriminate between these expressions.

A second approach stems from the work of Meltzoff and Moore (1977), who have investigated whether infants can imitate different facial and bodily movements. In their experiment, infants of between 12 and 21 days in age were exposed to a number of movements (lip protrusion, mouth opening, tongue protrusion and sequential finger movement). Each movement was demonstrated four times in a 15-second presentation followed by a 20-second response period in which the experimenter resumed a passive face. Videotapes of the babies' behaviour during the response period were scored by students who were not informed of the nature of the preceding presentation period, and the results showed that the distribution of each movement 'peaked' following the experimental demonstration. Meltzoff and Moore argued against a reinforcement interpretation of these findings since the experimenter maintained a passive face when not demonstrating the movements, and there were no judged differences in his expressions by raters between the different conditions. Meltzoff and Moore argue instead that the infant has the ability to act on the basis of an abstract representation of the movement, and that this capacity is innate; the kind of imitation Meltzoff and Moore describe has been demonstrated with an infant who was only 60 minutes old.

Meltzoff and Moore's work is particularly important because it suggests that infants are capable of discriminating between different expressive movements virtually at birth. The question still of course remains at what time do infants recognize the meaning of different expressions, and whether this ability is innate or learned. As Darwin observed, it is extremely difficult to prove that the recognition of emotional expressions is innate, and whether this is so still remains an open question.

OTHER SOURCES OF INFORMATION ABOUT EMOTION

It has been argued that facial expression conveys information concerning at least six fundamental emotions, that gaze and pupil size convey information about emotional intensity, and that the evidence on posture and gesture is insufficient to establish whether it conveys information about intensity or category of emotion. Nevertheless, the significance attached to bodily cues and emotion varies according to the theoretical standpoint taken. Ethologists and psychologists have laid stress on innate determinants; according to this view, there are certain basic emotional expressions with universal meanings which override both culture and situational context. Structuralists and sociologists have argued that non-verbal cues are all learned forms of communication which cannot be adequately interpreted or understood outside the social context in which they occur. According to this view, social context is paramount and is necessary to understand the significance of particular cues; the cues themselves are ascribed relatively less importance in conveying information about emotion.

One type of evidence relevant to this question comes from studies in which comparisons have been made between bodily cues and other sources of information about emotion. Typically such studies have employed a decoding approach, investigating the relative importance which subjects attribute to different sources of information in judgements of emotion. The main alternative sources of information to bodily cues are speech content, paralanguage and situational context.

1. Speech Content

One comparative study of the decoding of facial expression and speech content was carried out by Friedman (1979), who systematically paired selected facial expressions of emotion with specific sentences, themselves of varying affect. The facial expressions were presented in photographs intended to convey happiness, surprise, anger or sadness, while the sentences were intended to vary on positiveness and dominance; both facial expressions and sentences were pre-rated independently of one another by a group of American high school students to ensure that they reached an adequate level of clarity. Another group of American high school students saw all possible combinations of facial expressions and sentences; they were told that the person in the picture was a teacher, and were asked to rate him on positiveness, sincerity and dominance. The results suggested that the facial expression carried most weight in the students' judgements, except in the case of the surprise expression, where the ratings of positiveness and dominance were a simple, direct function of the sentences employed. In the case of the other emotions, facial expressions outweighed speech content, although content still influenced the judgement. Thus, happy faces were seen as happy by more subjects when paired with positive than negative sentences, angry faces were seen as angry by more subjects when paired with negative than positive sentences, and sad faces were seen as sad by more subjects when paired with negative than with positive sentences.

2. Vocal Cues

There have been no studies comparing the relative importance of bodily and vocal cues in judgements of emotion. Nevertheless, there are a number of studies which show that intonation is perceived as conveying information about emotion. For example, Scherer (1974) employed a Moog synthesizer to vary pitch level and variation, amplitude level and variation, and tempo; he asked decoders to judge whether these artificially created tones resembled any of the emotions of interest, sadness, fear, disgust, anger, surprise, elation and boredom. Scherer found effects especially for pitch variation and tempo. For example, fast tempo is seen as indicative of interest, fear, happiness, anger and surprise; slow tempo as indicative of sadness, disgust and boredom. Scherer hypothesizes that the vocal expression of emotion, as well as its facial expression, may be innate, especially given the strong relationship between respiration and emotion.

Such a view gains some support from a study by Tartter (1980), who investigated the relationship between smiling and intonation. Shor (1978) noted that a side-effect of smiling is alteration of the vocal tract from its neutral position, widening the mouth orifice, shortening the vocal tract and enlarging its opening. On the basis of this observation, Tartter set out to investigate whether the effects of smiling might be audible. American high school and college students heard sentences and nonsense syllables uttered in a smiling and unsmiling version, and were asked to guess in which version the speaker was smiling (speakers were specifically instructed not to sound happy during the smiled versions). Results showed that the subjects were able to guess in which version the speaker was smiling at a level significantly above chance. Acoustic analysis of the tapes showed that smiling has the effect of raising the pitch and in some cases of increasing the amplitude. Tartter's results are particularly interesting, in that they suggest a close relationship between facial expression and intonation. In view of this, if the facial expressions of emotion are innate, then it is quite likely that the patterns of intonation associated with different emotions may also be innate. Such a view might suggest that intonation is as important as facial expression in conveying information about emotion, although direct tests of this hypothesis have yet to be performed.

3. Situational Context

Most comparisons of bodily cues and other sources of information concerning emotion have concentrated primarily on facial expression and situational context. Clearly, such studies are of relevance to the claim by structuralists and sociologists that situational context is essential to understand the meaning of particular bodily cues. Ekman, Friesen and Ellsworth (1972) reviewed a number of studies in which decoders were given pictures of facial expressions and verbal descriptions of situational contexts, and were asked to make judgements about the emotion they considered the person was experiencing. Ekman, Friesen and Ellsworth criticized these studies because of their failure to judge face and context separately, so that each source of information can be matched for comparable clarity. Watson (1972) carried out a study which did involve such a pre-test. She used facial expressions to represent sadness, happiness, anger and a neutral expression, as well as a number of verbal descriptions of situational contexts (e.g. 'He is told that a close friend, stricken with leukemia, has died'—intended to evoke sadness). To match the clarity of each source, facial expressions and situational contexts were rated separately by a group of American students, and only those which achieved at least 80 per cent agreement on the emotion judged were included in the main part of the study. Another group of American students then rated the combinations of facial expressions and situational contexts on a number of categories commonly used to describe emotion, and also on scales designed to measure the probability or improbability of each combination of facial expression and context. For combinations judged as probable, the average shift away from the context line judged alone was almost twice as large as that away from the facial expression judged alone; for combinations judged as improbable, it was almost three times as large.

Watson's study clearly suggests that when facial expression is set in conflict with the emotion people expect someone to experience in a particular situation, then the facial expression will predominate. At the same time the methodology employed in this experiment can still be criticized on the grounds that the two sources of information were presented in different modalities; thus the results might indicate a more powerful effect for visual than for verbal information, rather than for facial expression over context. In another study, it might be possible to present both contextual information and facial expression on videotape to control for this possible source of bias. Moreover, even if Watson's data are inconsistent with the view that situational context predominates over facial expression in the judgement of emotion, this does not mean that situational context is unimportant. For example, if the description, 'He is told that a close friend, stricken with leukemia, has died', is paired with a happy facial expression, Watson's results would suggest that subjects are more likely to judge the emotion as happy than sad. Nevertheless, one might expect that people would want to know a great deal more about the situational context to explain the apparent discrepancy between the emotion one might expect someone to display in that situation, and the actual emotion displayed.

SUMMARY

In Chapter 1, it was argued that there should be evidence of both encoding and decoding before a behaviour can be regarded as communicative. The evidence reviewed in this chapter shows that there is a high degree of consistency in the way particularly in which facial cues are decoded as conveying emotion. If the evidence of cross-cultural universals in decoding is taken as evidence of universal encoding (regardless of whether the encoding of emotion is innate or learned), then we would clearly be justified in regarding facial cues as a means of non-verbally communicating emotion. However, at present direct evidence on the encoding of emotion is still very sparse.

The innate hypothesis of emotional expression is much more important in evaluating the significance of facial cues expressing emotion. If the innate hypothesis is accepted, that certain facial cues represent part of the physiological response of emotion, then this give those cues a special status in conveying information about emotion. The available evidence is consistent with this view but by no means conclusive. Evidence from cross-cultural studies shows that the facial expressions associated with six emotions are decoded in the same way by members of both literate and pre-literate cultures. Children born deaf and blind show the same kinds of basic facial expressions in appropriate situational contexts, thus ruling out visual or auditory communication as necessary conditions for learning these particular expressions. Infants are born with the capacity to produce almost all the adult facial movements, and show some of the combinations of muscular movements associated with adult expressions, although it is still not clear how the expressions come to be associated with particular emotions. Comparative studies of different kinds of bodily cues suggest that the face is perceived as most important in conveying information about what emotion is being experienced, gaze and pupil size conveying information primarily about emotional intensity; little is as yet known about how much information concerning emotion is conveyed by posture, gesture and interpersonal distance, and how important this is in relation to the face. Studies comparing bodily cues with other sources of information concerning emotion suggest that the face is perceived as more important than speech content and verbal descriptions of situational context; there is no evidence directly comparing its relative importance with paralanguage, although facial expression and intonation may well be closely related to one another in conveying information about emotion.

Chapter 3

Body Movement and Speech

In Chapter 2, it was proposed that there are innate facial and pupillary responses associated with at least six fundamental emotions, and that these cues are important in communicating information about emotion. But it would be wrong to assume that the only information bodily cues convey concerns emotion. Research has also shown that there is a strong correspondence between bodily cues and speech. Condon and Ogston (1966) from a frame-by-frame analysis described how the body of the speaker moves closely in time with his speech, a phenomenon which they called self-synchrony. They also described how the body of the listener appears to move in time with the speech and bodily movements of the speaker, a phenomenon which they called interactional synchrony. Condon and Ogston's observations were not simply confined to hand gestures; it is movements of all parts of the body which they found to be closely synchronized with speech. At the same time, it does not appear to be the case that every bodily movement is related to discourse. For example, Freedman and Hoffman (1967) carried out a study of the hand and arm movements of two patients undergoing psychotherapy, which were scored according to whether observers intuitively judged the movements as related to speech, and according to whether the movements involved touching or stimulating some part of the body. The results showed that it was hand movements which did not involve touching the body which for the most part appeared to be related to speech.

The way in which bodily cues can be described as speech-related has been examined in terms of the syntactic, semantic and phonemic clause structure of speech. Lindenfeld (1971) set out to investigate whether bodily movement is related to the syntactic structure of speech. She carried out an analysis of the speech of a patient in a psychotherapy session, parsing it in terms of its deep and surface structure; surface structure refers to the actual form of sentences as they are heard when somebody speaks, deep structure to their abstract underlying form. Lindenfeld also made observations of the number of postural shifts, leg movements and foot movements, and noted whether or not they coincided with syntactic boundaries. A movement was scored as coinciding with syntactic structure if it took place within the duration of one clause, and as not coinciding

58

with syntactic structure if it took place across more than one clause. Lindenfeld found that most of the body movements she observed fell within syntactic boundaries, and hence argued that body movements are related to the syntactic structure of speech.

Discourse has a discernible structure based on strings of words which seem to be spoken as a unit. This unit was identified by Trager and Smith (1951), and named the phonemic clause. The phonemic clause consists of a group of words, averaging five in length, in which there is only one primary stress indicated by changes in pitch, rhythm or loudness, and which is terminated by a juncture, where these changes in pitch, rhythm and loudness level off before the beginning of the next phonemic clause. Some researchers have claimed that bodily cues appear to be closely related to phonemic clause structure. Pittenger, Hockett and Danehy (1960) observed that most speakers of American English accompany their primary stresses with slight jerks of the head or hand. Scheflen (1964) notes that Birdwhistell demonstrated that junctures are accompanied by a movement of the head, eyes or hands. These claims were criticized by Dittman and Llewellyn (1969), who carried out a study in which American male and female students participated in two 15-minute interviews with one of the experimenters. The bodily movements of the students were recorded by movement transducers attached to the head, to both hands and to both feet, while transcripts of their speech were segmented into phonemic clauses. Dittman and Llewellyn found that bodily movements occurred significantly more frequently at what they called start positions (the beginnings of clauses, non-fluencies within clauses and the start of speech following those non-fluencies) than at non-start positions. They criticize the observations of Scheflen and of Pittenger, Hockett and Danehy on the grounds that stress points and junctures occur at or towards the end of phonemic clauses, whereas their own data suggest that bodily movements occur mainly at the beginnings of clauses. They do, however, acknowledge that their own data show a significant relationship between body movement and stress and juncture, but maintain that the relationship is not sizeable and has been greatly exaggerated by Scheflen and by Pittenger, Hockett and Danehy. The basic problem with Dittman and Llewellyn's approach, however, stems from the use of movement transducers to record body movement which provide no details of the visual appearance of those movements, and hence of how the structure of those movements relates to the structure of discourse. If, for example, a person extends his forearm, index finger outstretched, to coincide with the stress point in a phonemic clause, he may well have flexed his forearm at the beginning of the clause in preparation for that movement; the action of flexing and extending the forearm can be seen as a single structural unit which reaches its apex on the stress point of the clause. Dittman and Llewellyn's method of recording body movement would presumably lead to the preparatory movement being scored as unrelated to the stress point in the phonemic clause, and hence their particular methodology may lead to an underestimate of the relationship between body movement and tonic stress. But whichever interpretation is valid, all the researchers discussed above concur in having demonstrated some kind of significant relationship between bodily cues and phonemic clause structure; their disagreements revolve around the extent of that relationship.

Scheflen (1964, 1973) has also maintained that posture is related to structural units larger than the phonemic clause. He discusses three such units—the point, the position and the presentation. When an American speaker uses a series of syntactic sentences in a conversation, Scheflen maintains that he changes the position of his head and eyes every few sentences. The attitude is held for a few sentences, and then shifted to another position; each of these shifts, Scheflen maintains, mark the end of a structural unit at the next level higher than the syntactic sentence. He calls the unit a 'point', because it corresponds roughly to making a point in a discussion. A sequence of several points go to make up a 'position', which corresponds roughly to a point of view that a person may take in a conversation; the position is marked by a gross postural shift involving at least half the body. The largest unit Scheflen employs is the 'presentation', which consists of the totality of one person's positions in a given interaction. Presentations may last from several minutes to several hours, and are terminated by a complete change in location.

Scheflen's observations find some support in a study by Kendon (1972), who carried out a detailed analysis of a film of a conversation in a London pub. Kendon found that the trunk and leg movements of one speaker occurred only with changes of what he called a 'locution cluster'; this refers to a change in what the speaker is talking about, and appears to be very similar to Scheflen's concept of the position. Bull and Brown (1977) also found some quantitative evidence in support of Scheflen's observations in a study of pairs of British male and female students in conversation with one another. Speech which introduced new information into conversation was found to be accompanied by significantly more changes in certain postures than speech which was less informative, a result which was interpreted as supporting Scheflen's concept of a 'programme', where new stages in social interaction are indicated by postural markers.

The research reviewed above suggests that bodily cues are related to speech in terms of its syntax, its phonemic clause structure and in terms of higher-order semantic units, such as topic change. According to the functions which they serve, speech-related bodily cues can be divided on the basis of a classification system proposed by Ekman and Friesen (1969a) into three main types, namely, emblems, illustrators and regulators. The terms 'emblems' they derived from Efron (1941) to refer to those non-verbal acts which have a direct verbal translation, such as nodding the head when meaning 'Yes', or shaking the head when meaning 'No'; their function is communicative, and is explicitly recognized as such. Illustrators are movements which are directly tied to speech, and it is maintained that they facilitate communication by amplifying and elaborating the verbal content of the message. Regulators are movements which guide and control the flow of conversation, influencing both who is to speak and how much is said.

EMBLEMS

Emblems are generally assumed to be specific to particular cultures or occupations, but there do appear to be pan-cultural emblems such as the 'eyebrow flash', where a person raises his eyebrows for about a sixth of a second as a greeting; Eibl-Eibesfeldt (1972) claims to have observed this in a wide number of differing cultures. Morris *et al.* (1979) have attempted to map the geographical distribution of 20 emblems by carrying out a series of standard interviews in 40 locations spread across western and southern Europe and the Mediterranean. Adult males were approached at random in public places, such as streets, squares or parks, and were shown drawings of the 20 gestures; they were asked if each gesture was used locally, and if so, what was its meaning. Their findings showed that whereas some emblems were specific to one culture,

Figure 13. The check-screw. (Based on a photograph in D. Morris *et al.* (1979), *Gestures: Their Origins and Distribution*, London: Jonathan Cape Ltd. Reproduced by permission)

other emblems showed a high degree of generality across cultures. For example, an emblem which they call the cheek-screw (see Figure 13), in which a straightened forefinger is pressed against the centre of the cheek and rotated, is primarily an Italian gesture of praise; it is little known elsewhere in Europe. Another gesture which they call the nose-thumb (see Figure 14), in which one hand is raised so that the thumb touches the tip of the nose, with the fingers spread out in a fan and pointing upwards, is widely known throughout Europe as a form of mockery. A gesture which they call the ring (see Figure 15), where the hand is held up with the palm facing away from the encoder, thumb and forefinger touching to form a circle, means in Britain something is good, in parts of France something is worthless, while in Sardinia it is a sexual insult! Similarly, what Morris *et al.* call the palm-back V-sign (see Figure 16), where the hand is raised in front of the body, with the palm towards the encoder's face and the forefinger and middle finger extended to form a V shape, in Britain carries the meaning of a sexual insult, whereas on the Continent no distinction is made between the palm-front and palm-back forms of the gesture, both meaning victory or peace.

Clearly the function of emblems is communicative, and they constitute a form of non-verbal communication of which people have explicit awareness. The question arises, however, why emblems should have emerged as an alternative form of communication to speech. Ekman and Friesen argue that their particular importance stems from the fact that they are often used when

Figure 14. The nose-thumb. (Based on a drawing in D. Morris *et al.* (1979), *Gestures: Their Origins and Distribution*, London: Jonathan Cape Ltd. Reproduced by permission)

Figure 15. The ring. (Based on a photograph in D. Morris *et al.* (1979), *Gestures: Their Origins and Distribution*, London: Jonathan Cape Ltd. Reproduced by permission)

speech is difficult or impossible, and hence function as an alternative system to speech. For example, the policeman directing the traffic on point duty, or the deaf-and-dumb person using sign language can both be said to be using emblems in situations where verbal communication is not possible. A number of the emblems described by Morris *et al.* are insults; the advantage of insulting people at a distance is presumably that it is more difficult for the insulted person to retaliate! Emblems are also sometimes used in conjunction with speech, in which case they could be said to serve the functions of illustrators; there are a number of ways in which illustrators can be considered to enhance and elaborate the verbal message, and these are discussed below.

ILLUSTRATORS

Illustrators are movements which are directly tied to speech, and it is maintained that they facilitate communication by amplifying and elaborating the verbal content of the message. One way of examining this hypothesis concerning illustrators is to examine a situation where a person talks but cannot be seen,

Figure 16. The palm-back V-sign. (Based on a photograph in D. Morris
et al. (1979), *Gestures: Their Origins and Distribution*, London: Jonathan
Cape Ltd. Reproduced by permission)

as in the case of a telephone conversation. Such an experiment was carried out
by Cohen and Harrison (1973), who asked male American students to give
directions to another person on how to reach a place on the university
campus over an intercom and face to face. Cohen and Harrison found
significantly more illustrators were used when conversing face to face, and
argued accordingly that hand gestures are certainly intended to facilitate the
process of communication.

Whether illustrators do in fact facilitate communication was tested in an
experiment by Rogers (1978). Rogers prepared a silent film of various actions
being performed, such as a car making a series of turns, or a tennis ball bouncing
into a corner. Eight male and female American students were asked to view
these actions, and to describe them to another person who was unable to see
the film. These descriptions were videotaped and shown to another group of
students either with sound and vision, with sound only or in a condition where
the vision was altered by reducing contrast to obliterate details of the eyes and

the mouth. This latter condition was included to investigate the effect of illustrators when information was not readily available from the movements of the speaker's lips. The tapes were presented under four signal-to-noise ratios which pre-testing had shown varied from being very easy to hear to being very difficult to hear; the noise was produced by a white noise generator. The students who were shown the videotapes were asked a series of five comprehension questions about each incident. The results showed that comprehension was significantly better in the audio-visual than in the audio-only condition. When those items which strongly differentiated between the audio and audio-visual condition were re-analysed on their own, a significant difference was also found between the modified audio-visual condition and the audio-only condition, thus suggesting that illustrators do facilitate speech comprehension independently of the information obtained from lip-reading. Results also showed a significant interaction between visibility and signal-to-noise ratio, the advantage of being able to see the speaker increasing as interference from noise increased.

Rogers' findings suggest that illustrators do assist the process of communication, in that they appear to facilitate the comprehension of speech. A variety of reasons have been proposed for why this should be the case. The most obvious answer is that visual information can be conveyed more easily through visual means. It is often easier or quicker, for example, to point to an object, rather than to describe it verbally. Similarly, some gestures are like representative pictures in that they attempt to represent the visual appearance of an object, spatial relationship or bodily action (called 'physiographic' by Efron, 1941). Graham and Argyle (1975b) in fact tested the hypothesis that visual information is communicated more easily through hand gestures in an experiment in which English and Italian male students were asked to communicate information about two-dimensional shapes to other male students from their own culture both with and without the use of hand gestures. The decoders drew what they thought the shapes were, and these were rated by English and Italian judges for their similarity to the originals. The results showed that when gesture was permitted, the drawings were judged as significantly more accurate; this effect was also significantly more pronounced for the Italian subjects, thus providing some evidence in support of the popular view that gesture is of particular importance in Italian culture.

But the hypothesis that bodily cues are particularly useful in communicating visual information would not seem to be applicable to all forms of illustrator. A number of alternative hypotheses have been proposed for why illustrators should facilitate comprehension, although none of these hypotheses have been subjected to any form of direct testing through experiment. For example, the relationship between bodily cues and points of stress in the phonemic clause documented by Pittenger, Hockett and Danehy (1960) and Dittman and Llewellyn (1969) suggests that bodily cues convey information about emphasis by supplementing the information on stress communicated by changes in intonation. The question naturally arises why this duplication should occur.

One hypothesis is that the bodily cues simply make the stress patterns more clear. A second possibility is that whereas changes in intonation carry the primary stress in spoken English, illustrators can be used as a way of communicating greater intensity; a speaker can pick out particular words or phrases which may be important in his communication, and highlight them with some kind of illustrative body movement.

The relationship between bodily cues and the syntactic and semantic structure of speech documented by Lindenfeld (1971) and Scheflen (1964, 1973) would also suggest that illustrators may be useful in communicating information about the structure of speech. Efron (1941) described certain movements as 'ideographic', in that they traced the logical stages or direction of a line of thought. By demarcating whether a speaker is making a new point, or changing the topic of conversation, it may be easier for the listener more readily to discern the structure of speech.

Rogers (1978) discusses a number of other possible explanations for ways in which illustrators may facilitate the comprehension of speech. One possibility is that they simply increase the listener's level of attention by providing greater stimulation. Another possibility is that they create a richer bimodal sensory image which better stimulates memory processes during the decoding of speech. Again, Rogers suggests that illustrators may serve as a visual tracking signal for the flow of speech, although it is not clear how this explanation would differ from the argument that illustrators convey useful structural or semantic information (which Rogers includes as a separate hypothesis).

All of the hypotheses described above are based on the notion that illustrators in some way facilitate the comprehension of speech. An alternative hypothesis is that the prime function of illustrators is not to make the message more comprehensible, but to convey information about the speaker's emotions and attitudes, both towards the content of his own message and towards other people. So, for example, Ekman and Friesen (1974a, p. 215) cite a study by Kiritz (1971) in which he observed the number of hand movements at the hospital admission and discharge of a number of female psychiatric in-patients, and found that people suffering from psychotic depression used significantly more hand illustrators at discharge than at admission; Ekman and Friesen argue that hand illustrators are used to convey greater enthusiasm and involvement on the part of the speaker. Similarly, Mehrabian and Williams (1969) found that when American male and female students were asked to present a message persuasively, they used significantly more gesture than when asked to present the message in a neutral fashion. What these studies suggest is that illustrators may qualify the verbal message by indicating the speaker's attitude towards it, for example, whether he is interested or bored by what he is saying, whether he is confident or diffident about it and so forth. If such messages are decoded appropriately by the listener, then this may affect his reception of the message in quite significant ways. If the speaker conveys great interest in his topic, the listener may attend more carefully; if the speaker conveys great confidence in his argument, the listener may be more easily persuaded. According to this view, illustrators convey stylistic features which may have an important effect on the reception of a message.

All the hypotheses discussed above share the basic assumption that illustrators communicate information additional to speech. A totally different explanation of their function has come from those who have attempted to relate body movement to speech encoding. Dittman and Llewellyn (1969), in the study referred to above (p. 59), argued that body movements occur more frequently at the beginnings of phrases because of difficulties of speech encoding; such difficulties are hypothesized to create tension which leads to greater bodily movement. It is, however, difficult to evaluate this hypothesis in the absence of more direct information on the visual appearance of the body movements recorded by Dittman and Llewellyn.

A. A. Cohen (1977) argued that illustrators are not substitutes for failure or inability to communicate, but rather facilitators or such activity; according to this view, the encoder 'creates' the illustrators as if 'drawing a map' of the situation, while encoding the message verbally. To test this hypothesis, Cohen carried out an experiment in which male and female Israeli students were asked to give directions on how to get to one place from another from a map. Subjects were asked to give instructions either face to face, or over an intercom or alone; in the alone condition, subjects were asked to record themselves on tape on their own as a form of practice. It was argued that if, as in the previous study by Cohen and Harrison (1973), subjects used more illustrators face to face, this would be consistent with a decoding view of the functions of illustrators. The tasks were also varied in terms both of familiarity and complexity, it being argued that if illustrators facilitate speech encoding, then there should be more illustrators when the task was unfamiliar and complex. In the familiar condition, the subjects (who were from the Hebrew University of Jerusalem) were given map segments of a part of Jerusalem; in the unfamiliar condition, another group of subjects was given the same map segments, but they were told the map depicted a fictitious Israeli town called Hadera. Task complexity was varied according to the number of decision points necessary to give instructions on how to get to one place from another.

When illustrators were analysed in terms of a rate based on the number of hand illustrators used per second, the results showed a significant main effect for the form of communication, with most illustrators being employed in the face to face condition; this, Cohen argued, was consistent with the decoding hypothesis that illustrators are intended to facilitate communication. The results also showed a significant main effect for task complexity, with more illustrators being used with more complex maps; this, Cohen argued, was consistent with the hypothesis that illustrators facilitate speech encoding. There were no significant effects associated with task familiarity.

If illustrators do facilitate speech encoding, then it might be expected that if people are restrained from using gesture, this would interfere with speech encoding. Graham and Heywood (1975) asked British male students to communicate information about two-dimensional shapes, having explicitly instructed them in one condition to keep their arms folded so as to prevent them from gesturing. Graham and Heywood found that of the 13 measures of speech they used, only 3 discriminated between the gesture and no-gesture conditions, and 2 of these were measures of speech content; when gesture was prohibited, phrases and words describing spatial relations within the pictures were used significantly more frequently, while significantly less use was made of demonstratives (e.g. 'like this', 'like so'). The only measure of speech fluency to discriminate between the gesture and no-gesture conditions was the measure of pausing; subjects did pause significantly more frequently in the no-gesture condition. Graham and Heywood's results would suggest that if gesture does facilitate speech encoding, its use is certainly not of any great importance.

REGULATORS

Regulators are movements which are assumed to guide and control the flow of conversation. Regulators have typically been discussed in relation to how people take turns to speak in conversation (turn-taking), but it is also possible to include under this heading greetings and farewells, referred to by Goffman (1972) as access rituals. By access rituals Goffman means signals which indicate a change in the amount of access which people will have to one another, so that a greeting usually signals the beginning of a period of increased access, while farewells signal the start of a period of decreased access.

1. Greetings

Kendon and Ferber (1973), from films of a birthday party, thanksgiving party and a wedding, described what they considered to be the sequence of greeting behaviours between Americans who are already acquainted with one another. The participants must first sight one another to greet, then follows a distance salutation with an explicit display, for example, of waving. Participants break eye contact by lowering the head, approach one another, then resume mutual gaze before making a close salutation, smiling, setting their head in a certain position and offering an open palm. The greeting ceremony itself then ensues, with a handshake, an embrace or no bodily contact. Greeting rituals differ widely between cultures, but it has been argued by Eibl-Eibesfeldt (1972) that there is a universal pattern of greeting which he calls the 'eyebrow flash', where the eyebrows are raised for a maximum of one-sixth of a second; Eibl-Eibesfeldt has filmed this in Europeans, Balinese, Papuans, South American Indians and Bushmen. He argues that the eyebrow flash signals that people are willing to interact with one another.

Nevertheless greetings do not necessarily indicate a willingness to converse. Acquainted people may meet by chance, acknowledge one another and continue on their way without further conversation, or they may stop and talk; it seems likely that a willingness to converse may be indicated by certain parts of the greeting ritual which may be omitted if the participants do not wish to converse.

For example, in the sequence of behaviours described by Kendon and Ferber, one might expect only the distance salutation to occur if the participants do not wish to converse; if they do wish to converse, this might be indicated by the approach movements and close salutation. Such a view would suggest that bodily cues are of considerable importance in communicating whether people do in fact wish to converse with one another.

Amongst the unacquainted, Goffman (1963) has proposed that the fundamental rule is what he calls civil inattention, whereby people give one another an initial look followed by withdrawal of attention. Cary (1978) investigated the role of gaze in the initiation of conversation by videotaping American male and female students in a waiting room. One student was already in the waiting room, and as another student entered, almost all of the pairs looked at one another. An additional mutual look following the initial look while moving away from the door significantly increased the chance of continuous conversation occurring, and Cary argued that these findings support Goffman's suggestion that the desire to converse can be signalled through violations of the norm of civil inattention.

2. Turn-taking

Once two or more people are engaged in conversation, the major issue of conversational management relates to the assignment of speaking turns. The most intensive set of studies of turn-taking have been carried out by Duncan and his associates (e.g. Duncan, 1972; Duncan and Niederehe, 1974; Duncan and Fiske, 1977). Within his theoretical framework, Duncan has identified a number of different cues, which he refers to as turn-yielding cues, attempt-suppressing signals, back channels, within-turn signals and speaker-state signals.

Turn-yielding cues offer a speaking turn to the other person, and Duncan (1972) has identified six such cues—a rise or fall in pitch at the end of a clause, a drawl on the final syllable, the termination of hand gestures, stereotyped expressions such as 'but uh' and 'you know', a drop in pitch or loudness associated with one of these stereotyped expressions, and the completion of a grammatical clause. Duncan's initial (1972) analysis was based on videotapes of two pairs of Americans in conversation with one another, one an interview between a male psychotherapist and a female client who were previously unacquainted, the other a casual conversation between two male psychotherapists who had been friends for 10 years. Duncan found that as more turn-yielding cues were displayed in combination with one another, the probability of a turn-taking attempt by the listener increased in a strictly linear fashion. In a replication study, Duncan and Fiske (1977) analysed another six conversations between pairs of Americans; four of these conversations were between mixed-sex pairs of students who were previously unacquainted, one conversation was between two female research assistants who had known each other for about two years, and the other conversation was between two male college students who were previously unacquainted with one another. This study failed to replicate the linear relationship between the number of turn-yielding cues and the probability of a turn-taking attempt, but did show a correlation of 0.98 between the number of turn-yielding cues and a smooth switch between speakers; this replicated a comparable correlation of 0.99 in the Duncan (1972) study. Thus Duncan and Fiske argue that there is a linear relationship not between the number of turn-yielding cues and the probability of a turn-taking attempt, but between the number of turn-yielding cues and a smooth switch between speakers.

Attempt-suppressing signals are used by the speaker to prevent a listener taking over the turn when the speaker wishes to continue talking. Duncan (1972) identifies only one such cue, that of hand gesticulation; he found that if the speaker continues to gesture, this essentially eliminated attempts by the listener to take over the turn. In the study by Duncan and Fiske (1977), this finding was replicated.

The term 'back channel' was introduced by Yngve (1970) to refer to short messages such as 'yes' and 'uh-huh' employed by the listener, which do not constitute a claim to the turn. Duncan (1972) identified five such cues—sentence completions, requests for clarification, brief phrases such as 'uh-huh', 'yeah' and 'right', and head nods and head shakes. The listener's use of the back channel is generally taken to indicate continuing attentiveness to the speaker's message. Brunner (1979) has argued that smiling can also be considered a back channel, since from an analysis of four of the conversations used in the Duncan and Fiske (1977) study, he found that smiles tended to occur at similar points in conversation as the other forms of back channel described by Duncan. Using the videotapes from the Duncan (1972) study, Duncan and Fiske also found that back channels are typically preceded by a shift in head direction towards the partner and the completion of a grammatical clause. Duncan and Fiske refer to these cues as within-turn signals, which mark appropriate points in conversation for a listener back channel, in the same way as turn-yielding cues mark appropriate points for the listener to take the turn.

If back channels do not constitute an attempt at taking the turn, how can a speaker distinguish between a back channel and a turn-taking attempt by the listener? Duncan and Niederehe (1974) argued that there are four signals which mark out a speaking turn from a listener back channel—a shift away in head direction, starting to hand gesture, an audible inhalation of breath and what they refer to as 'paralinguistic overloudness'. Duncan and Niederehe found that in the conversation between the two psychotherapists, these four cues were displayed significantly more often at the beginnings of turns than at back channels. But in the conversation between a psychotherapist and a client, they found that only turning the head away and gesticulation distinguished the beginning of turns from back channels. In the replication study, Duncan and Fiske (1977) again found that only those two cues were significantly associated with beginning a turn. Hence, turning the head away from the other and beginning to gesture are regarded as constituting the speaker-state signal.

Most other research on turn-taking can be subsumed within Duncan's theoretical framework. Matarazzo et al. (1964) carried out a number of

45-minute interviews with American Civil Service applicants. The interviews were divided into three 15-minute periods; in the second period, each time the interviewee began an utterance, the experimenter nodded his head repeatedly throughout the whole utterance. Both experimenters were careful not to introduce other cues such as smiling or saying 'mm-hmm', and kept their utterances to a consistent length of five seconds throughout the interview. Matarazzo *et al.* found that the interviewees talked for significantly longer during the second phase of the interview. This is of course consistent with what would be expected from the concept of a back channel, which is regarded not as a claim to a speaking-turn but as signalling continued attentiveness to what the speaker is saying, i.e. encouraging the speaker to continue talking. Matarazzo *et al.* interpret this finding in terms of learning theory, where head-nodding is regarded as a reinforcer which increases the amount a person says. They do not, however, discuss why head nodding should function as a reinforcer, although the answer in Duncan's theoretical framework would of course be that head-nodding is a communicative signal, which indicates to the speaker that the listener is attending to him and does not wish to take over the turn.

Another line of research on turn-taking stems from Kendon's (1967) observations on the regulatory functions of gaze. Kendon's observations were based on seven pairs of British students (drawn from ten men and three women), who were left together and simply asked to get to know one another, while their conversation was recorded. Kendon found that the students typically looked less while speaking than while listening. He hypothesized that a speaker typically looks at the other when he wishes the listener to take over the turn, and the listener typically looks away to signal that he has accepted the turn; in Duncan's terms, looking at the listener is a turn-yielding cue, looking away at the start of a turn is speaker-state signal. From a further analysis of two conversations, Kendon found that utterances which terminated with an extended look were followed by either no response or a delayed response significantly less frequently than those which ended without the speaker looking at the listener, a finding which supports his hypothesis that gazing at the listener functions as a turn-yielding cue.

Kendon's hypothesis that the listener signals he has accepted the turn by gazing away from the other is certainly consistent with the data reported by Duncan. Duncan and Fiske (1977) found that turning the head away from the listener was one of the two cues they identified as constituting the speaker-state signal (Duncan took observations of head turn rather than gaze, because he considered the definition on his tapes inadequate to score gaze). But Kendon's hypothesis that gaze directed at the listener functions as a turn-yielding cue is certainly not consistent with Duncan's observations. Duncan and Fiske (1977) in fact maintain that turning the head towards the listener is a within-turn signal requesting a back channel; they did not find it to be a turn-yielding cue.

Of course it is possible that this discrepancy might simply represent a cross-cultural difference in turn-taking between the Americans and the British, but other British studies have also cast doubt on Kendon's hypothesis that gaze directed at the listener functions as a turn-yielding cue. Rutter *et al.* (1978)

examined conversations between same-sex pairs of British students, and found only a low level of eye contact at the ends of utterances, whereas they maintained that there should be a high level of eye contact if gaze is being employed as a turn-yielding signal. Beattie (1978) examined four conversations between pairs of British men; three were tutorials (involving a graduate tutor and a student), the fourth was a conversation between two university staff members. Beattie found that utterances terminating with extended gaze were associated with significantly longer switching pauses than utterances terminating without gaze, which he maintained is precisely in the reverse direction from Kendon's original hypothesis. However, in another study of tutorials, Beattie (1979) did find that hesitant phases of speech terminating in gaze were associated with significantly shorter switching pauses. Beattie argues that during speech hesitations gaze aversion typically occurs as a consequence of cognitive planning, and hence that gaze may function as a turn-yielding cue but only in contexts typically associated with low levels of other-directed gaze (such as speech hesitations). Hence, according to this view, gaze would function as a turn-yielding cue at best only in very specific linguistic or social contexts.

Similarly, support for a highly restricted regulatory function for gaze in conversation comes from a study by Hedge, Everitt and Frith (1978). They investigated whether gaze and turn-taking in conversation conformed to a first-order Markovian process, in which information on the immediately preceding event is sufficient to predict the current event without requiring further information on earlier events. Hedge, Everitt and Frith sampled gaze and speech of same-sex pairs of friends and strangers in conversation with one another at 0.3 second intervals, recording who was speaking and the direction of gaze of both participants. The results showed that for conversations between strangers, speech in the immediately preceding 0.3 second was sufficient to predict the next state of the dialogue without reference to gaze; but for friends both speech and gaze had to be taken into account. Hence Hedge, Everitt and Frith argued that gaze has an important function in controlling the dialogues only of friends.

Finally, there have been studies in which turn-taking has been investigated in situations where subjects cannot see one another, such as talking over the telephone. If gaze has an important regulatory function in conversation, then it might be expected that situations where visual communication is not possible will be characterized by a lack of synchronization. Beattie and Barnard (1979) sampled 700 directory enquiry conversations monitored at a British trunk telephone exchange, which they compared with face-to-face conversations video-recorded in different university contexts at Cambridge. Their results showed no significant differences in the time taken for speaker and listener to exchange roles, nor in the number of times simultaneous claiming of the turn occurred. Rutter and Stephenson (1977) arranged for same-sex pairs of British students previously unacquainted with one another to discuss items on a questionnaire on which they had disagreed both over an intercom and face to face. Rutter and Stephenson in fact found that the duration and frequency of simultaneous speech were significantly greater in the face-to-face condition. Hence both studies clearly failed to support the hypothesis that where visual communication is not possible the synchronization of conversation will be impaired, thus providing further support for the view that gaze is only of limited importance in regulating conversation.

However, the fact that Rutter and Stephenson found a significantly greater occurrence of simultaneous speech in face-to-face conversation is an interesting finding which deserves explanation. According to their interpretation, interruptions occur more often face to face because in that situation visual signals can be employed to prevent conversational breakdown. This interpretation would certainly seem to be quite consistent with the results reported by Duncan. When the turn is not in dispute, as in the case where turn-yielding cues or back channels are in use, then visual cues do not seem to be of great importance. For example, of the six turn-yielding cues described by Duncan, only one (ceasing to gesture) is a visual cue, and Duncan regards each of these six cues as of equal importance, exerting an additive effect on whether a smooth transition takes place between speaker and listener. But when the turn is in dispute, as in the case where an attempt-suppressing signal is employed, then the only cue identified by Duncan is the visual cue of hand gesturing. Similarly, the only cues which distinguish the speaker-state from a back channel (another potential source of conflict) are the visual cues of gesturing and turning the head away from the other person. Hence it would seem that on present evidence the importance of bodily cues in regulating dyadic conversations lies in handling conflicts over who should take the speaking turn; where visual communication is not possible (as in telephone conversations), people avoid such conflicts by avoiding simultaneous speech.

Duncan has provided a useful theoretical framework in which to understand turn-taking, and a detailed description of the turn-taking system. Nevertheless, questions must obviously be raised concerning the generality of Duncan's findings. One issue is whether the turn-taking signals which Duncan describes operate independently of speech content. Duncan provides no analysis of speech content, but a study by Thomas and Bull (1981) suggested that there may be a relationship between turn-taking cues and speech content. Thomas and Bull examined conversations between mixed-sex pairs of British students, coding speech according to the different ways in which information is exchanged. They found that prior to asking a question, the students typically either raised the head or turned the head towards the listener; prior to answering a question, the speaker typically turned his head away from the listener. Thomas and Bull suggested that these changes in head posture associated with questions and answers (which 'offer' and 'accept' the floor respectively) may be components of the turn-taking system. They also argued that the particular relationships found between body postures and speech activity suggest that the relationship between speech content and the turn-taking system may be much more specific than has been hitherto realized.

A second question which arises with respect to the generality of Duncan's findings stems from the fact that all of the studies described above took place between pairs of people, and it may well be the case that in larger groups different rules for turn-taking apply. Studies of larger groups do in fact suggest that where there are more than two people involved in conversation, seating position plays an important role in turn-taking. According to one hypothesis, the person in a central position initiates and receives more communications from others (Harris, 1949). According to another hypothesis, centrality will only have this effect if it gives the person greater visual accessibility (Hare and Bales, 1963). Research findings seem to support the second of these hypotheses. Steinzor (1950) took records of the seating positions of two 10-person groups of American students and counsellors which met regularly over a period of weeks, and found that people sitting in positions which allowed them to observe more of each other's behaviour tended to follow one another in conversation with significantly greater frequency than those with inferior visibility. Michelini, Passalacqua and Cusimano (1976) observed three-person groups of American students and townspeople conversing in public places such as snack-bars and cafés, where they were either sitting on three sides of a table, or two people were sitting alongside one another and opposite a third. The person in the centre in both seating arrangements tended to initiate speech significantly more frequently, but he only received significantly more communications when he was both central and visible (when the other two were sitting alongside one another). Silverstein and Stang (1976) took observations of three-person groups of American students on campus, and found that one person sitting opposite two others tends to talk significantly more; they also asked the students how long they had known one another to investigate whether length of acquaintanceship affected speech participation, but without any significant findings, so that seating position in this study appeared to override length of acquaintanceship.

But seating position does not appear to override the effects of status on speech participation. Hearn (1957) observed Canadian male students in six-person groups, where in each case the investigator was the sixth member of the group; in half the groups he offered directive leadership, in the other half he offered non-directive leadership. Where his leadership was non-directive, Hearn's findings replicated those of Steinzor, with people conversing significantly more with those at a greater distance but more in their line of vision. Where his leadership was directive, the reverse was found, with people addressing significantly more of their comments to people on one side than to those sitting opposite. Similarly, Caproni *et al.* (1977) found that in a 13-person student group, students seated in positions of high visibility (directly opposite the instructor) participated significantly more often than students in positions of low visibility (seated to one side of the instructor); the instructor varied his own seating position from session to session, so that there were no significant differences in the proportion of time students spent in areas of differing visibility to the instructor.

The effects of status point to another variable which may affect the generality of Duncan's findings on turn-taking. Duncan has studied conversations between friends and strangers, and between same-sex and mixed-sex pairs, but with the possible exception of the conversation between a psychotherapist and a client, all of Duncan's findings are based on conversations between pairs of equal status. Since priority in speaking is often one of the prerogatives of higher status, differences in status might well be expected to have marked effects on the turn-taking system. Again, with the exception only of the conversation between a psychotherapist and a client, all of Duncan's findings are based on informal conversations; there may be marked differences in the turn-taking system in more formal conversations such as interviews, where the task of the interviewer is to collect information about a person's suitability for a job, or his medical history, or his guilt or innocence in respect of a crime.

Finally, there is the question of subcultural and cross-cultural differences in turn-taking. There has been practically no investigation of this with the exception only of the work of LaFrance (1974) and LaFrance and Mayo (1976). LaFrance and Mayo carried out a frame-by-frame analysis of two conversations, one between two American blacks, the other between a black and a white American. They found that whereas the white person looked at the other more when listening (replicating Kendon's (1967) finding), the blacks looked more at the other when speaking. In a second study with a much larger sample, LaFrance and Mayo observed black American and white American pairs in conversation in a number of social settings (e.g. college cafeterias, hospital and airport waiting-rooms), and found that blacks looked significantly less at one another than whites while listening; looking while listening occurred least frequently in pairs of black males and most frequently in pairs of white females. LaFrance and Mayo argue that these differences in gaze patterns may well mean there are important differences in the turn-taking system in black culture; certainly it is to be expected that turn-taking varies according to language and culture, and hence needs to be documented accordingly.

3. Partings

When people wish to bring a conversation to a close, there is some evidence to suggest that they use bodily cues for this purpose. Lockard et al. (1978) observed pairs of Americans standing and conversing with one another in a variety of settings (e.g. shopping centres, zoo, airport). They found that at the beginning of a conversation, the most common stance was one where equal weight was placed on both feet; towards the end of the conversation, the most common stance was one where more weight was placed on one foot than the other, and shifting the weight from one foot to the other occurred significantly more towards the end of the conversation. Weight-shifting was particularly pronounced in conversations in which one member of the pair departed separately, from which Lockard et al. argue that it may function as a social signal to indicate imminent departure.

Knapp et al. (1973) carried out a study in which American students were asked to conduct an interview as quickly as possible with another person who was in fact a confederate of the experimenter. The confederate was either a student or a university lecturer (to investigate the effects of status) and was either well acquainted or unknown to the student subject (to investigate the effects of relationship); the confederate was instructed not to give any leave-taking signals himself. Knapp *et al.* examined the behaviour of each subject which occurred up to 45 seconds before the subject rose from his chair, and all the behaviour which occurred while leaving. The four most frequently occurring bodily cues they found prior to leaving were breaking eye contact, pointing the legs and feet towards the door, leaning forward and head-nodding; none of these behaviours interacted significantly with status or acquaintanceship with the confederate. The four most frequently occurring forms of speech were listener responses (such as 'yeah', 'right'), which were used significantly more frequently by subjects in acquainted pairs and pairs differing in status; statements concerned with the subject's professional role, which were used significantly more frequently by subjects in pairs of equal status; 'buffing' (short words or phrases used to 'bridge' thoughts or change the topic under discussion), which was used significantly more by subjects in pairs differing in status; and statements of appreciation at having enjoyed the conversation.

Knapp *et al.* argue that the main communicative functions of behaviours associated with leave-taking are to convey both inaccessibility and supportiveness in the relationship. Some behaviours may signal future inaccessibility, such as breaking eye contact and pointing the legs and feet towards the door; other behaviours convey supportiveness, such as leaning forward and head-nodding, although such behaviours might convey future inaccessibility too. Hence the task of leave-taking is to convey that the interaction is terminated, but that the relationship continues—unless the person wishes to communicate that the relationship as well as the interaction is also at an end!

SUMMARY

Bodily cues are related to speech in terms of its syntactic, semantic and phonemic clause structure. Three main types of speech-related bodily cue have been distinguished, and their social functions discussed. Emblems refer to those non-verbal acts which have a direct verbal translation; their function is communicative and explicitly recognized as such. Illustrators are movements which are directly tied to speech; there is some evidence to show that they facilitate the comprehension of discourse, thus suggesting that they too function as a form of communication. They have also been related to the emotions and attitudes of the speaker, and to the process of speech encoding. Regulators are movements which guide and control the flow of conversation, and it has been argued that bodily cues play a role in initiating and terminating interactions, and in turn-taking, thus again suggesting that they too function as a form of communication.

Chapter 4

Individual Differences

In Chapters 2 and 3, it has been argued that bodily cues communicate information about emotion and speech. It is also widely assumed that bodily cues encode significant information about the personalities of others, that people in some way project information about themselves through their expressive style. In fact studies of body movement and the encoding of individual differences have been carried out not only on personality but also with regard to sex, psychopathology and culture. Studies investigating such encoding differences typify what Duncan (1969) calls the external variable approach (see Chapter 1, p. 12–13). Whether such differences exist is a question of considerable theoretical importance, since if it can be established that bodily cues encode information about individual differences, this would demonstrate another type of information which they convey in addition to information about emotion and speech; to discuss this possibility is one purpose of this chapter.

Individual differences in decoding constitute a second important theoretical issue. A number of studies have been carried out to investigate whether groups differ in their decoding ability, whether, for example, women are superior to men in this respect, or whether psychiatric patients are disadvantaged in comparison to the normal population. The importance of these studies with regard to the encoding/decoding distinction is that although bodily cues may encode information about emotion, speech and individual differences, such information may not always be accurately decoded; if certain groups of people fail to decode bodily cues appropriately, then the significance of those cues as a communication system may be confined to certain sectors of the population. Hence individual differences in decoding constitute the second main theme of this chapter: they are discussed with reference to differences in age, culture, personality, psychopathology and sex.

STUDIES OF ENCODING

1. Culture

Cross-cultural differences in bodily cues have already been discussed in Chapters 2 and 3 with respect to the encoding of information about emotion and speech. The view has been proposed that there are at least six emotions with innate facial expressions, which can be modified by display rules learned through culture; it has also been argued that emblems, illustrators and regulators are learned and vary between cultures. The anthropologist Edward Hall has suggested that cultures may also differ in that what he calls 'contact cultures' are characterized by a higher degree of physical contact and closer interpersonal distances than 'non-contact cultures'; he cites Arabs and Latin Americans as typical examples of contact cultures (Hall, 1959, 1966), and North Americans as an example of a non-contact culture. To test this observation, Watson and Graves (1966) compared American and Arab students studying at a Midwestern American university; they were asked to converse in pairs for five minutes with a friend from their own culture. Differences between the two groups were statistically highly significant. As well as sitting closer and touching one another more, the Arabs also faced each other more directly, looked at one another more and spoke more loudly. In another study, Watson (1970) again arranged for foreign students to converse in pairs with a member of their own culture, but on this occasion he studied a wider range of cultures. He divided the students into two groups, one representing what are hypothesized to be contact cultures (Arabs, Latin Americans and South Europeans), the other representing what are hypothesized to be non-contact cultures (Asians, Indians–Pakistanis and North Europeans). Differences between the two groups were again statistically highly significant. Watson found that members of the contact cultures faced one another more directly and looked at one another more. Members of all the contact cultures sat closer to one another than did the North Europeans, the Arabs sat closer to one another than did the Asians, and the Latin Americans sat closer to one another than did the Indians and Pakistanis. The Arabs touched one another more than did the students from the non-contact cultures, while the South Europeans touched one another more than did the North Europeans. The Arabs talked more loudly than did members of the non-contact cultures, and the Latin Americans talked more loudly than did the Asians.

Watson and Graves appear to have produced a considerable amount of evidence in support of Hall's observations, but there are a number of difficulties with their research. One problem is that their findings have not been replicated. Forston and Larson (1968) carried out a similar kind of study to those performed by Watson and Graves, in this case comparing North American and Latin American students studying in a United States university; they found no cultural differences of any statistical significance. Lomranz (1976) investigated cultural variations in interpersonal distance between Argentinian, Iraqi and Russian male students who had been studying in Israel for approximately a year. The students were asked to arrange silhouettes to represent the distance at which they would each converse with a friend, a stranger, a person of their own culture and an Israeli. From a significant statistical interaction between culture and interpersonal relationship, Lomranz found that the Argentinians preferred a greater distance when conversing with a stranger than the Russians, who in turn preferred a greater distance than the Iraqis. Lomranz criticizes the global use of the terms 'contact' and 'non-contact' cultures, since the Argentinians, who are supposed to come from a contact culture, used the greatest interpersonal distance.

A second difficulty is that the groups of Watson and Graves may have differed in respects other than those of culture. Watson (1970) administered a questionnaire in which the students were asked, for example, about their experience of town living, their experience of travel abroad, and how well acquainted they were with their conversational partner. Results did show that some of the groups differed from one another on these dimensions; for example, the Arabs were significantly better acquainted with one another than were the North Europeans. This is a serious problem, since all the significant differences found between the Arabs and the North Europeans might simply be an artefact caused by their closer acquaintanceship.

Finally, there is the problem that Watson and Graves' observations are all based on foreign students studying abroad. The difficulty here is that people may not behave in the same way to people of their own culture abroad as they would do at home. The only real answer to this criticism is to observe people within their own culture in situations which can be compared between cultures. Mazur (1977) attempted to do this by making observations of the interpersonal distances between male strangers seated on park benches in Spain and Morocco (contact cultures) and in the United States (a non-contact culture), but found no significant differences in interpersonal distance. Shuter (1976) observed pairs of people in conversation in San José (Costa Rica), Bogota (Colombia) and Panama City (Panama). His results showed that people stood significantly further apart and touched and held one another significantly less as one travels from Central to South America, a finding which Shuter uses to question the notion of a homogeneous contact culture. In another study, Shuter (1977) observed pairs of people in conversation in Venice (Italy), Heidelberg (West Germany) and Milwaukee (USA), and again found that his results failed to support Hall's concept of contact and non-contact cultures. For example, Shuter found that female pairs and mixed-sex pairs in Italy did not differ significantly in touch, orientation or interpersonal distance from the equivalent pairs in Germany, although Italy is supposed to be a contact culture, Germany a non-contact culture. Shuter argues contrary to Hall that each of the cultures he has examined is so behaviourally diverse that it cannot be simply classified as either a contact or a non-contact culture, and this view would certainly seem consistent with most of the evidence reviewed above. Hence Hall's distinction between contact and non-contact cultures cannot be said to provide a firm basis for distinguishing between cultures according to the way in which they encode bodily cues.

2. Personality

The most extensive study on the encoding of personality through non-verbal cues has been carried out by Duncan and Fiske (1977); they investigated the relationship between a large number of non-verbal behaviours and a wide range of personality variables. Other research on personality and bodily cues has been focused on whether a particular personality dimension is characterized by particular bodily cues; four main dimensions of personality have been studied, namely, extraversion/introversion, field dependence/independence, affiliation and dominance. A third approach stems from the hypothesis that there are global personality differences in the way in which people make use of non-verbal cues: one such possibility stems from research on what have been called internalizers and externalizers (Jones, 1960); another possibility stems from the concept of self-monitoring (Snyder, 1974). Each of these different approaches to the encoding of personality through bodily cues is discussed in turn.

(i) The Duncan and Fiske Study

In their study of the relationship between personality and non-verbal behaviour, Duncan and Fiske (1977) employed 88 American students, who each had a conversation with a person of the same and the opposite sex. These conversations were recorded on videotape, and observations were taken of head nodding, smiling, gaze, gesture, self-adaptors, foot movements and postural shifts, as well as a number of measures of speech. The students were also asked to complete three personality questionnaires: the Adjective Check List (Gough and Heilbrun, 1965), the Thorndike Dimensions of Temperament (Thorndike, 1966) and Schutz's FIRO scales (Schutz, 1958). In the Adjective Check List, the subject is asked to indicate from a list of 300 adjectives in alphabetical order covering a wide range of personality dispositions those adjectives which he considers to be self-descriptive. The Thorndike Dimensions of Temperament is intended to measure rates and patterns of energy discharge. The FIRO scale is intended to assess people's desire to be included in social groups as expressed in their own actions and their preferences for such actions by others.

In analysing the data, Duncan and Fiske divided the students into four groups formed by sex and the order in which they met their conversational partners. Hence, one group comprised females who conversed initially with a female and then with a male, another group comprised females who conversed initially with a male and then with a female; the other two groups were the corresponding groups of males. Duncan and Fiske present data both on the correlations between the behavioural observations and self-report questionnaires, and between the same behaviours across the two conversations. Clearly the latter measure is important, since if bodily cues are an attribute of personality, they should show some consistency between different conversations.

In general, the results did not show a strong relationship between bodily cues and self-descriptive measures; in fact none of the significant correlations which were found replicated across all four groups. For example, in the case of gaze, although there were some significant correlations of over 0.30 with a particular personality measure, there was no consistency across groups either of the same or of the opposite sex. The measures of gaze were frequency of gaze, duration of gaze and mean length of gaze; these measures were analysed separately for each person while speaking, while listening and for the whole conversation, thus deriving nine measures of gaze. The stabilities of these gaze measures across the two conversations ranged from 0.21 to 0.57, the duration measures tending to have greater stability across the two conversations than the mean lengths of gaze.

Smiling was measured in terms of the total number of smiles within each conversation, since this was relatively stable across conversations (0.54). Nevertheless, there were no significant correlations between smiling and self-report measures which were found for both sexes. Frequency of smiling for men was significantly associated with self-reports of being sociable, affiliative and nurturant, and both wanting and expressing inclusion within the group. For females, frequency of smiling was significantly related to self-reports of being tender-minded or feminine, although this relationship was more pronounced for conversations with men. Other correlations of over 0.30 were confined to one group only.

Since hand gestures occurred almost exclusively during speech, the rare instances observed while listening were not included in the analysis. Hand gesturing was measured in terms of the total time spent gesturing, the total time gesturing divided by total speaking time, the total time spent gesturing divided by the number of gesturing periods, and the number of gesturing periods divided by the total speaking time; these measures were moderately stable across conversations, showing correlations of between 0.31 and 0.49. For both male groups, the total gesturing time had significant negative correlations with self-reports of self-control and deference, and significant positive correlations with aggression. These relationships were in part a function of the relationship between the total time spent gesturing and the total time spent talking; the total time spent talking had similar but lower correlations with self-ratings of deference and aggression. When gesture time was measured as gesture extent (by dividing total gesturing time by total speaking time), the only consistent significant relationship for the male groups was the negative correlation with self-control. The other measures of gesture had no replicated relationships.

Self-adaptors included all forms of self-manipulation—touching clothing, accessories, the face and other parts of the body. Self-adaptors were analysed according to the total time and number of periods of self-adaptors, the proportion of time spent in self-adaptors while speaking and listening, and the mean length of time spent in self-adaptors for the whole conversation and while speaking and listening. These variables had correlations of between 0.20 and 0.57 across the two conversations. In the male group where the students conversed first with other males, there were significant negative correlations between self-reports of autonomy and all but one of the self-adaptor variables, while the trend in the other male group was in the same direction. There were also significant negative correlations in both male groups between the proportion of time spent in self-adaptors and self-reports of exhibition; in the two female groups, there were significant positive correlations between this measure and self-reports of being gloomy and sensitive. For females there were also significant positive correlations between the mean length of self-adaptors while listening and self-reports of defensiveness.

Foot movements included all movements of either foot, except the movements necessarily involved in shifting leg position. They were measured according to the time spent moving a foot, the number of times the person moved a foot and the mean duration of such foot movements. These variables were comparatively stable across conversations, with correlations ranging from 0.39 to 0.63. For males, there were significant positive correlations between the mean length of foot movements and self-reports of dominance and significant negative correlations with counselling readiness. For this same measure, the males and females whose first conversations were with males showed significant positive correlations with self-reports of affiliation, personal adjustment and the number of favourable adjectives selected.

Postural shifts included changes of both leg and seat position. These were measured according to the total number of times postural shifts took place, and according to whether they took place while speaking or listening; these were analysed for leg and seat positions separately, and for when changes of leg and seat position took place simultaneously, giving nine separate measures. But no consistent relationships were found for these variables.

Overall the range of results from this study of personality and non-verbal behaviour is not impressive. Duncan and Fiske make no attempt to conceal the sparseness of significant findings; in fact they use that sparseness to buttress Duncan's argument that studies of non-verbal communication should focus on structural rather than external variable approaches, on the grounds that it is in the sequential ordering of non-verbal cues that their effective significance lies, rather than in their relation to underlying personality dispositions.

(ii) Single-trait Approaches

Other research on personality and bodily cues has been focused on whether a particular personality dimension is characterized by particular bodily cues; four main dimensions of personality have been studied, namely, extraversion/ introversion, field dependence/independence, affiliation and dominance.

(a) Extraversion/Introversion.

Research on extraversion/introversion has not shown a strong relationship with bodily cues. Argyle and Cook (1976) reviewed five studies in which the relationship between gaze and extraversion was investigated, using the Extraversion scale of the Eysenck Personality Inventory. The findings are rather conflicting, in that while all the studies have found some relationship between extraversion and the amount of gaze, the precise relationship has varied according to each situation. The most strongly confirmed result is that extraverts gaze more frequently, especially while talking. Some of the studies have also found that extraverts look for a greater percentage of time and with longer glances, but these results have sometimes been found only for women or same-sex pairs. But Campbell and Rushton (1978) found that extraversion was associated with looking significantly less at a conversational partner amongst British female students.

It has also been hypothesized that extraverts prefer closer interpersonal distances. Pedersen (1973c) found some evidence for this in a study with American students who completed the Maudsley Personality Inventory and were asked to approach another student, stopping at the distance at which they felt uncomfortable; a significant positive correlation was found between a preference for closer distances and extraversion. Williams (1971) employed three procedures to investigate the relationship between interpersonal distance and extraversion. In one study, Canadian male students were administered a questionnaire concerning their interpersonal distance preferences, which showed that extraverts estimated they would allow people to get significantly closer to them for the minimal distance for a comfortable conversation, and also that they preferred dancing cheek to cheek significantly more than introverts! In a behavioural test, an experimenter approached each student, who was asked to tell the experimenter when to stop at the minimum, optimum and maximum points for a comfortable conversation. Extraverts did allow the experimenter to get significantly closer to them than did the introverts in the minimum-distance condition. But when the students each engaged in conversation with a male confederate, having first been asked to carry a chair into the room and place it where they wanted, there were no significant differences in the interpersonal distance between introverts and extraverts. In view of this latter finding, which approximates more closely to ordinary conversation than the other procedures adopted, it seems questionable whether there are any differences in the preferred distances between extraverts and introverts.

(b) Field Dependence/Independence. The concept of field dependence/independence stems from the work of Witkin et al. (1962/1974), who maintained that the way in which people perceive the world can be seen as reflecting a stable personality disposition. They distinguished between field-dependent people, who tend to rely more on cues from the environment (including other people), and field-independent people, who govern themselves more by internal cues, and tend to be less influenced by others. If field-dependent people are more dependent on information from others, then one might expect them to gaze at other people more. This hypothesis was investigated by Ruble and Nakamura (1972), who arranged for American children (aged between 7 and 10 years) to play two experimental games, one a concept-identification task, the other an object-assembly task; field-dependent children were found to look at the experimenter significantly more than field-independent children. But Kendon and Cook (1969) arranged for adults to converse in pairs, and found that those who were field dependent actually gazed significantly less at the other person while speaking, a finding in the reverse direction of what might have been predicted from the theory of field dependence.

Other studies have been carried out to investigate whether there are particular postures or gestures which may be associated with field dependence/independence. Witkin *et al.* (1962/1974) arranged for photographs to be taken of 10-year-old American boys, who were given no instructions as to the pose to adopt. The postures shown in these photographs were rated by judges on a 4-point scale with the face on each photograph blotted out so as to avoid influencing the judges' response. The 4-point scale ranged from one extreme, described as an active–assertive stance, to the other extreme, which was described as a passive stance. The active–assertive stance was characterized by good body balance, with weight evenly distributed; secure stance with feet slightly apart, or active, challenging pose; body and head generally erect, yet without obvious tension; relaxed or purposeful, intentional positioning of arms and hands. The passive stance was characterized by slouching, tight unbalanced stance, feet turned in or twisted, rigidity, tension of posture, head drooping, hands hidden, tense extending of arms from body, twisting, curling or extending of the fingers. The two intermediate points on the scale were defined with reference to these two extremes. More field-independent boys were judged as showing a significant tendency to display the more assertive, relaxed stance. Freedman *et al.* (1972) found that field-dependent American female students tend to make more body-focused gestures; in interviews they were more prone to use hand-to-hand movements (rubbing and squeezing their hands together) while they speak, and they also made more pointing or groping movements when at a loss for words. Sousa-Poza and Rohberg (1977) also found that field-dependent Canadian male students made greater use of body-touching movements. This greater use of self-adaptors seems broadly consistent with the rather diffident self-ratings found by Duncan and Fiske, where people who made greater use of self-adaptors described themselves as more gloomy, sensitive, defensive and lacking in autonomy and exhibition. Greene (1976) found in a study of American women who were attending a weight-reduction clinic that a field-independent group made significantly greater use than a field-dependent group of behaviours which were interpreted as showing greater psychological distance, namely, arm and leg crossing, shoulder shrugging, absence of forward lean and absence of smiling. Shennum (1976) showed pictures (previously judged to be pleasant or unpleasant) to American female students, whose facial expressions were filmed while they looked at the pictures. These films were then decoded by other observers, and the facial expressions of the field-dependent group were found to be significantly less expressive than the field-independent group.

(c) Affiliation. Expressive behaviour associated with affiliation has been studied most intensively by Mehrabian and Ksionsky (1974). They hypothesized that affiliation can be understood in terms of a two-dimensional scheme, comprising those who expect positive reinforcement from others (affiliative tendency), and those who expect negative reinforcement from others (sensitivity to rejection). They devised questionnaires to measure these two dimensions, which were administered to American male and female students who took part in conversations in pairs. These conversations were rated for 26 selected

measures of verbal and non-verbal behaviour which Mehrabian and Ksionsky claimed and shown unambiguous significance in other studies. A factor analysis of these ratings showed a factor which was interpreted in terms of affiliation, and which showed significant positive correlations with high scores on the affiliation questionnaire; this factor included gaze, facial pleasantness and hand gestures, as well as amount of talk and positive verbal content. But Duncan and Fiske in the study referred to above found no significant relationship between affiliation and gaze and hand gesturing, although they did find that for men frequency of smiling was significantly associated with self-reports of being sociable, affiliative, nurturant and both wanting and expressing inclusion within the group. Mehrabian and Ksionsky found a second factor from their factor analysis which they interpreted in terms of tension; this factor consisted of symmetrical body postures and a lack of sideways lean, and showed a significant positive correlation with the sensitivity to rejection scale.

(d) Dominance. There has also been some research on the relationship between gaze and dominance, based on the assumption that a highly dominant individual will be able to outstare a less dominant individual. Strongman and Champness (1968) found a perfect transitive relationship between gaze in a study of British male and female students. If C broke off gaze first when conversing with B, and B broke off gaze first when conversing with A, then C would break off gaze first when conversing with A. The question still remains, of course, whether this does in fact reflect a trait of dominance. Snyder and Sutker (1977) administered three self-report scales of dominance (Bernreuter Personality Inventory, Gough 60 Point Dominance Scale and the California Psychological Inventory) to American male students to investigate the relationship of gaze to dominance. In one procedure, the students were seated opposite one another in pairs, but were blocked from each other's view by a frame which included a draw-string curtain. Without explanation the curtain was drawn, and observers recorded which of the pair broke eye contact first. The curtain was closed again, and the experimenter explained that when it was opened for a second time, the students were to try and outstare one another. Although the three questionnaire measures of dominance yielded a reasonably high level of intercorrelation ($r = 0.65$), Snyder and Sutker report that the relationship between dominance scores and 'winning' was significant only in two of the four hypothesis-testing situations for the Bernreuter, one of the four for the California Psychological Inventory and none of the four for the Gough. Duncan and Fiske, in the study referred to earlier (pp. 80–82), found a significant positive correlation for the mean length of foot movements with self-reports of dominance, but no significant relationships were found between gaze and dominance.

(iii) Global Personality Differences

An alternative view to the single-trait approach is that personality differences in encoding take the form of global differences in the way in which people make use of bodily cues: one such possibility stems from research on what have been called internalizers and externalizers (Jones, 1960); another possibility stems from the concept of self-monitoring (Snyder, 1974).

(a) Internalizers and Externalizers. Jones (1960) observed with infants that there is sometimes an inverse relationship between their expressive behaviour and the galvanic skin response. Jones carried out a series of experiments with a group of adolescents, having first selected the 20 per cent who were most reactive and the 20 per cent least reactive in their galvanic skin response. These two groups were then instructed to classify a series of words and phrases in terms of their emotional significance, while their galvanic skin response was measured. Jones claimed to find two distinct patterns of response, and he labelled the groups internalizers and externalizers. Internalizers show high galvanic skin responsiveness, but their outward behaviour is restrained, and they are judged to be calm and poised in their social relationships. Externalizers show little galvanic skin responsiveness, but they tend to be talkative and animated, and display a great deal of motor activity.

In Chapter 2 (pp. 37–38), a number of studies were reviewed in discussing the regulation of emotion which also provide independent support for Jones' concept of internalizers and externalizers. In these studies, an encoder is typically exposed to a number of emotionally arousing events while a decoder judges from his expression what event he is observing; the sender's heart rate or skin conductance are both continuously monitored during the stimulus presentation (e.g. Lanzetta and Kleck, 1970; Buck *et al.*, 1972). The results of these studies consistently indicate that decoders are most accurate with the least physiologically aroused encoders, and least accurate with the most physiologically aroused encoders. This is entirely consistent with Jones' concept of internalizers and externalizers, which is also supported by other studies which have included direct observations of the amount of facial expressiveness, and found significant negative correlations with physiological arousal (Buck, 1977; Notarius and Levenson, 1979).

(b) Self-monitoring. A second basis for general differences in encoding stems from Snyder's (1974) concept of self-monitoring. Snyder constructed a questionnaire which was intended to measure the extent to which individuals observe and control their own expressive behaviour and presentation, and which was validated in a number of ways. One study of American male students showed a significant positive correlation between how they responded to the questionnaire and how they were rated in terms of self-monitoring by their peers. Another study showed that when American male and female students were asked to pose a number of different emotions, then the poses of high self-monitors were decoded more accurately (in terms of the poser's intentions) on the basis of both facial and vocal expression than the poses of low self-monitors. Studies of different occupational groups also support the validity of the scale; for example, actors, who might be expected to obtain high scores on self-monitoring, did in fact obtain significantly higher scores than a

comparison group of American students. Both the concept of internalizers and externalizers and the concept of self-monitoring suggest that there may be overall personality differences in the encoding of non-verbal cues, although whereas Jones regarded high physiological arousal as a consequence of the inhibition caused by internalizing emotion, Snyder regards self-monitoring as a more conscious process in which the encoder adopts a particular self-presentation which is appropriate to the situation in which he finds himself.

(iv) Personality Differences in Encoding: Summary

Overall the range of results from studies of the encoding of personality through bodily cues is not impressive. Even where significant correlations have been found between a particular personality dimension and particular bodily cues, the results often do not replicate. Significant findings which have been replicated are remarkably few, and can be summarized as follows. Extraverts tend to gaze at other people more. Field-dependent people make greater use of self-adaptors, which are also used more by people who describe themselves as more gloomy, sensitive, defensive and lacking in autonomy and exhibition. People with a high need for affiliation tend to show greater facial pleasantness and smile more. General differences in encoding non-verbal cues may be related to the self-monitoring and internalizing/externalizing personality dimensions. The sparseness of these findings (given the intensity of the research effort) suggests that the belief that body movement encodes significant information about personality may well be an example of a decoding error.

3. Psychopathology

Hill (1974), in a discussion of the role of non-verbal behaviour in mental illness, comments that psychiatrists of an earlier generation commonly believed that they could diagnose the likely mental state of their patients simply by observing their behaviour. Hence, for example, the tense obsessional might display rigid bodily postures and use very precise movements, while the retarded depressive used slow movements and displayed an immobile facial expression. Hill comments that such observations were all part of the diagnostic procedure, and were mentioned in the major textbooks of psychiatry; but at the time at which Hill was writing, it would be hard to find such illustrations in any textbooks of psychiatry published in the last 30 years. In recent years, however, there have been a number of more systematic studies intended to investigate the relationship between different bodily cues and psychopathology, in particular anxiety, depression, schizophrenia, autism, psychopathy and delinquency; these studies will be reviewed in turn.

(i) Anxiety

Waxer (1977) took videotapes of psychiatric patients while they were orally responding to a questionnaire designed to measure anxiety (the Spielberger

State-Trait Anxiety Inventory). The patients constituted a heterogeneous sample in terms of age, ethnic background and psychiatric categorization. The ages ranged from 18 to 54, ethnic backgrounds included two Italians, two Hungarians, one Scot, one French-Canadian and three Americans, the remainder being English-speaking Canadians. Psychiatric diagnoses included agitated depression, belle indifference, reactive depression, anxiety reaction, schizoid reaction, alcoholism and drug addiction. Videotapes of the patients were shown without sound to Canadian students, who were asked to judge on a 10-point scale the level of anxiety of the patients. Results showed a significant positive correlation between their ratings and the patients' degree of anxiety, as measured by the anxiety questionnaire. From the comments of the raters, certain key areas were investigated for the specific bodily cues associated with anxiety. Patients were divided into a high and low anxious group on the basis of their responses to the questionnaire. Hand movements were divided into signalling movements (e.g. pointing) and non-signalling movements (e.g. stroking oneself, hand tremors); non-signalling movements were found to be used significantly more by high anxious patients, while low anxious patients made significantly greater use of signalling movements. There was no difference in the frequency of glances at the interviewer between high and low anxious patients, but high anxious patients did show significantly shorter length of glances. Finally, high anxious patients smiled significantly less frequently. This evidence for both encoding and decoding suggests that anxiety can be communicated through bodily cues.

(ii) Depression

In a similar design, Waxer (1974) showed silent films to Canadian students and faculty members of five depressed and five non-depressed psychiatric patients; Waxer found that the judges were able to identify the depressed patients from the bodily cues alone. In another study, Waxer (1976) showed Canadian students a silent videotape of depressed and non-depressed psychiatric patients, and compared the decoders' judgements with the scores obtained by the patients on the depression scale of the Minnesota Multiphasic Personality Inventory (MMPI). Results showed a significant positive correlation between judgements of depression from the videotapes and intensity of depression as shown by the MMPI scores. The particular cues which judges reported as identifying depression were a lack of eye contact, downward angling of the head, a drooping mouth and a lack of hand movement.

Other studies have provided some support for these observations. Ekman and Friesen (1974a, p. 215) describe a study by Kiritz (1971; discussed in Chapter 3, p. 66) in which hand movements of American female psychiatric in-patients were observed at hospital admission and discharge. All hand movements were classified as either illustrators or self-adaptors, and it was hypothesized that the number of illustrators would increase with enthusiasm and involvement. Observations were taken of people suffering from psychotic depression, neurotic depression and schizophrenia, and it was found that those suffering from psychotic depression showed the fewest number of illustrators at admission; there was, however, a significant increase in their use of illustrators from the admission to the discharge interview.

A number of studies have been carried out with British patients on the relationship between gaze and depression. Rutter and Stephenson (1972a) gave a standardized interview to 20 men and women suffering from depression, who had just been admitted to hospital. They were compared with a control group of patients suffering from chest illnesses, who were matched for sex, age, socio-economic status and length of hospital stay since admission. The interview was standardized by reading printed questions from a sheet of paper; the interviewer looked at the paper while asking the questions, and looked continuously at the interviewee as the interviewee made his reply. The people suffering from depression spent significantly less time looking at the interviewer than did the control group, regardless of whether they were speaking or listening. In a second study, Rutter and Stephenson (1972b) repeated the same procedure, but with a group of psychiatric patients not diagnosed as schizophrenic or depressive (mainly male alcoholics). These patients did not show significantly less gaze than the control group, but did look significantly more than the group diagnosed as suffering from depression. Hinchcliffe, Lancashire and Roberts (1971) conducted a standardized interview with patients suffering from depression and with patients who had recovered from depression, matched for age, sex and social class. The recovered patients spent significantly more time gazing at the interviewer than did those still suffering from depression.

It appears, then, that depression is associated with a lack of eye contact, downward angling of the head, a drooping mouth and a lack of hand movement. Rutter and Stephenson (1972b) argued that since reduced gaze is not associated with all psychiatric patients, then an interpretation in terms, for example, of stigma is ruled out. The behaviours which encode depression seem to involve a lack of interest in or rejection of other people; they would seem likely to maintain the social isolation of a person suffering from depression, given that Waxer (1974, 1976) has shown that observers can identify depressed patients on the basis of bodily cues alone, thus suggesting that depression can be communicated through bodily cues.

(iii) Schizophrenia

In their standardized interview referred to above, Rutter and Stephenson also compared men and women who had recently been admitted to psychiatric hospital suffering from schizophrenia with the control group of patients suffering from chest illnesses, matched for sex, age, socio-economic status and length of hospital stay since admission. The schizophrenic patients looked significantly less at the interviewer than did the control group, both while talking and listening; they also differed from the depressive patients, in that they looked at the interviewer in significantly shorter glances. When compared with the psychiatric control group (mainly male alcoholics), they also spent significantly less time gazing at the interviewer. But in a subsequent study, Rutter (1976) investigated whether this effect might be specific to the psychiatric interview. In one experiment, he compared recently admitted male and female schizophrenic patients in two free conversations, one with a person also suffering from schizophrenia, the other with a psychiatrically normal person. Their behaviour was compared with three control groups—depressive patients, patients suffering from neurotic and personality disorders and psychiatrically normal patients suffering from chest illnesses. The results showed no significant differences in gaze between the schizophrenic and psychiatrically normal groups; in fact there was a trend for the schizophrenic patients to look significantly more at the interviewer than the patients suffering from neurotic and personality disorders. In a second experiment, Rutter compared a group of chronic, long-stay schizophrenic patients (mainly male) with a group of recently admitted schizophrenic patients matched for sex and age; each person took part in a conversation with a psychiatric nurse, and the results showed no significant differences in gaze between the two groups. But when compared with the schizophrenic patients in the first study, these patients did look significantly less at their conversational partner, a finding which Rutter interpreted in terms of the associated speech content. In the first study, the patients were asked to discuss an item from the Choice Dilemmas Questionnaire (Kogan and Wallach, 1964); in the second study, they tended to discuss their personal history and problems with the psychiatric nurse, which was also the content of the original interview study (Rutter and Stephenson, 1972a). Consequently, Rutter argues that people suffering from schizophrenia do show gaze avoidance, but only when talking about personal matters; their gaze is quite normal when the topic is not of immediate personal relevance.

Subsequently, Rutter (1978) has re-analysed a number of his earlier studies of schizophrenic gaze (Rutter, 1976; 1977a; 1977b), and compared the timing of gaze in relation to changes in speaker. Rutter found no significant differences in the timing of gaze between schizophrenic and normal groups in relation to switches of speaker. Hence Rutter concluded that although there is evidence that schizophrenic patients do show gaze avoidance, there is no evidence that they time their looks abnormally. He interprets the gaze aversion which has been demonstrated simply in terms of embarrassment, arguing that schizophrenic patients are embarrassed by personal conversations about their symptoms and case histories, and respond by averting their gaze.

It has also been argued that people suffering from schizophrenia adopt greater interpersonal distances than normals in relation to others. Horowitz, Duff and Stratton (1964) asked American male and female schizophrenic patients to approach a hat-rack, imagining that it was a person, until they felt they were at a comfortable interpersonal distance; their results showed that the schizophrenic patients adopted a significantly greater distance than a control group of people with no history of psychiatric disturbance. Aronow, Reznikoff and Tryon (1975) compared the interpersonal distances adopted by American males suffering from process and reactive schizophrenia with a control group of hospital employees. They used a number of techniques to measure preferred interpersonal distances, including a measure of seating distance from a target person, and a projective technique, which involved placing felt figures at preferred distances, one figure of which is intended to represent the subject of the experiment (the Kuethe technique). Their results showed no significant differences in interpersonal distance preferences between the schizophrenic patients and the hospital employees, and in view of the marked artificiality of the technique employed by Horowitz, Duff and Stratton, the hypothesis that schizophrenic patients adopt abnormally large interpersonal distances can scarcely be said to have been satisfactorily demonstrated.

One study which has shown a difference in the encoding of bodily cues between schizophrenics and normals was carried out by Winkelmayer *et al.* (1978). Winkelmayer *et al.* arranged for normal and schizophrenic women, closely matched for age and educational level, to relate three personal experiences, one which evoked happiness, another which evoked anger and another which evoked sorrow. A film was made of these accounts, and was shown without sound to male American, British and Mexican students, who were asked to identify the emotion being described. The results showed a significant statistical interaction between diagnostic category and nationality of the judges, with American and British judges performing significantly better at guessing the emotions encoded by the group of normal women. This finding that the schizophrenic women were relatively poorer at encoding information about emotion provides some support for the traditional description of schizophrenia as characterized by 'flattened affect' (Bleuler, 1950). Flattened affect refers to a relative impoverishment of emotional expressiveness, a concept which is highly similar to that of poor encoding demonstrated in this study.

(iv) Autism

Hutt and Ounsted (1970) have argued that gaze avoidance is the key distinguishing feature of autism. They arranged for five models of faces (happy, sad, blank, face of a monkey, face of a dog) to be placed on stands and to be distributed around the room. Autistic and non-autistic children of the same age group from a British hospital were studied, and the results showed that the autistic children looked significantly less at happy and sad faces, and significantly more at environmental features. Similarly, Richer and Coss (1976) compared a group of British autistic boys and girls (mean age seven years seven months) with local primary schoolchildren matched for sex and age, and found that the autistic children would look significantly more at an adult, and were significantly less inclined to run away when the adult covered his eyes. The autistic children also looked significantly less when both eyes were exposed rather than one, thus supporting the belief that it is the eyes which provoke gaze aversion.

Hutt and Ounsted argue that gaze aversion has the effect of reducing arousal, maintaining that the autistic child may be chronically over-aroused. Similarly, Clancy and McBride (1969) argued that the autistic child shows a whole number of behaviours which help to maintain his social isolation. Case histories they reviewed typically revealed a pattern in the first year of life characterized by a lack of smiling, by quiet undemanding behaviour when left alone but by irritation when disturbed, and by a lack of responsiveness to the human voice but by selective responsiveness to other sounds. According to Hutt and Ounsted, gazing at other people is essential for social interaction, and so gaze aversion can be seen as a form of communication serving to maintain the isolation of the autistic child.

(v) Psychopathy

It has also been hypothesized that violent offenders are characterized by exceptionally large zones of personal space, and may feel provoked into violence if others come too close to them. Kinzel (1970) compared preferences for interpersonal distance between violent and non-violent prisoners; an experimenter walked towards them from a number of different positions, and they were asked to say when he came 'too close'. The results showed that the violent offenders preferred significantly greater interpersonal distances, particularly when approached from the rear, a finding which Kinzel interpreted in terms of homosexual anxiety. Kinzel (1972) argued that the dislike of physical closeness by violent prisoners is due to a failure to cope with extreme stranger anxiety during development; he maintains that isolating such prisoners will only exacerbate their condition. Roger and Schalekamp (1976) criticized these findings on the grounds of the possible confounding effects of imprisonment; it may be that violent offenders are only intolerant of close interpersonal distances during a period of institutionalization. They avoided this problem by using ex-prisoners (male Cape Coloured South Africans) who had previously served sentences for either violent or non-violent offences. When approached from the front, sides and rear, the distance preferences of the violent ex-prisoners were significantly greater than those of the non-violent group from all the directions of approach, thus suggesting that Kinzel's results were not an artefact of institutionalization. The finding has in fact been replicated on a number of occasions with American male prisoners (Hildreth, Derogatis and McCusker, 1971; Booraem et al., 1977; Curran, Blatchley and Hanlon, 1978). But Kinzel's finding that violent offenders are particularly sensitive to approaches from the rear has not been replicated (Hildreth, Derogatis and McCusker, 1971; Curran, Blatchley and Hanlon, 1978). Wilds (1973), however, failed to find any significant differences in personal space preferences between violent and non-violent male American offenders.

Similar studies have also been carried out with delinquent adolescents. Duke and Fenhagen (1975) administered the Comfortable Interpersonal Distance Scale to coloured and white American adolescent females who had been placed in a detention unit of a county juvenile court (primarily for running away from home); they were compared with a control group of non-delinquent girls who had attended a nearby high school. The results showed that the delinquent girls preferred significantly greater interpersonal distances. Newman and Pollack (1973) compared a group of American male adolescents who had been placed in a special class because of their aggressive behaviour with another group who had been placed in a special class because of academic under-achievement. When approached by an experimenter, the aggressive group preferred significantly greater interpersonal distances than the control group. But Beck and Ollendick (1976) compared American male adolescent delinquents who had been referred to a special school by a court with a control group from a normal school, and found no significant differences in the distance they allowed an experimenter to approach towards them.

Beck and Ollendick suggest that their failure to replicate Newman and Pollack's findings might stem from the effects of institutionalization on the delinquents, Sommer (1967) having suggested that one of the effects of institutionalization is a reduction in the requirements for personal space. This is of course the opposite of the argument put forward by Roger and Schalekamp (1976), who argued that Kinzel's findings might only have occurred within an institutional context. Roger and Schalekamp's findings with violent ex-prisoners suggested that this was not the case, and in fact the failures to replicate greater distance preferences with violent offenders (Wilds, 1973) and adolescent delinquents (Beck and Ollendick, 1976) both come from studies of institutional populations. Hence the evidence suggests that violent offenders and adolescent delinquents do have abnormally large zones of personal space, but that this preference may be mollified by the existence of institutionalization.

One study in which the role of other bodily cues has been investigated in relation to psychopathy was carried out by Rimé et al. (1978). They divided Belgian male adolescents from a private institution into two groups of psychopaths and non-psychopaths on the basis of ratings by counsellors who worked at the institution. All the boys took part in a non-directive interview with a male interviewer, who was unaware of the group in which each boy had been placed. The results showed a number of significant differences in bodily cues between the psychopathic and non-psychopathic group. Those in the psychopathic group spent a longer period of time hand gesturing, leaning forward and gazing at the interviewer's eyes, but smiled less frequently. Rimé et al. interpret these differences as showing a greater intrusiveness in interpersonal behaviour, which they relate to the hypothesis (e.g. Hare, 1970) that psychopathy is related to cortical under-arousal, and that as a result the psychopath actively seeks stimulation with active or exciting qualities. They support this argument from their observations of the interviewer's behaviour, which showed only one significant difference, in that the interviewer spoke significantly less with the psychopathic than the non-psychopathic group. They interpret this difference in speech participation as a response to the psychopaths' greater intrusiveness; but it is of course equally possible that the interviewer may have been responding in this way to some other aspect of the psychopaths' behaviour, and that they in turn responded by displaying greater intrusiveness. Rimé *et al.* also fail to discuss the apparent contradiction between the interpersonal distance research, which suggests that adolescent delinquents prefer greater distances from others, and their own argument that psychopaths are more intrusive, using behaviours (such as leaning forward) which reduce the distance between themselves and others.

(vi) Psychopathological Differences in Encoding: Summary

There do appear to be a number of encoding differences in bodily cues systematically related to psychopathology. People suffering from anxiety make greater use of non-signalling hand movements, use shorter glances and smile less frequently; observers can identify differences in the self-reported degree of anxiety on the basis of bodily cues alone, thus suggesting that anxiety is communicated through bodily cues. People suffering from depression show a lack of eye contact, downward angling of the head, a drooping mouth and a lack of hand movement; observers can also identify depressed patients on the basis of bodily cues alone, thus suggesting that depression, too, is communicated through bodily cues. Autistic children show marked gaze aversion, which has been regarded as a form of communication serving to maintain the social isolation of the autistic child. The hypothesis that people suffering from schizophrenia show marked gaze aversion does not appear to be supported by more carefully controlled studies; instead it appears that they avert their gaze only when talking about their own personal problems. In addition, they appear to be relatively poor encoders of emotion. Studies of psychopathy and delinquency are more confusing and contradictory, but it appears that violent offenders and delinquent adolescents have abnormally large personal space preferences, which are possibly modified by the effects of institutionalization.

4. Sex

Hall (1979) was able to find 26 studies in which comparisons were made of sex differences in encoding through facial expression, body movement or content-free speech. In these studies, groups of judges varying from 2 to 200 in number were asked to make judgements from either posed or spontaneous non-verbal expressions; if the judges were able to accurately identify the non-verbal expression, then the sender was regarded as a 'good' encoder. In the case of posed expressions, the task of the decoders was to judge the expression in terms of its meaning (emotional or otherwise), or degree of friendliness, or honesty; the criterion of 'good' encoding was whether that judgement concurred with the poser's intentions. In the studies of spontaneous expressions, the experimenters surreptitiously recorded the encoders' faces on film or videotape while they were viewing emotionally arousing incidents (on slides, videotape or in person); the criterion of 'good' encoding was whether the decoders could guess the particular incident viewed by the encoder. The ability of people to encode through posed and spontaneous expressions appears to be positively correlated; for example, Zuckerman *et al.* (1976) found a significant correlation of 0.46 between posed and spontaneous encodings.

The results of the 26 studies reviewed by Hall show a clear advantage in favour of women. Nine of the studies show a significant gender difference, and eight of these showed that women were better encoders, a proportion which is significantly greater than the 50 per cent which would be expected by chance. To make the studies statistically comparable, the size of effect was calculated in terms of standard deviation units (d); d is the difference between the mean of the two groups divided by their common standard deviation (J. Cohen, 1977). The mean effect size for visual studies was 0.88 standard deviation unit, while the mean effect size for vocal studies was only 0.01 standard deviation unit, a difference which is marginally significant $(p = 0.067)$. Hence it appears that the female non-verbal encoding advantages is essentially confined to visual cues.

A number of specific sex differences in the encoding of bodily cues have also been documented, and these are discussed below.

(i) Gaze

One finding commonly reported in the literature is that women gaze at other people more than men. For example, Exline (1963) arranged for groups of American students to take part in discussions in groups of three people of the same sex; he found that the women spent significantly more time looking at one another both while speaking and while listening, and exchanged significantly more mutual glances. Exline, Gray and Schuette (1965) arranged for American students to be interviewed by either a male or female graduate student, who was instructed to look continuously at the subject throughout the interview. Half of the subjects were asked personal questions which were intended to be embarrassing, the other half were asked questions intended to be innocuous. The students were further subdivided into one half who were asked to conceal their feelings, the other half being given no such instructions. Exline, Gray and Schuette found that the women looked at the interviewer for a significantly longer proportion of time regardless of the interviewer's sex. The difference was found while speaking to the interviewer, during periods of silence and while listening to the interviewer (for the students who were given instructions to conceal their feelings). Subsequently Exline (1972) has reported that women look significantly more at others than men in all the studies in which he has measured sex differences in interpersonal gaze.

Sex differences in gaze have in fact been reported with young children and even with infants. Kleinke, Desautels and Knapp (1977) carried out a study with American children aged between three and five; they were asked to play a word game (using familar words from the vocabulary test of the Wechsler Intelligence Scale for Children) in which the experimenter read each vocabulary item which the child was then expected to define. Experimenters either looked down while reading each vocabulary item and gazed at the child for the duration of each answer (80 per cent gaze), or gazed at the child only during the answer to every seventh item (20 per cent gaze). The experimenters were two female college students who were unaware of the hypotheses of the experiment, and were trained to be consistent in facial expression, body posture and tone of voice. The girls gazed for a significantly longer percentage of time than the boys, regardless of whether the experimenter gazed 80 per cent or 20 per cent of the time. Hittelman and Dickes (1979) arranged for new-born infants to listen to periods of taped speech of an adult, while the adult gazed continually at the infant. The infants were arranged in four different postures: supine in bassinet, cradled flat, partially cradled and upright. The results showed that in the upright postures, the girls looked significantly longer at the adult.

Nevertheless, not all investigators have replicated sex differences in inter-personal gaze. Schneider, Coutts and Garrett (1977) reported a study of Canadian students who met in groups of three, made up of one female confederate, one male confederate and one male or female experimental subject. The confederates were instructed to gaze continuously at the subject, while the subjects were asked to talk about their future interests and goals for a period of three minutes. The results showed no significant differences in either frequency, duration or mean duration of the subjects' gaze, regardless or whether they were addressing a male or a female confederate. Schneider, Coutts and Garrett conclude that group size may moderate the influence of sex upon patterns of gaze, but in view of the study by Exline (1963) on same-sex groups of three discussed above, it is possible that it is only mixed-sex groups which moderate the influence of sex on patterns of gaze.

(ii) Facial Expression

The major reported sex difference in facial expression is in the frequency of smiling. For example, Duncan and Fiske (1977) arranged for 88 American male and female students to each have a conversation with a person of the same sex and of the opposite sex. Duncan and Fiske found that the women both smiled significantly more frequently and spent a significantly higher proportion of time smiling. Bond and Ho (1978) arranged for Japanese male and female students to participate individually in interviews with male and female graduate students, who were instructed to standardize their behaviour across the interviews. Bond and Ho found that the female students smiled significantly more frequently. Freedman (1979, pp. 174–175) reports an unpublished study by DeBoer (1974), who observed smiling in two-day-old black American infants. Smiles were classified into three types: full smiling (at least one second), assymetrical smiling and fleeting smiles. Girls showed more smiles of all types, and significantly more fleeting smiles.

(iii) Posture and Gesture

Birdwhistell (1971) has argued that body movement can be used as what he calls a gender identification signal. From his own observations in seven different societies (Chinese, middle and upper-class London British, Kutenai, Shushwap, Hopi, Parisian French and American), both male and female informants were able to distinguish not only between male and female behaviour, but also between 'feminine' males and 'masculine' females. This has been tested more formally by Lippa (1978). Videotapes were made of male and female encoders as they role-played being junior high school maths teachers. The encoders also completed the Bem Sex Role Inventory (Bem, 1974), according to which it is possible to identify any person of either sex as possessing either masculine qualities, feminine qualities or as androgynous, with the latter possessing masculine and feminine traits in roughly equal proportions. The videotapes were rated by American students on a number of 7-point rating scales, including dimensions of masculinity and femininity. The results showed not surprisingly a significant main effect of sex on ratings of masculinity and femininity, but they also showed a significant main effect for sex-typing (irrespective of the sex of the encoder), with masculine sex-typed persons being perceived as more masculine than feminine sex-typed persons, the androgynous group being perceived as intermediate between the other two groups. In a second study, Lippa arranged for similar ratings to be made by a new group of judges under five different conditions: from the vision only, the body only, the head only, the voice only and from a still photograph. Significant effects for sex-typing occurred only in the vision-alone and body-alone conditions, suggesting that cues from the body are of particular importance in judging sex-typing. The results also suggested that physical appearance or clothing is unimportant, since there was no significant effect for sex-typing when judgements were made from photographs alone. These findings are of particular interest in that they suggest that information about sex-role indentification is communicated through bodily cues.

Birdwhistell (1971) has described what he considers to be some American gender identification signals. For example, he maintains that the American female moves with arms closer to the whole body than the male, and may present the entire body from neck to ankle as a moving whole, whereas the male moves the arms independently of the trunk. There has, however, been little systematic documentation of sex-typing in posture and gesture. One form of sex-typing in posture which has been demonstrated is the way in which books are carried. Jenni and Jenni (1976) distinguished between two methods of carrying books. In Type 1, one or both arms are wrapped around the books, the forearm on the outside of the books supports them. In Type 2 the books are supported by one hand and arm at the side of the body (see Figure 17). Jenni and Jenni's initial finding that 92 per cent of the women at the University of Montana employed Type 1 and 95 per cent of the males used Type 2 was confirmed in a number of locations throughout North and Central American (Ontario, New York, El Salvador and Costa Rica). Jenni and Jenni also carried out a development study with children at kindergarten and first grade school, but found that at this age children of both sexes carried books like mature males.

Rekers, Amaro-Plotkin and Low (1977) have, however, shown that some sex-typed movements are displayed by children as young as four or five. In a previous study (Rekers, 1977), they had observed in gender-disturbed boys

Figure 17. Sex differences in book-carrying. (Based on a drawing in D. A. Jenni and M. A. Jenni (1976), Carrying behaviour in humans: analyses of sex differences. *Science*, **194**, 859—860. Reproduced by permission. Copyright 1976 by the American Association for the Advancement of Science)

eight gestures which they categorized as effeminate; in this study, they set out to investigate whether these gestures were used more often by normal girls than by normal boys. They observed American children in two age groups (4- to 5-year-olds and 11- to 12-year-olds) playing a game with a beanbag, and found that the sexes did differ with respect to three of the 'effeminate' movements used by gender-disturbed boys. These were what they call the limp wrist, flutters (a rapid succession of up and down movements of the forearm and/or upper arm while the wrist remains relaxed), and walking with a flexed elbow (where the angle between the upper arm and forearm is between 0° and 135°); these movements were used significantly more frequently by girls irrespective of age. In another study with a larger sample of American children (aged 4 to 5, 7 to 8 and 10 to 11 years), Rekers and Rudy (1978) replicated these findings, and in addition found that the girls irrespective of age made significantly greater use of what they called a hand clasp (touching the hands together in front of the body) and palming (touching the palm to the back, front or sides of the head above the level of the ears).

(iv) Interpersonal Distance

An early study by Sommer (1959) reported sex differences in interpersonal space. Sommer arranged for a confederate of the experimenter to be seated at a table, while staff and inmates of an American hospital were asked to go into the room in turn to converse with the confederate. With a female confederate, women preferred to sit alongside or at the corner of the table; men overwhelmingly preferred opposite seating, regardless of the sex of the confederate. Sommer interpreted this finding as showing that women prefer closer interpersonal distances amongst themselves than do men, and this hypothesis has been supported by other research. Giesen and McClaren (1976) arranged for groups of male and female American students to discuss a social issue (abortion or vasectomy) in three-person same-sex groups under the guidance of either a male or female group leader. Giesen and McClaren found that women chose significantly closer seating distances amongst themselves, and that students of both sexes sat significantly closer to a female than to a male group leader.

Baxter (1970) made observations of pairs of people looking at animals in a zoo; the members of each pair were standing together and hence presumably acquainted with one another. Baxter found that for both white and black Americans, mixed-sex pairs stood significantly closer than female pairs, who in turn stood significantly closer than male pairs; for Mexican Americans, female pairs stood significantly closer than mixed-sex pairs who in turn stood significantly closer than male pairs. Baxter's observations included children (estimated between 5 and 10 years of age) as well as adolescents and adults, and he found that for Mexican Americans, pairs of girls stood closer than other pairs, but black American girls stood further apart than other pairs; for white American children, there appeared to be no sex differences in interpersonal distance. Beach and Sokoloff (1974) observed white American children (aged between four and five years) playing together in groups of three, and in fact found that the girls kept a significantly greater distance apart than the boys. Thus it appears that in American society it is the adult norm for women to adopt closer interpersonal distances amongst themselves than men.

(v) Sex Differences in Encoding: Summary

There do appear to be significant and reliable sex differences in the encoding of bodily cues. Women appear both to encode more clearly than men, and also to look more at others, show a preference for closer interpersonal distances with each other, smile more and use particular kinds of sex-typed posture and gesture (although these studies are based mainly on American society). Sex-typing as measured by questionnaire can be ascertained by observers from bodily cues alone, thus suggesting that sex differences in encoding communicate significant information about a person's sex-role identification, what Birdwhistell (1971) has called 'gender identification signals'.

STUDIES OF DECODING

The most extensive set of studies on individual differences in decoding non-verbal cues have been carried out by Rosenthal *et al.* (1979), using a test which they call Profile of Nonverbal Sensitivity (abbreviated to PONS). This test comprises a 45-minute black-and-white film, in which a number of short scenes are posed by a young American woman. The information available to the decoder includes both bodily cues (pictures of the face and body from the neck to the knees) and speech, especially processed by electronic filtering or randomized splicing to disguise the actual words spoken but to retain vocal information, such as tone of voice, pitch and affect. Electronic filtering involves filtering all the speech frequencies above a certain level, so that the content of speech is rendered unintelligible; the result of this filtering process sounds like 'a kind of mumble as heard through a wall' (Starkweather, 1956). Randomized splicing is a technique developed by Scherer (1971), which involves cutting a stretch of recording tape into pieces and splicing them back together in random order, which makes the speech almost totally unintelligible; randomized splicing preserves the full voice spectrum, which is its major advantage over electronic filtering, but of course destroys any paralinguistic information which is dependent upon the original speech sequence.

In the PONS, the information from the face, the body, electronically-filtered speech and randomized-spliced speech is presented both separately and in all possible combinations for 20 different situations to the decoders, whose task is to judge which situation is being depicted. For each scene, the decoder is given two alternate descriptions, one of which is correct, e.g. whether the encoder is nagging a child or expressing jealous anger. The criterion of accuracy is based on a combination of what message the encoder intended to send, and what message the researchers, the encoder and a panel of judges decided the encoder had in fact sent; the items which achieved the highest level of agreement were included in the final test. Clearly, this particular criterion of accuracy raises a number of problems, in that it is assumed that the original judges are reasonably perceptive, since even if they agree amongst themselves, this is no necessary guarantee of their accuracy. The criterion is particularly questionable if the innate hypothesis of emotional expression is accepted as valid. If non-verbal cues are a learned, culture-specific code, then the agreement of a number of representative judges of that culture is a relatively good criterion against which to evaluate people's performance. But if the expression of emotion is innate, then inter-observer agreement may be totally irrelevant, representing popular stereotypes about the particular non-verbal cues associated with different emotions, rather than the actual responses themselves. Nevertheless, Rosenthal *et al.* argue in defence of the test that it does have what is referred to as construct validity (Cronbach and Meehl, 1955), that the results obtained from the suggest that it is measuring what it is supposed to measure. For example, studies of occupational groups show that the sort of people who might be expected to perform well on such a test do obtain high scores; the best three groups tested have been actors, students of visual arts and students on courses in non-verbal communication (Rosenthal *et al.*, 1979). In fact the best score ever obtained on the test was achieved by a group who had enrolled for a course on non-verbal communication *before* they had started the course! The test has also been compared with self-ratings and ratings by other people of the decoders' sensitivity to non-verbal cues. Ratings by others show consistent significant positive correlations with performance on the test, with a median correlation coefficient of 0.22. But when people rate themselves on their sensitivity to non-verbal cues, their ratings do not correlate highly with test performance, suggesting that people are not good judges of their own interpersonal sensitivity. Rosenthal *et al.* have in fact carried out a whole series of studies relating performance on the PONS to differences in age, culture, personality, psycho-pathology and sex, and argue from the results obtained that the test does have a high degree of construct validity. These studies are reviewed in the remainder of this chapter, alongside other studies of individual differences in decoding non-verbal cues.

1. Age

In Chapter 2 it was argued that there is no real evidence to support the view that the decoding of emotional expression is innate, although the capacity to discriminate between different expressions is present virtually from birth. Charlesworth and Kreutzer (1973), in a review of the literature on facial expression and recognition of emotion in infants and children, have argued that in comparison to emotional expression, emotional recognition may require greater cognitive and perceptual development, as well as greater social experience. Evidence from decoding studies certainly supports the view that decoding skills improve with age. Rosenthal *et al.* (1979) have administered the PONS to Americans of differing ages, and found that accuracy increased in a linear fashion between the ages of 8 and 25. They also found significant statistical interactions between age and the decoding of bodily cues, the younger children performing at a relatively greater disadvantage when visual cues are present. This finding confirms the results of two studies by Bugental, Kaswan and Love (1970) and Bugental *et al.* (1970) in which they compared the relative importance of facial cues with speech content and intonation for Americans of differing ages. Adult encoders presented messages which were intended to be friendly or unfriendly, where there was always a conflict between the facial, verbal and vocal channels; these channels were rated independently of one another prior to the main experiment to check that they conformed to the experimenters' intentions. Bugental, Kaswan and Love (1970) found that whereas young children perceived as negative a woman making a negative statement in a negative tone of voice contradicted only by a smile, adults most commonly perceived the same combination as joking. Bugental *et al.* (1970) in fact found a general trend for children to be more influenced than adults by verbal or vocal than by visual channels. When the younger decoders were divided into three age groups (5 to 8, 9 to 12, 13 to 18), a significant increase with age was found in the importance attached to the visual channel.

Rosenthal *et al.* suggest three possible hypotheses for the relative disadvantage of young children at decoding visual cues. One possibility is that it is simply due to their size; adult facial expressions are relatively inaccessible to them. But this would not explain their inferiority in respect of decoding cues from the body. A second hypothesis draws on a study by Bugental, Love and Gianetto (1971), who found that whereas fathers tend to smile in conjunction with positive verbal statements, mothers show no such relationship between smiling and speech content. Rosenthal *et al.* suggest that younger children may ignore female facial expressions because they are not always accurate reflectors of female emotions. A third hypothesis is that as children become more verbally oriented, either the social pressure to pay attention to verbal messages or the effort required to comprehend them leads to a relative inattention to visual cues. A somewhat similar suggestion was made by Bugental *et al.* (1970), who suggest the inferiority of children in decoding visual cues may be due to inadequate intersensory integration; they cite the work of Birch and Belmont (1965), who have found clear evidence of developmental trends in intersensory judgements.

2. Culture

Cross-cultural studies of decoding represent an interesting test of the interactionist hypothesis, where certain facial expressions of emotion are seen as innate, while display rules, emblems, illustrators and regulators are seen as learned and variable across culture. Rosenthal *et al.* (1979) have administered the PONS test to nationals from 20 different countries. They argue that it overcomes some of the shortcomings of earlier cross-cultural research, in that film has been used instead of static photographs, and non-verbal cues have been depicted through several channels (face, body, paralanguage), rather than confining the test to facial expression alone. They also argue that the results could support at least three different interpretations of the role of culture in non-verbal communication. Since the PONS is an American test, if only Americans score significantly above chance, this would support the view that non-verbal cues are specific to a particular culture. Conversely, if members of all cultures scored significantly above chance and did equally well on the test, this would support a universalist view that non-verbal cues can be accurately interpreted irrespective of culture. But if members of other cultures scored significantly above chance but their performance was still inferior to that of the Americans, this would support an interactionist position where some cues are universal and some specific to particular cultures.

In fact the results of cross-cultural studies with the PONS overwhelmingly support the interactionist position. Non-American samples perform significantly better than chance, but significantly worse than Americans. The different cultural groups were also rated by judges for their similarity to

American culture; for example, Canadian students were rated as more similar than students from Hong Kong. When these ratings were compared with performance on the PONS, the results showed significant positive correlations between test performance and rated similarity to American culture. Another way of rank ordering the cultures is in terms of linguistic similarity. The cultures represented were divided into four language groups according to their similarity to American culture—Germanic languages (English, German Dutch, Swedish), Italic and Hellenic (French, Spanish, Portuguese, Italian, Greek), Slavic (Polish, Czech, Serbo-Croatian) and non-Indo-European (Chinese, Hebrew, Turkish, New Guinea). Rank-ordered for linguistic similarity in this way, there was again a highly significant positive correlation between cultural similarity to the USA and performance on the PONS. Rosenthal *et al.* also used a number of other measures to establish degrees of cultural similarity and cultural contact, consisting of measures of modernization (steel consumption, motor vehicles, doctors, all per capita), communications development (energy consumption, newsprint consumption, telephones, televisions, radios, all per capita), and measures of contact with the United States (ratio of American imports to total imports, ratio of touring Americans to total tourists, ratio of foreign letters received to total domestic mail; a measure of American mail to total domestic mail was unavailable). All of these measures showed significant positive correlations with performance on the PONS, with the exception only of the number of doctors per capita, the ratio of American imports to total imports and the ratio of foreign letters to domestic mail. Thus the results of decoding studies of cross-cultural differences using the PONS are highly consistent with the interactionist model of non-verbal communication formulated by Ekman and Friesen (Ekman, 1972; Ekman and Friesen, 1969a).

3. Personality

The work of Rosenthal *et al.* (1979) is the main source of information for the study of personality differences in decoding. Rosenthal *et al.* compared the performance of a number of groups on the PONS with their responses to a number of different personality tests, and the results of these studies are described below.

The California Psychological Inventory is intended to measure a number of different dimensions of personality (Gough, 1957); this test was administered to American and Australian students. Of the 18 variables which this test measures, 3 showed significant positive correlations with the PONS in at least two of the five samples tested; those who scored higher on the PONS scored on the California Psychological Inventory as significantly more confident, more socially mature and more typical in terms of the way people respond to this particular personality test.

The Personality Research Form (Jackson, 1967) is another personality questionnaire which is intended to measure a number of different dimensions of personality. This test was administered to American clinical psychology graduate students, teachers and doctors. Few systematic trends emerged from these studies, although amongst doctors the nurturance scale correlated significantly positively with the PONS scores.

The Least Preferred Coworker Scale was developed by Fiedler (1967) as a way of measuring leadership style. This test requires the subject to describe the person with whom he has found it most difficult to work on a number of bipolar adjective scales; people who obtain a low score on this test by describing their least preferred co-worker in highly unfavourable terms are considered to be more concerned with task performance and less concerned with interpersonal relationships. Rosenthal *et al.* report that Johnson administered this scale to Canadian students, and found that low scorers on the scale (assumed to be more task-oriented) tended to perform significantly better on the PONS.

The Dogmatism Scale was developed by Rokeach (1960) as a way of identifying people with a closed way of thinking, an intolerance towards those with opposing beliefs and an acceptance only of those with similar beliefs. This scale was administered to American students and doctors, and in both groups a significant tendency emerged for less dogmatic people to score more highly on the PONS.

The Marlowe–Crowne Social Desirability Scale was developed by Crowne and Marlowe (1964) to identify individuals with a high need for approval. This test was administered to the same American students who took the Dogmatism Scale, as well as to institutionalized alcoholic patients. For students, there was no significant relationship between this test and performance on the PONS, whereas for alcoholic patients the scores were significantly negatively correlated, indicating that alcoholics with a lower need for social approval were more likely to score higher on the PONS. But the Good Impression Scale of the California Psychological Inventory and the Desirability Scale of the Personality Research Form also appear to measure the need for social approval, and in the studies referred to above there were no significant correlations between these scales and PONS scores. It would seem that there is no consistent relationship between need for approval and performance on the PONS.

The Machiavelli Scale was developed by Christie and Geis (1970) to identify individuals who are capable of manipulating others; many of the items are derived from the unscrupulous political maxims of the Renaissance Florentine, Niccolo Machiavelli. This test was administered to American high school students, college students and adults, but the results showed only a small significant negative correlation between machiavellism and performance on the PONS.

In two samples of students of dance therapy, the extraversion–introversion factor of the Myers–Briggs Type Indicator (Myers, 1962) was correlated with the PONS. In another study, industrial personnel managers rated themselves on a 9-point scale of introversion, and these self-ratings were compared with performance on the PONS. The results showed no consistent trends in the relationship between extraversion/introversion and scores on the PONS.

Snyder's (1974) Self-Monitoring Scale (which is intended to measure differenes in the extent to which individuals can and do observe and control their self-presentation and non-verbal display of emotion) was administered by Rosenthal *et al.* to two groups of American students, two groups of doctors, a group of business executives and a group of teachers of nursing. The results showed no sizeable correlations for these groups between scores on the PONS and the Self-Monitoring Scale.

Thus studies of personality differences in decoding have for the most part produced negative results. There is some suggestion that people who score highly on the PONS are more confident, more socially mature, more typical of the way people respond to personality tests, more nurturant, less dogmatic and more task-oriented in their leadership style. But there is no consistent relationship between PONS scores and extraversion, need for approval, machiavellism and self-monitoring.

4. Psychopathology

Rosenthal *et al.* (1979) have investigated the performance of psychiatric patients on the PONS. Their sample came from psychiatric hospitals in Northern Ireland, America and Australia, these groups showing no significant differences between each other in their overall scores or on any of the different channels or combinations of channels of communication in the test. Rosenthal *et al.* also obtained scores on the PONS from a sample of American alcoholic patients. They compared the performance of these groups with the scores of American high school students, and found that although the scores of the alcoholic and psychiatric patients were similar to one another, they were significantly lower than the scores of the high school students. Rosenthal *et al.* also calculated the mean level of accuracy with or without information from the face, the body and tone of voice, and found that for both groups adding information significantly increased their accuracy, but in each case the normal group benefited significantly more than the psychiatric and alcoholic patients. They also found that the psychiatric patients were unable to benefit from practice with the PONS. Whereas the high school students and the alcoholic patients showed a gain of a full standard deviation in going from the first half to the second half of the test, the psychiatric patients showed no improvement whatsoever.

Most other work supports the finding that psychiatric patients are inferior to normal groups in the decoding of non-verbal cues. Dougherty, Bartlett and Izard (1974) compared the performance of American female schizophrenic patients with that of a normal group of women on judging photographs of facial expressions intended to represent Izard's eight fundamental emotions (discussed in Chapter 2, pp. 41–43). The criterion of accuracy for the judgements was the modal category for each picture as determined by previous cross-cultural research. The subjects completed both an emotion recognition task, in which they had to choose the appropriate label from a list of emotion categories provided by the experimenter, and a free response task, in which they could describe the picture in their own words. The free response data were categorized by judges according to whether they fell into Izard's eight emotion categories. Both tasks showed significantly better results for the normal group; the schizophrenic patients had particular difficulty with the depictions of disgust–contempt and shame–humiliation, making much greater use of enjoyment–joy descriptions. Muzekari and Bates (1977) compared the performance of American male and female schizophrenic patients with a normal control group, drawn from students at a local community college with no previous history of psychiatric disorder. The subjects were asked to judge posed photographs and videotaped scenes of facial expressions intended to convey happiness, sadness, anger and fear, and again they were given emotion-recognition and free-response tasks. The criterion of accuracy was agreement with a panel of four psychologists; the results showed again that the normal group performed significantly better than the schizophrenic patients, and also that there were no significant effects associated with the sex of the decoders.

Other studies also suggest that in comparison to normal groups, psychiatric patients attribute less importance to non-verbal cues than to speech content. Reilly and Muzekari (1979) had a videotape made of an actress delivering ten messages, five of which were negative in verbal content but positive in vocal tone and facial expression, the other five being positive in verbal content and negative in vocal tone and facial expression. The tapes were shown to four different groups of American subjects: chronic schizophrenic male patients, male night-school students, disturbed boys and normal boys (mean age of both groups of boys was eight years old). The subjects were asked to rate on 7-point scales how they considered the woman felt about the person to whom she was talking. The results showed a significant statistical interaction, with the normal adults calling the non-verbally positive messages positive and the non-verbally negative messages negative, while all the other groups showed the reverse pattern, allowing their judgements to be influenced predominantly by the speech content. Argyle *et al.* (1970) carried out a study in which verbal and non-verbal signals for inferior, equal and superior attitudes were compared. British students were asked to rate videotapes of a female encoder reading messages where the speech content was intended to convey and inferior, equal or superior attitude in an inferior, equal or superior non-verbal style. These messages and styles had been rated by another group of students to match the relative strength of speech content and style. When judged in combination, the non-verbal cues had a much more powerful effect on perceived attitude, but significantly less so for students who scored highly on the neuroticism scale of the Maudsley Personality Inventory.

The repeated finding that psychiatric patients are significantly inferior to normal groups in the decoding of non-verbal cues, and that they attribute significantly less importance to non-verbal cues is consistent with the view put forward by Argyle (e.g. 1969) that a lack of social perceptiveness may be a causal factor in mental illness. But there are difficulties with the studies reviewed above, which suggests that such a conclusion needs to be treated with caution. In particular, these studies typically make use of posed expressions and a criterion of accuracy based on the agreement of a panel of judges, who also constitute a normal group of the population. What this means in effect is that, as LaRusso (1978) points out, consensual validation by a sample from the normal group is being used to establish the standard of accuracy. Since by reason of diagnosis, the psychiatric population has already been found in certain respects to function outside the boundaries of consensual validation, then not surprisingly their performance is inferior on these decoding tasks.

In order to avoid these problems, LaRusso (1978) designed an experiment with an objective criterion of decoding accuracy. Videotapes were made of two male and two female encoders as they watched two lights serving as signals. In one condition, electric shock was administered to the encoder when a red light went off, but none after a white light; in the other condition, encoders were simply asked to pose their expectations in response to the lights without actually receiving the shocks. The task of the decoders was to judge whether in each case the encoder did or did not expect to receive a shock; hence the criterion of decoding accuracy was entirely objective. The subjects were a group of Canadian male and female patients diagnosed as suffering from paranoid schizophrenia; they were compared with a control group who had had no previous history of psychiatric disorder, and were roughly matched for social class and intelligence. The results of the study showed that when the encoders were actually subjected to electric shocks, then the paranoid schizophrenic patients were in fact significantly better at judging from the videotaped facial expressions whether the encoder was about to receive a shock. But when the encoders were posing their expectation, then the normal group were significantly better at judging what the poser intended to communicate. Half of the subjects in each group experienced a sample electric shock before making their judgements, but this had no significant effect on their decoding performance.

The findings thus indicated that patients suffering from paranoid schizophrenia are more sensitive than normal people to facial cues which communicate a particular stress or relief from that stress. LaRusso notes that the results from the posed expressions are much more difficult to interpret. In this condition a response was scored as correct if it corresponded with the intent of the pose, but that was in fact a distortion of reality since the actual situation was one in which an electric shock was never received or expected by the encoder. A truly accurate response in this condition would have been to judge all the expressions as not associated with receiving shock, but the paranoid schizophrenic patients and the normal group did not significantly differ in their absolute number of no-shock judgements in this condition. LaRusso argues instead that the paranoid schizophrenic patients were simply confused by this situation, unable to accept it at face value, but also unable to penetrate the deception which was being practised upon them. Consistent with this view is the finding that their responses were significantly slower in this condition than those of the normal group, whereas no such difference was found in the condition where the encoders were actually expecting to receive the shock.

It would be unwise to make too much of the findings of this one experiment, since they are based on one particular task with one particular psychiatric group. Nevertheless, it does suggest that generalizations about the inferior non-verbal decoding skills of psychiatric patients should be regarded with some caution, since they are based essentially on studies of posed expressions where the criterion of accuracy is agreement with another group of judges who are not drawn from a psychiatric population. LaRusso's experiment suggests the alternative possibility that psychiatric patients are less able to accept conventionalized expressions at face value. Clearly, further research on the performance of psychiatric patients in decoding non-verbal cues requires tasks which evoke spontaneous non-verbal expressions and provide objective criteria of accuracy.

5. Sex

Hall (1978) has reviewed 75 studies in which the decoding accuracy of men and women has been compared; these studies have shown a pronounced advantage for women. In these studies, judgements were made of the face, body or voice, either separately or in combination, presented in a variety of media (drawings, photographs, films, videotapes, standard-content speech, randomized-spliced speech and electronically-filtered speech). In the method of standard-content speech, the encoder recites meaningless or emotionally ambiguous material, while varying the vocal expression to convey the intended emotion. The most common tasks for the judges were either to guess the emotion which the encoder intended to pose, or to guess the situation in which the expression had occurred. Of the 75 studies reviewed by Hall, 24 showed a significant sex difference, 23 of which were in favour of women, a proportion which is statistically highly significant. In terms of standard deviation units, the mean effect size in favour of females is 0.40, a finding which again is statistically highly significant; the mean effect size when auditory and visual cues are presented together is significantly greater than the effects of the two modes when presented separately. In studies using the PONS, Rosenthal et al. (1979) have compared schoolchildren of different ages with college students and older adults, and have found females to be significantly superior to males at all the ages studied, with no significant statistical interactions with age.

EXPLANATIONS OF SEX DIFFERENCES IN NON-VERBAL CUES

The finding that women are superior to men in decoding non-verbal cues is interesting in view of the finding reported earlier in this chapter that women gaze more than men at other people (see pp. 95–96). The reasons for sex differences in non-verbal cues have been investigated in a number of studies; these will be discussed both with reference to sex differences in decoding and with reference to the sex differences in encoding reviewed earlier in this chapter (that women look more than men at other people, show a preference for closer interpersonal distances with each other, smile more, use particular kinds of sex-typed posture and gesture and encode more clearly than men; see pp. 94–99). Hall (1979) has proposed five possible explanations for sex differences in non-verbal cues, and these are discussed below.

(i) Empathy

Hoffman (1977) has reviewed the literature on empathy, and concluded that a number of studies show women to be more empathic than men; this might in turn account for their superior encoding or decoding of non-verbal cues. Various questionnaires have been constructed to measure empathy, three of which were used by Hall (1979) in two studies intended to investigate whether empathy is significantly related to non-verbal communication skills. Hall compared the Mehrabian (1972), Jackson (1976) and Hogan (1969) scales of empathy with performance on encoding and decoding tasks, including items from the PONS; the subjects were American male and female students. She found that the three empathy scales were significantly positively intercorrelated, and that women also reported themselves as significantly more empathic than men on Jackson's scale; but there were no significant correlations between empathy scores and decoding or encoding of non-verbal cues. Thus it appears that there is no direct relationship between empathy and non-verbal skills, nor need there necessarily be so; to be skilled at perceiving someone else's emotional states does not necessarily involve sharing their emotional experience. However, Hall argues that it is still possible that girls' earlier empathic awareness of emotions might be a precursor to the development of superior encoding and decoding skills, and hence that empathy may be indirectly related to these skills in a manner not revealed by the studies discussed above.

(ii) Social Roles

A second possibility is that women differ in non-verbal cues as a function of their social role; they are expected to acquire certain kinds of behaviours, and consequently do so. To test the hypothesis that women's decoding skills might be related to social role, Hall (1979) reviewed 11 previously unpublished studies of decoding. All of these studies involved the use of one or more measures of ability to decode non-verbal cues from the face, the body or content-free speech, as well as one or more measures of masculinity and femininity measured on separate unipolar scales. Unipolar scales measure masculinity and femininity as two separate dimensions (e.g. the Bem Sex Role Inventory, Bem, 1974); they were developed to answer the criticism that masculinity and femininity are not opposites (as they would be on a bipolar scale, with masculinity at one end of the scale, femininity at the other), but can be seen as constituting two independent dimensions. The subjects in all of these 11 studies reviewed by Hall were Americans ranging in age from pre-school children to adults. In the main, Hall found only insubstantial correlations between the tests of non-verbal perceptiveness and the questionnaires intended to measure aspects of social role. The only significant correlation was in the reverse direction of that predicted by the social-role hypothesis, in that there was a significant positive correlation of 0.25 between the decoding of visual cues and masculinity scores for adult subjects. But precisely the same criticism can be made of these studies as of the studies of empathy; sex differences in decoding skills may be a consequence of traditional role expectations inculcated early in life, regardless of any subsequent changes in sex-role attitudes.

Of course the possibility also exists that role expectations may account for sex differences in encoding. In the study referred to earlier (p. 102), Bugental, Love and Gianetto (1971) hypothesized and confirmed that fathers are more likely to use the smile in conjunction with positive speech than mothers, who they maintained would use the smile simply as part of their culturally assigned role. LaFrance and Carmen (1980) arranged for American students to complete the Bem Sex Role Inventory, according to which they were categorized as sex-typed or androgynous. The students took part in a seven-minute conversation with another person of the same sex; the members of each pair were either both sex-typed, both androgynous or sex-typed and androgynous. LaFrance and Carmen found that androgynous men and women tended to be intermediate between sex-typed men and women in terms of amount of gazing and smiling; women gazed for a significantly larger proportion of time than men while speaking, and smiled for a significantly longer period of time than men while listening. Hence these studies do suggest that differences in the encoding of bodily cues can be related to sex-role attitudes.

(iii) Differences in Power

English (1972) and Weitz (1974) have both hypothesized that women's superior decoding skills may be due to their inferior position in society; because of restrictions on their overt exercise of power, they become more alert to the behaviour and moods of more powerful others, and develop more subtle means of exercising social influence. Similarly, Frieze and Ramsey (1976) have argued that the non-verbal cues encoded by women are those associated with low status, and hence serve to maintain their inferior position in society.

Hall (1979) has attempted to test the hypothesis relating decoding skills to inferior status in three studies, two involving married people who had children and one involving grade-school children. Hall compared decoding performance with responses to questionnaires intended to measure attitudes towards women's role in society, and hypothesized that if the 'oppression' hypothesis was valid, then women with more traditional attitudes towards sex roles should perform better at decoding non-verbal cues. In fact she found the reverse result, with a significant positive correlation between more egalitarian sex-role attitudes and decoding of both auditory and visual cues. In another study, she attempted to relate decoding skill to the division of labour within the home of married women; she found a significant negative correlation between the amount of housework a woman said she performed and her decoding of auditory non-verbal cues, i.e. a woman who adopted the traditional division of labour within the home was less likely to be skilled at decoding non-verbal cues. Hall argued that the findings of both these studies are in the reverse direction of what might be expected if the superior decoding of women was due to their inferior position in society. But the same criticism can be applied to these studies as to those intended to test the empathy and social-role hypotheses, namely, that superior decoding skills might be acquired as a consequence of an early experience of an inferior position in society, regardless of any subsequent change in sex-role attitudes.

(iv) Practice Effects

Another hypothesis Hall (1979) discusses is also based on the assumption that women have to play a more passive role, but states that their greater decoding skills develop not out of a need to cope with social inferiority but as the inevitable result of woman's predominant role as an observer. This would of course be consistent with the finding that women look more at others than do men, which gives them greater opportunity to observe and learn from the reactions of others, but to date there has been no specific test of this hypothesis.

(v) Accommodation

Rosenthal and DePaulo (1979) have proposed that women are socialized to be accommodating towards others. The accommodating person, they argue, wants to understand what others are trying to communicate and wants to make his or her own messages easy to understand; consequently the accommodating person decodes more accurately and encodes more clearly. But Rosenthal and DePaulo also argue that skill at decoding non-verbal cues may be detrimental to satisfactory social relationships under certain circumstances, especially if the encoder unwittingly conveys information that he actually does not wish to communicate. Consequently, Rosenthal and DePaulo argue that if women's superiority in decoding non-verbal cues is due to a desire to be accommodating, they will not show such an advantage in respect of unintentional communications. Rosenthal and DePaulo tested this hypothesis in three different ways. In one set of 10 studies, they showed American adults, college students and high school students scenes of visual cues with very brief exposures, arguing that very brief signals may be less controllable by the sender and hence carry more unintended messages. To do this, they administered a special version of the PONS using scenes of visual cues with median exposure lengths of only 250 milliseconds. These studies showed no significant advantage for women, irrespective of age. A re-analysis of the studies reviewed by Hall (1978) showed that only 7 per cent of the studies using briefly exposed cues showed a significant advantage for women, whereas 4 per cent of the studies using cues of longer duration showed a significant female advantage, a difference which is statistically significant.

In a second set of studies, Rosenthal and DePaulo rank ordered non-verbal cues according to the degree which they considered they might give off unintended information. They argued that the face gives the most information, and is best controlled by the sender. From studies of deception carried out by Ekman and Friesen (1969b, 1974b) (see Chapter 5, pp. 153–154), they argued that less attention is paid to the body which may reveal more unintended information. Tone of voice, they maintained, is less controllable than cues from the face or body, and hence may give information about deception or stress. Very brief exposures of the face or body may offer further unintended cues which may be more difficult to control. Finally, they maintained that discrepant messages may be the most difficult to control, because they involve simultaneous communication in two different channels which may involve problems of co-ordination. These measures of sensitivity to non-verbal cues were administered to American high school and college students, and the results showed that female advantage decreased significantly with cues which were hypothesized to be more difficult to control. A re-analysis of previous studies where a comparison was possible between these different types of information showed that female decoding superiority decreases with a change from face to body to tone of voice.

Finally, in a third series of studies, Rosenthal and DePaulo arranged for American male and female college students to be videotaped while describing a person they liked, one they disliked, one about whom they were ambivalent, one to whom they were indifferent, a person they really liked as though they disliked him or her and a person they really disliked as though they liked him or her. Thus the first two encodings were of clear affects, the second two of mixed affects and the final two of deceptive affects. Each of the encoders also acted as a decoder who rated the performance of half of the encoders on liking, disliking, ambivalence, discrepancy, tension and deception. The accuracy of decoding was defined in terms of ratings of liking and disliking for liking and disliking communications, in terms of ratings of ambivalence for ambivalent communications and in terms of ratings of deception for deceptive communications. According to this analysis, results showed that women were significantly more accurate than men for the perception of liking and disliking, but that their advantage decreased significantly and linearly with the transition from ordinary to ambivalent to deceptive cues; this would again be consistent with the accommodation hypothesis.

(vi) Explanations of Sex Differences in Non-verbal Cues: Summary

Rosenthal and DePaulo have presented a considerable degree of evidence in support of their accommodation hypothesis, at least with respect to decoding; these findings they interpret in terms of female sex-role socialization. One interesting feature of their findings is the implication that there may be different types of skill in decoding non-verbal cues; the person who is skilled at decoding what the encoder intends to communicate may not necessarily be skilled at decoding what the encoder does not wish to communicate, for example, in detecting when the encoder is being deceitful. Another interesting feature of Rosenthal and DePaulo's findings is that most of the observed sex differences in non-verbal cues can be related to differences in accommodation. Hence the superior encoding of women can be seen as more accommodating in that it makes their messages easier to understand, and their greater use of gaze, smiling and closer interpersonal distances can be seen as encoding a more receptive, affiliative attitude to others. The problem, of course, is that many of these findings can also be explained in terms of empathy, differences in power, practice effects or simply in terms of what is expected as part of the female social role; the failure to find evidence in support of these alternative hypotheses from empathy and sex-role attitude questionnaires does not rule out the possibility that non-verbal behaviours are learned early in life irrespective of subsequent changes in empathic ability or sex-role attitudes. In fact it cannot even be said that the hypothesis that sex differences in non-verbal cues are due to sex-role socialization has been substantiated; the possibility that there are innate differences in social interest between the sexes cannot be ruled out, especially in view of the findings referred to earlier from studies of neonates (p. 96) that infant girls both smile significantly more and gaze significantly longer at others. Certainly what has been demonstrated is that there are substantial differences between the sexes in the use of non-verbal cues; but what is still very much open to question is the explanation of those differences.

SUMMARY

In this chapter, studies have been reviewed with respect to whether the encoding and decoding of bodily cues are systematically related to differences in culture, age, sex, psychopathology and personality.

The hypothesis that bodily cues encode significant information about culture or personality cannot be said to be strongly supported by the evidence. Thus, cross-cultural studies have failed to support Hall's distinction between contact and non-contact cultures, and little evidence has been found to substantiate the widespread belief that body movement reveals a great deal about personality. Those personality differences in encoding which do appear to be reasonably well substantiated are that extraverts tend to gaze at other people more, that people with a high need for affiliation show greater facial pleasantness and smile more, that field-dependent people make greater use of self-adaptors, which are also used more by people who describe themselves as more gloomy, sensitive, defensive and lacking in autonomy and exhibition, and that general differences in encoding non-verbal cues may be related to the self-monitoring and internalizing/externalizing personality dimensions. The sparseness of these findings suggests that the belief that body movement encodes significant information about personality may well be an example of a decoding error.

There do, however, appear to be a number of encoding differences in bodily cues systematically related to psychopathology. People suffering from anxiety make greater use of non-signalling hand movements, use shorter glances and smile less frequently; observers can identify differences in the self-reported degree of anxiety on the basis of bodily cues alone, thus suggesting that anxiety is communicated through bodily cues. People suffering from depression show a lack of eye contact, downward angling of the head, a drooping mouth and a lack of hand movement; observers can also identify depressed patients on the basis of bodily cues alone, thus suggesting that depression, too, is communicated through bodily cues. Autistic children show marked gaze aversion, which has been regarded as a form of communication serving to maintain the social isolation of the autistic child. The hypothesis that people suffering from schizophrenia show marked gaze aversion does not appear to be supported by more carefully controlled studies; instead it appears that they avert their gaze only when talking about their own personal problems. In addition, they appear to be relatively poor encoders of emotion. Studies of psychopathy and delinquency are more confusing and contradictory, but it appears that violent offenders and delinquent adolescents have abnormally large personal space preferences, which are possibly modified by the effects of institutionalization.

There are also significant and reliable sex differences in the encoding of bodily cues. Woman appear both to encode more clearly than men, and also look more at others, show a preference for closer interpersonal distances with each other, smile more and use particular kinds of sex-typed posture and gesture (although these studies are based mainly on American society). Sex-typing as measured by questionnaire can be ascertained by observers from bodily cues alone, thus suggesting that sex differences in encoding communicate significant information about a person's sex-role identification, what Birdwhistell (1971) has called 'gender identification signals'.

It can thus be seen that bodily cues can be regarded as communicating information about individual differences, at least with regard to psychopathology and sex. Studies of decoding non-verbal cues have also shown marked individual differences. Developmental studies have shown that decoding non-verbal cues clearly improves with age, and children appear to be particularly disadvantaged at decoding information from visual cues. Cross-cultural studies of decoding are consistent with an interactionist hypothesis, where some cues are regarded as innate, others as learned and variable across culture. Personality studies have provided some evidence that people who are more skilled at decoding non-verbal cues are more confident, more socially mature, more typical of the way people respond to personality tests, more nurturant, less dogmatic and more task-oriented in their leadership style. Psychiatric patients are inferior to normal groups in the decoding of posed non-verbal cues, and they attribute less importance to such cues than do normal groups. Sex is clearly related to decoding, in that women have been found to be consistently better than men at decoding non-verbal cues; it has been argued that this is because women are socialized to be more accommodating towards others. The theoretical importance of these substantial individual differences in decoding is that the extent to which non-verbal cues function as a communication system will vary substantially according to the decoding skills and cultural similarity of the communicators.

Chapter 5

Specific Contexts

The argument has been advanced that bodily cues encode information about emotion, speech and individual differences; it has also been demonstrated that there are substantial individual differences in decoding non-verbal cues. But if certain general functions of bodily cues have been established, their significance can only be ultimately ascertained within a particular context. A given context can be examined in terms of the relationship between the pariticipants, the goals for which they meet in a given situation and the medium through which they communicate; each of these factors will be discussed in turn.

RELATIONSHIPS

Condon and Ogston (1966), in the frame-by-frame analysis of conversation discussed in Chapter 3 (p. 58), described a phenomenon which they called interactional synchrony, whereby the speaker and listener appear to move in close harmony with one another. Condon and Ogston (1971) maintain that interactional synchrony occurs constantly during normal human interaction, and that it is a fundamental, universal characteristic of human communication evident from the day of birth (Condon, 1975). Condon (1975) hypothesized that interactional synchrony provides constant feedback from the listener to the speaker concerning the listener's level of attention and interest; hence interactional synchrony may be seen as an indicator of rapport within a relationship.

Condon and Ogston's far-reaching claims for the significance of interactional synchrony have been criticized by McDowall (1978). McDowall filmed a conversation between six Australian students (three men and three women), and investigated whether all possible combinations of two or more people in that conversation were characterized by interactional synchrony. Observers analysed the film for initiations, terminations and changes of direction in movement; rather than examining the film frame by frame, they used a three-frame unit as their basic unit of analysis, since McDowall regarded the inter-observer reliability which he obtained at the single frame level as unacceptably low. Interactional synchrony for all the various possible combinations of participants was compared with what would be expected by chance, and in only one case out of the 57 comparisons was there significantly more interactional synchrony than would be expected by chance. There was also no significant difference in interactional synchrony between various combinations of friends and strangers in the group, which might have been expected if interactional synchrony is an indicator of rapport.

A similar concept to interactional synchrony is that of postural congruence, elaborated by Scheflen (1964). Postural congruence refers to similarity of posture, which, Scheflen argues, indicates similarity of views or roles in a group; non-congruence of posture, Scheflen maintains, indicates marked divergence in attitude or status. But whereas the concept of interactional synchrony refers to simultaneous movement, the concept of postural congruence refers only to people maintaining the same postures at a given point in time, irrespective of how they came to take up those postures (LaFrance, 1979). Scheflen's observations are based on a natural history procedure (see Chapter 1, pp. 11–12), in which he maintains the investigator through repeated viewing of a tape learns to recognize patterns of repetitive behaviour which can be compared with other similar patterns and evaluated in their social context.

Figure 18. Postural congruence. The pair in the foreground are showing identical postures, the pair in the background mirror-image postures

Scheflen calls this technique Context Analysis, and it is best exemplified in the book *Communicational Structure* (Scheflen, 1973), in which a psychotherapy session has been transcribed and examined in this kind of elaborate detail.

Other researchers have attempted to test Scheflen's hypotheses concerning postural congruence using quantitative methods. Charny (1966) analysed a film of a psychotherapy session between a male therapist and a female patient. Charny categorized postures into congruent and non-congruent postures; he also distinguished between mirror-image congruent postures, where one person's left side is equivalent to the other's right, and identical postures, where right matches right and left matches left (see Figure 18). But since identical postures rarely occurred, only mirror-image postures were included in the final analysis. Lower body postures (hips and lower limbs) were also excluded from the final analysis, since these could not be scored with adequate reliability. Charny found that as the interview progressed, there was a significant trend towards spending more time in upper-body mirror-congruent postures. There was also a significant difference in speech content between periods where mirror-congruent and non-congruent postures were employed, the speech during mirror-congruent periods being scored as more positive; Charny argues from these results that mirror-congruent postures may be taken as indicative of rapport or relatedness.

Trout and Rosenfeld (1980) set up an experiment to investigate the perception of postural congruency in simulated therapist–client interactions. They arranged for two male American graduate students to play the roles of therapist and client, and to adopt either mirror-congruent or non-congruent postures; there was no sound-track, and the faces were blocked out of the tape. The tapes were judged by American male and female students on a number of rating scales (e.g. the therapy relationship was unharmonious–harmonious), and averaged to yield an overall score of rapport. The results showed that the mirror-congruent postures were rated as indicating significantly more rapport than the non-congruent postures.

Dabbs (1969) investigated how postural congruence would affect the ratings of an interviewee in a simulated interview. Dabbs arranged for pairs of American male students to interview an experimental confederate who was in fact a trained actor, and had been instructed to mimick the postures and gestures of one of each pair of students selected randomly by the experimenter. At the conclusion of the 'interview', the students completed a questionnaire evaluating the confederate. They showed no awareness of the mimicry, nor did the mimicked students rate the confederate as significantly more similar in postures and gestures. But the confederate was evaluated significantly more favourably by the mimicked students; in particular, they considered he 'thought more like they did', and said that 'identified' with him. Dabbs' findings are clearly consistent with Scheflen's hypotheses concerning postural congruence, although Dabbs made no effort to distinguish between mirror-image and identical postures.

LaFrance (LaFrance and Broadbent, 1976; LaFrance, 1979) has investigated whether postural congruence is related to rapport in American college seminars.

In one study, LaFrance and Broadbent (1976) asked students to complete a questionnaire made up of ten 6-point bipolar scales reporting their assessment of the seminar. Of these ten items, the dimensions apart–together, involved–disinterested and rapport–no rapport were judged to be particularly relevant to the measurement of rapport, which was assessed in terms of the sum of these scales. The postures of the students were coded according to whether they were non-congruent, identical or mirror-congruent. The results showed a significant positive correlation between mirror-congruent postures and the measure of rapport, a significant negative correlation between non-congruent postures and rapport, and no significant relationship between identical postures and rapport, although the correlation was positive. In a second study, LaFrance (1979) measured posture and rapport during the first week (time 1) and the final week (time 2) of a six-week seminar course to investigate the probable direction of causality between mirror-congruent postures and rapport, using a method of statistical analysis known as the cross-lag panel technique (Kenny, 1975). To use this technique, mirror-congruent postures at time 1 were correlated with rapport at time 2, and rapport at time 1 was correlated with mirror-congruent postures at time 2. The difference between these two correlations can then be used to investigate which of the two variables has casual priority over the other. For example, if postural congruence determines rapport, then the correlation between postural congruence at time 1 and rapport at time 2 should exceed the correlation between rapport at time 1 and postural congruence at time 2. In fact the results did not show a significant difference between these two correlations, although the direction of the effect suggested that postural congruence may be influential in establishing rapport. There were also significant positive correlations between postural congruence and rapport both at time 1 and time 2.

LaFrance has reported one other study which failed to show a relationship between postural congruence and rapport. In this study, LaFrance and Ickes (1981) arranged for American male and female students who were unacquainted with one another to meet in same-sex pairs while ostensibly waiting for an experiment. Afterwards the students completed questionnaires concerning perceptions of their own and the other's behaviour. Mirror-congruent postures were coded and showed a non-significant but negative correlation with self-ratings of rapport ($r = -0.17$). LaFrance and Ickes attempt to explain this finding by arguing that postural congruence is a means of establishing rapport, rather than an indicator that rapport has already been established; hence a failure to find a relationship between posture-mirroring and rapport amongst strangers in a waiting room might simply mean they had had insufficient time to establish a satisfactory level of rapport.

There is for the most part a considerable degree of experimental support for Scheflen's hypotheses concerning the significance of postural congruence. If bodily cues convey information about interpersonal relationships, they may convey such information either to observers of the relationship or to the participants themselves. Whether observers can judge the relationship between people on the basis of bodily cues alone has been tested in a number of experiments. Benjamin and Creider (1975) arranged for eight Americans (two men and two women, aged about 25, and two boys and two girls, aged about 9) to talk to each other in pairs on topics of their own choice. Each person talked to each other person, and their facial expressions during the conversations were videotaped. The tapes of each encoder alone were shown without sound to a group of adult observers and a group of boys (aged eight to nine), who were asked to make judgements about the identity of the unseen conversational partner. Results showed that both groups of observers were able to perform this task successfully in terms of age, sex and acquaintanceship. From an analysis of the videotapes, Benjamin and Creider identified certain differences in facial expression according to the relationship. When adults talked to children, their muscle tonus was low, the skin beneath the eyes and over the cheekbones hanging loosely down except during broad smiles, whereas when adults talked to other adults, their skin was bunched and raised. There also appeared to be significant differences in the activity rates between same-age and different-age conversations, conversations between people of the same age appearing to be much more animated.

Studies by Abramovitch have shown that even very young children are capable of accurately discerning the relationship between people from bodily cues alone. Abramovitch (1977) carried out two experiments in which children aged between three and five were shown videotapes of their own and unknown mothers conversing with strange and familiar people. They saw only the mother's face and upper torso, without the sound-track. In the first experiment, the children were able to guess at a level significantly above chance whether their own mother was conversing with a friend or a stranger. In a second experiment, the children were also able to guess at a level significantly above chance the sex of the other person, but only when they were able to guess acquaintanceship as well. These videotapes were also shown to American students, who were capable of discriminating conversations between friends and strangers at a level significantly above chance. In another study, Abramovitch and Daly (1979) showed videotapes to four-year-old children of classmates and unknown peers; each child conversed with his own mother, a mother who was a stranger, a peer friend and a peer who was a stranger. The observers saw only the face and upper torso of the videotaped children with no sound. Results showed that the children were significantly better than chance at identifying the age and acquaintanceship of the person with whom their classmates were conversing, but were not successful when the videotapes were of unfamiliar peers. Students viewing the same videotapes scored significantly better than chance in identifying age and familiarity of the unseen partner, even though all the children were strangers to them.

The results of these studies by Benjamin and Creider, Abramovitch and Abramovitch and Daly show that even quite young children are capable of discerning the relationship between people in terms of age, acquaintanceship and sex on the basis of bodily cues alone. The results of these studies demonstrate that in addition to communicating information about emotion, language and individual differences, bodily cues also communicate information about inter-personal relationships to observers of the relationship.

Of course a much more fundamental question is the role which bodily cues play for the participants within a particular relationship. One way in which interpersonal relationships can be discussed is in terms of broad dimensions. For example, Kiesler (1979) has argued that there are three major dimensions of interpersonal relationships, namely, affiliation (love or hate), status (domi-nance or submission) and inclusion (degree of importance in one's life); Kiesler argues that these issues are continually negotiated between people in the course of a relationship. Another way in which interpersonal relationships can be discussed is in terms of the social roles which people occupy. The number of role relationships is virtually limitless, but since most non-verbal communication research in this context has been focused on mother–infant and husband–wife relationships, these are the two role relationships which will be discussed, preceded by a review of the significance of bodily cues in the context of particular relationship dimensions.

1. Dimensions of Interpersonal Relationships

In terms of Kiesler's three main dimensions of interpersonal relationships, there has been virtually no research on bodily cues with regard to the dimension of inclusion. The only reference to inclusion appears to come from Scheflen (1964), who suggested that inclusiveness within a group may be indicated by posture; if people are seated in a line, those at each end may turn inward and extend an arm or a leg across the open space as if to limit access in and out of the group, an effect Scheflen calls 'bookending'. However, the dimensions of affiliation and dominance have been quite extensively researched, so these relationships will be discussed in some detail.

(i) Affiliation

Argyle, Alkema and Gilmour (1972) carried out a study in which verbal and non-verbal signals for friendliness and hostility were compared. British students were asked to rate videotapes of a female student reading friendly, neutral and hostile messages in a friendly, neutral or hostile non-verbal style. These messages and non-verbal styles had been previously rated by another group of students to match the relative strength of speech content and non-verbal style. The encoder used a warm, soft tone of voice, open smile and relaxed posture to convey friendliness, a harsh voice, frown with teeth showing and a tense posture to convey hostility, and an expressionless voice and a blank face to convey a neutral attitude. Both speech content and non-verbal styles were approximately equal in judged friendliness/hostility when rated independently of one another; when judged in combination, non-verbal cues accounted for 12.5 times as much of the variance as speech content, and produced 5.7 times as much shift on the rating scales. On the basis of this experiment, it would seem that non-verbal cues are of considerable importance in the decoding of affiliation.

Other research has been focused on the specific bodily cues associated with affiliation. Exline and Winters (1965) arranged for American male and female students to have separate conversations with two different people, both of the same sex as themselves, and then asked them which person they liked better; they found that the students looked for a significantly longer period of time at the person to whom they were more attracted. Mehrabian (1968a, 1968b) and Mehrabian and Friar (1969) carried out a series of encoding studies using a role-play design. In these studies, American male and female students were asked to imagine they were conversing with someone, and to adopt the positions they would employ to convey different attitudes towards different people varying in sex and status; the location of the person with whom they were to imagine they were conversing was indicated by a coat-rack. In one study, the students were instructed to convey different attitudes while standing (Mehrabian, 1968a); in the other two studies, they were instructed to convey different attitudes while seated (Mehrabian, 1968b; Mehrabian and Friar, 1969). All three studies showed some kind of relationship between affiliation and gaze. Mehrabian (1968a) found that men gazed significantly more at the coat-rack when asked to imagine a person they liked than when asked to imagine a person they disliked. Mehrabian and Friar (1969) replicated this finding for men, and also found that women showed significantly less gaze for disliked men than for women and men they liked. Mehrabian (1968b) asked the students to adopt the positions they would employ for five different levels of affiliation (intense dislike, moderate dislike, neutral, moderate liking and intense liking). In this study, he also found a significant main effect for affiliation on gaze, which showed that irrespective of the sex of the encoder or the sex of the imagined recipient of the message, disliking was accompanied by the least gaze, a neutral attitude by the most gaze, which diminished slightly to a moderately high level for an attitude of intense liking.

Mehrabian also investigated the relationship of a number of bodily postures to affiliation in these studies. In the study of standing positions, Mehrabian (1968a) coded behaviour for relaxation, body openness, body orientation, arm position and up–down head tilt. He found that disliking was significantly associated with the use of the arms akimbo position, and that female encoders used open-arm positions significantly more with liked than with disliked men (a closed-arm position being arms crossed). The studies of seated postures (Mehrabian, 1968b; Mehrabian and Friar, 1969) also included observations of backward and sideways lean. In both studies, it was found that irrespective of the sex of the encoder or the imagined recipient of the message, the angle of backward lean was significantly less for a liked than a disliked person. Mehrabian (1968b) found sideways lean to vary significantly according to the sex of the encoder. In the case of male encoders, intense dislike of another male was indicated by a lack of sideways lean, whereas intense dislike of a female was indicated by a greater degree of sideways lean. In the case of female encoders, dislike was indicated through greater sideways lean, irrespective of the sex of the imagined recipient of the message. In this study, Mehrabian also found significant differences for shoulder orientation; male encoders used less direct shoulder orientation for a person they liked very much, whereas female encoders used the least direct shoulder orientation for someone they intensely disliked, the most direct for someone for whom their feelings were neutral, and moderately direct shoulder orientation for someone they liked very much.

In all these studies, Mehrabian measured the distance between the encoders and the coat-rack which was intended to represent the imagined recipient of the message. In the studies of seated encoders (Mehrabian, 1968b; Mehrabian and Friar, 1969), significantly closer distances were adopted by the encoders in relation to liked than to disliked people, irrespective of the sex of the encoder or the person he was supposed to be addressing. In the study of standing encoders (Mehrabian, 1968a), it was found that men adopted significantly closer distances to a liked person regardless of the sex of the person with whom they were supposed to be communicating, whereas women adopted significantly closer distances to a liked person only in relation to other women.

Although all these studies were based on a highly artificial role-play procedure for observing encoding, they do nevertheless strongly suggest that certain bodily cues are closely related to affiliation. In one of these papers, Mehrabian (1968a) reports three experiments intended to investigate how these cues are decoded. In the first experiment, photographs were taken of American male and female students seated on a swivel chair either leaning forward or back at an angle of 20°, with either open or closed arm and leg positions (arms and legs crossed), and either tense or relaxed. In the second experiment, forward/backward lean and open/closed positions were varied in relation to the age of the encoder (two men and two women aged between 32 and 37, and two boys and two girls aged between 10 and 13). The final experiment was a study of standing encoders. The encoders were the children from the second experiment and adults the same age as students; the orientation and distance they adopted were systematically varied. In all three experiments, the encoders wore masks over their faces, so that judgements would not be influenced by their facial expressions; the photographs were rated by American male and female students, who were asked to imagine they were in conversation with the person in the photograph, and to indicate how positive they considered that person's attitude was towards them. Mehrabian summarizes the results of these three decoding studies as demonstrating that greater relaxation, forward trunk lean and smaller interpersonal distance are decoded as conveying a significantly more positive attitude. The attitude of women who use a more open body posture is also decoded as significantly more positive. A significant statistical interaction between body orientation and the identity of the encoder showed that direct body orientation was decoded as more positive than an indirect body orientation for male students and for the two girls, the reverse being the case for the female students and the two boys.

A number of other studies have been carried out on the decoding of bodily cues in relation to affiliation. Bond and Shiraishi (1974) arranged for Japanese male and female students to be interviewed by one of two Japanese male graduate students. The interviewer assumed either a forward or backward lean during the interview, and person perception ratings indicated that when the interviewers conducted the interview in a forward-lean position, they were judged as significantly more polite and 'flexible' than when they conducted it in a backward-lean position. Mehrabian (1967) arranged for pairs of American female students to meet another American female student, who was in fact a confederate of the experimenter. For half the pairs of students, the confederate oriented her head and body predominantly towards one member of each pair; for the other pairs, the confederate oriented her head primarily towards one student with her body oriented primarily towards the other student. The students were asked after the conversation to rate the confederate's attitude both to themselves and to the other member in the pair. When making judgements of the confederate's attitude towards themselves, the students judged her attitude as significantly more positive when she oriented both her head and body towards them. When making judgements of the confederate's attitude towards the other person, the students judged the confederate's attitude as significantly more positive only when she oriented her head predominantly towards the other person.

Waldron (1975) investigated the relative importance of facial expression and body posture in the decoding of affiliation. Photographs of a woman posing three facial expressions intended to convey liking, disliking and neutrality were superimposed in all possible combinations on photographs of two different body postures intended to convey liking and disliking. The body postures were derived from Mehrabian's encoding studies, and both facial expressions and body postures were rated independently of one another by a group of American female students to ensure that pictures could be selected which conveyed equal levels of liking and disliking. The superimposed photographs were then presented to another group of American female students, who had not seen the pictures before. Although significant effects on judgements of liking were found for both face and posture, a significant statistical interaction suggested that these judgements were dominated by the facial expression. However, the results did also show that posture can moderate the effects of facial expression. Thus, a positive facial expression with a positive posture was judged as conveying more liking than a positive facial expression and a negative posture, whereas a neutral facial expression with a positive posture was actually judged as conveying less liking than a neutral face with a negative posture. But since in this latter case the positive posture was presumably a trunk lean forward (although this is not actually made explicit in Waldron's article), it may well have been the case that forward lean with a neutral facial expression was seen to be rather aggressive, although there is no direct evidence on this point.

When taken together, these studies certainly suggest that bodily cues communicate information about affiliation. There is evidence from both encoding and decoding studies (mainly of American students) to suggest that leaning forward (or reducing backward lean), gazing and adopting a close interpersonal distance communicates a friendly attitude. There is also evidence to suggest that women communicate a positive attitude through open body positions. Arms akimbo has been related to the encoding of dislike, and differences in sideways trunk lean have also been related to the encoding of affiliation, but there have been no relevant decoding studies of either of these behaviours. The relationship of body orientation to affiliation is unclear; where studies have shown significant effects, they have usually involved rather complex statistical interactions with the sex or age of the encoder.

Mehrabian (e.g. 1972) has attempted to subsume the bodily communication of affiliation within the concept of immediacy. Immediacy refers to the degree of mutual sensory stimulation between people; leaning forward, gazing and adopting a close interpersonal distance result in an increase of mutual sensory stimulation, and hence according to Mehrabian result in greater immediacy and communicate a more positive attitude. According to this view, the communicative significance of these bodily cues is a by-product of the fact they increase mutual sensory stimulation. A different explanation of the relationship between gaze and affiliation has been proposed by Rutter and Stephenson (1979). They took observations of gaze from conversations between pairs of same-sex friends and strangers; their subjects were recruited from a British university and through a newspaper advertisement. They found that strangers tended to look at one another significantly more than friends, and used this finding not to question the relationship between gaze and affiliation but to argue that the function of gaze is primarily to collect information about others rather than to communicate affect. According to this view, friends look at one another less than strangers because they are more sure of each other's responses and do not need to check them so frequently. This would suggest that people look more at people to whom they are attracted not to communicate attraction but simply to gain more information; the communicative significance of gaze in relation to affiliation can be seen as a by-product of this information-gathering process.

The role which non-verbal communication plays in interpersonal attraction has been specifically discussed by Argyle and Dean (1965) and Mehrabian and Ksionsky (1974). The work of Mehrabian and Ksionsky has already been discussed in Chapter 4 (pp. 84–85) with reference to whether there are specific bodily cues associated with an affiliative personality, but it is also appropriate in this context since it embodies a specific theory about the role of bodily cues in affiliation. Mehrabian and Ksionsky hypothesized that affiliation can be understood in terms of a two-dimensional scheme, comprising those who expect positive reinforcement from others (affiliative tendency) and those who expect negative reinforcement from others (sensitivity to rejection). They devised questionnaires to measure these two dimensions, which were administered to American male and female students who took part in conversations in pairs. These conversations were rated for 26 selected measures of verbal and non-verbal behaviour which Mehrabian and Ksionsky claimed had shown unambiguous significance in other studies. A factor analysis of these ratings showed a factor which was interpreted in terms of affiliation, and which showed a significant positive correlation with high scores on the affiliation questionnaire; this factor included gaze, facial pleasantness and hand gestures, as well as amount of talk and positive verbal content. High scorers on the affiliative tendency questionnaire were also repeatedly found to perceive others in a more positive light, to see themselves as more similar to others and to be perceived more positively by others: they were better liked, evoked more behavioural affiliation from others and reported themselves as more popular and less lonely. Mehrabian and Ksionsky found a second factor from their factor analysis which they interpreted in terms of tension; this factor consisted of symmetrical body postures and a lack of sideways lean, and showed a significant positive correlation with the sensitivity to rejection scale. High scorers on the sensitivity to rejection scale did not tend to perceive others more negatively, but were found to be less confident when dealing with others, and were found to evoke less positive attitudes from others as well as greater behavioural tension.

As was discussed in Chapter 4, Mehrabian and Ksionsky's hypothesis that there are specific bodily cues associated with an affiliative personality has not found much support from other research. However, the concept of personality is not critical to their model of interpersonal attraction; what is important is that according to Mehrabian and Ksionsky, positive expectations of others lead to positive behaviours which are reciprocated by others and facilitate liking, whereas negative expectations of others leads to tense behaviour towards others which again is reciprocated, and which discourages future interaction. Hence, in Mehrabian and Ksionsky's model of affiliation, expectations of others linked to a principle of reciprocity play a critical role in interpersonal attraction.

This emphasis on reciprocity is particularly interesting in that Argyle and Dean's (1965) model of intimacy makes precisely the opposite assumption. Argyle and Dean proposed that there is an equilibrium level for intimacy, which represents a joint function of the approach and avoidance forces associated with such features as eye contact, physical proximity, intimacy of topic and smiling. They argued that if equilibrium for intimacy is disturbed along one of these dimensions, then attempts to restore it will be made by altering other behaviours. They reported an experiment in which conversations took place between pairs of British male and female students, one of whom in each case was a confederate of the experimenter. The students were explicitly told where to sit for each conversation, which took place with the participants either 2 feet, 6 feet or 10 feet apart at 90° to one another, seated around a table. The confederate was instructed to gaze continually at the partner during the conversation, in which the participants were given three minutes to make up a story for a picture (a Thematic Apperception Test card). Gaze was observed from behind a one-way screen, and the results showed that irrespective of the sex subject or the confederate, the total duration of eye contact was significantly shorter at closer interpersonal distances.

Stephenson and Rutter (1970) criticized Argyle and Dean's experiment on the grounds that their results might simply have been an artefact of the way in which gaze was measured. As the distance between two people increases, so the angle between one person's eye-to-eye gaze and gaze away from the other person's eyes becomes progressively finer and hence more difficult to judge. The experiment which Stephenson and Rutter performed (described in Chapter 1, pp. 17–18 with reference to the measurement of gaze) did in fact show that as the distance between the conversational partners increased, so too did the tendency of observers to overestimate their mutual gaze. Subsequently, Stephenson, Rutter and Dore (1973) devised an experiment to overcome what they considered to be the shortcomings of the Argyle and Dean study. They arranged for conversations to take place between same-sex and mixed-sex pairs of British students, and used a zoom lens to videotape each student's face so that the observers would not be affected by distance in their judgements of gaze. The methodology employed by Argyle and Dean was also modified in two other ways. Argyle and Dean used a continually gazing confederate as one of the conversational partners, and since continuous gaze is very unusual in naturally occurring conversations, this might well have produced spurious results; Stephenson, Rutter and Dore avoided this problem by simply not using confederates and by not trying to constrain the gaze of the students in any way. Each of the students also participated in only one conversation at one of the three distances, so that the distance manipulation was not made salient as it was in the Argyle and Dean study. Nevertheless, with these modifications duration of eye contact was still found to increase significantly with greater interpersonal distance.

This relationship between gaze and interpersonal distance has been replicated on a number of occasions. Cappella (1981) made an extensive review of studies relevant to the intimacy–equilibrium hypothesis, and most of those which have measured proximity and gaze have found an inverse relationship between the two. The studies reviewed by Cappella also indicate compensatory relationships between proximity and a number of other behaviours: increased proximity by one member of a pair leads the other to reintroduce normal social distances, to adopt a more oblique body orientation, to move more, to have faster reactions, to leave or to speak less. But the Argyle and Dean model also predicts compensatory relationships between other behaviours apart from proximity which are not supported in the studies reviewed by Cappella. For example, there is no real evidence to suggest that an increase in gaze by one member of a pair is likely to lead to compensatory behaviour by the other person.

There are also some studies which have failed to replicate the inverse relationship between proximity and gaze, and some which have in fact showed a positive relationship between proximity and gaze. Aiello (1972) arranged for American male and female students to have a conversation with a male or female confederate at one of three distances (2 feet, 6 feet or 10 feet); the confederate was given no specific instructions with respect to gaze, but was asked to talk for approximately 50 per cent of the time. A significant statistical interaction between distance and sex of subject showed that whereas the duration and mean length of glances by male students increased with increasing distance, the duration and mean length of glances by female students were at their highest at 6 feet, intermediate at 2 feet, and least at 10 feet. Subsequently, Aiello (1977) has replicated this finding in another study of American students using interpersonal distances of 2.5 feet, 6.5 feet and 10 feet, and an examination of the data in Stephenson, Rutter and Dore's study with British students suggests a curvilinear trend in the relationship between gaze and the three interpersonal distances for females, but a linear trend for males. Aiello maintains that large interpersonal distances lack the necessary reinforcement value for women, and hence they simply withdraw from the interaction.

A study which showed a positive relationship between proximity and gaze was carried out by Patterson, Mullens and Romano (1971). They arranged for American male and female students sitting alone at a table in a university library to be approached either by a male or a female experimenter, who sat down in the adjacent seat, or the opposite seat, or two seats adjacent or three seats adjacent. The response of the students to this intrusion was observed, measurements being made of gaze, leaning or sliding away from the experimenter and what were called blocking responses, in which the student placed a hand or elbow in front of the experimenter. The results showed that leaning, blocking and gazing at the experimenter increased significantly in a linear fashion the closer the seat adopted by the experimenter during the first five minutes after arrival. Patterson, Mullens and Romano proposed that the students may have looked more either out of curiosity or vigilance at an intruder who approached them too closely; equally their response could be seen as an act of self-assertion in response to the intrusion. The problem here for Argyle and Dean's hypothesis is that increased gaze is not simply associated with affiliation; as was argued in Chapter 2, it may be associated with a whole range of emotions, not all of which are by any means positive for the recipient of the gaze.

Nevertheless, proximity has been found to be positively related to gaze in a situation where the affect expressed appears to be unmistakably positive. Chapman (1975) arranged for groups of seven-year-old British children to listen to humorous stories over headphones at one of two interpersonal distances (chairs were secured to the floor either 2.7 feet apart or 5.5 feet apart). Chapman found that children at the closer distance engaged in significantly more laughter, smiling and eye contact, in direct contradiction of Argyle and Dean's hypothesis. Chapman used these data to criticize the intimacy–equilibrium hypothesis on the grounds that it is based on an invalid assumption, namely, that levels of intimacy remain static during an interaction.

Patterson (1976) has attempted to reconcile these conflicting findings and viewpoints. Patterson proposes that in an interaction, changes in one person's intimacy behaviours precipitate a change in arousal in the other person. Depending upon factors such as the social setting and the type of relationship, this change in arousal may be labelled by that person as either a positive or negative emotional state. Positively labelled states facilitate reciprocal or enhancing reactions to the other person's intimate behaviours, while negatively labelled states facilitate compensatory reactions. Hence if a person is happy for greater intimacy to develop, he may reciprocate the affiliative behaviours expressed by the other person in the way hypothesized by Mehrabian and Ksionsky. If he does not wish for greater intimacy to develop, then he may respond in the compensatory fashion described by Argyle and Dean. According to this view, reciprocal or compensatory behaviours can be seen as contributing either to the development of greater intimacy, or to the maintenance of the status quo or indeed to a developing estrangement. The problem is of course to specify under what conditions each of these responses takes place.

(ii) Dominance

Kiesler uses the term 'status' to refer to a relationship characterized by dominance or submission; in fact the terms can be distinguished from one another, for example, in the case of the 'power behind the throne', where a person of lower formal status exerts a dominating influence over another person who is in fact his nominal superior. In the ensuing discussion, the term 'dominance' will be used to refer to a dimension of interpersonal relationships, whereas the term 'status' will be used to refer to specific roles in which relationships of dominance and submission have been formalized. Although dominance and status can be distinguished from one another in this way, nevertheless they are discussed together, since it has been argued that non-verbal cues relating to dominance and submission may become ritualized in formal status hierarchies.

Certainly it would appear that non-verbal cues are perceived as conveying important information about interpersonal attitudes of dominance and submissiveness. Argyle *et al.* (1970) carried out a study (discussed in Chapter 4, p. 106), in which verbal and non-verbal signals for inferior, equal and superior attitudes were compared. British students were asked to rate videotapes of a female encoder reading messages where the speech content was intended to convey an inferior, equal or superior attitude in an inferior, equal or superior non-verbal style. The non-verbal styles employed by the encoder for a superior attitude were an unsmiling facial expression, head raised and loud, dominating speech; for a neutral attitude, the encoder employed a slight smile with head level and neutral-to-pleasant speech; for an inferior attitude, the encoder employed a nervous, deferential smile, head lowered and nervous, eager-to-please speech. Both speech content and non-verbal styles were approximately equal in judged inferiority/superiority when rated independently of one another; when judged in combination, non-verbal cues accounted for 10.3 times as much of the variance as speech content, and produced 4.3 times as much shift on the rating scales.

Other research has been focused on the specific bodily cues associated with dominance and status. In a study described in Chapter 2 (pp. 45–46), Graham and Argyle (1975a) arranged for British students to rate on 20 rating scales confederates of the experimenter who had been asked to pose all four possible combinations of two facial expressions (frowning or smiling) and two gaze patterns) 10 or 90 per cent looking). Gaze affected rating scales which were interpreted in terms of a dimension of potency; 90 per cent gaze was perceived as more strong, aggressive and dominant. Van de Sande (1980) arranged for male and female students to rate for dominance 36 four-minute conversations between pairs of male and female students, which had been recorded on videotape to show a head-and-shoulders picture of the participants. The observers also measured 11 variables relating to speech and gaze, and these observations were factor analysed along with the ratings of dominance. Results showed that most of the variance in the dominance ratings was accounted for by a factor of duration of speech activity and another factor of word adoption (the number of times a keyword which has been introduced by one conversational partner is used by the other); the only measurement of gaze which showed a significant relationship to perceived dominance was that of gaze aversion while listening. Van de Sande does not regard his study as contradicting the finding that high levels of gaze are perceived as conveying dominance, commenting simply that such levels of gaze are unusual in normal social interaction; hence when naturally occurring conversations are judged, the level of gaze does not have such a marked effect on the perception of dominance.

The relationship of gaze to status was investigated by Mehrabian in his role-play studies of encoding which were described in the previous section on affiliation (pp. 121–122) (Mehrabian, 1968a, 1968b; Mehrabian and Friar, 1969). In these studies, in addition to investigating the bodily cues associated with affiliation, American male and female students were also asked to demonstrate the positions they would adopt when communicating with someone of higher and lower status. In the study of standing encoders, Mehrabian (1968a) found that the students looked more at a person of higher status, the effect being particularly pronounced for male encoders. In a study of seated encoders, Mehrabian and Friar (1969) found that the students used significantly less gaze with a person of lower status, that male encoders used significantly more gaze with a person of higher status and that female encoders used significantly less gaze with a disliked person of lower status.

Mehrabian's studies of encoding suggest that people look more at another person when he is of higher rather than lower status. This finding is interesting in view of a hypothesis put forward by Chance (1967) that the patterning of gaze (which Chance calls the structure of attention) provides important clues to the dominance hierarchy within groups of subhuman primates. Chance notes that the traditional definition of dominance is that attribute of an animal's behaviour which enables it to obtain an object when in competition with others. He suggests instead a definition of dominance according to which the dominant individual is the focus of attention of those holding subordinate status within the group, and that it is the attention-binding characteristics of a particular animal which establishes its dominance.

Abramovitch (1976) tested this hypothesis with a group of American children, aged between three and five years. She took measures of rank on the basis of the number of individuals with whom fights were won and lost, dividing the children into three groups of high, middle and low rank; in addition, she took observations of the number of times each child glanced at each other child. Abramovitch's data showed that high-ranked children glance at low-ranked children significantly less than would be expected by chance, whereas low-ranked children glanced at high-ranked children significantly more than would be expected by chance.

Spiegel and Machotka (1974) investigated the perception of dominance in a study in which American male and female students were shown a set of four pictures, where the gaze of three background figures was systematically varied between two foreground figures, one seated and one standing (see Figure 19). The results showed that as the background figures were oriented more towards the standing figure, they made him appear (in terms of Spiegel and Machotka's rating scales) more superordinate, important and initiating; the effect of head orientation was more marked than that of body orientation. As the background figures were more oriented towards the seated figure, they made him appear more haughty, important and initiating; again, the effect of head orientation was more marked than that of body orientation. The orientation of the background figures had no effect on how they themselves were rated; they were consistently seen as inferior to the foreground figures. Thus, there is a certain

Figure 19. Gaze and the perception of dominance. (Reprinted by permission of Macmillan Publishing Co. Inc. and from J. P. Spiegel and P. Machotka (1974), *Messages of the Body*. New York: Free Press. Copyright © 1974 by the Free Press, a Division of Macmillan Publishing Co., Inc.)

degree of support from human studies for Chance's hypothesis concerning the structure of attention and dominance, and it does appear that the structure of attention functions as a means of non-verbally communicating dominance in human groups.

Studies of posture suggest that a number of body positions are associated with status and dominance. The data from Mehrabian's encoding studies showed significant relationships between status and head, trunk, arm/hand and leg positions. In his study of standing encoders, Mehrabian (1968a) found that the head was raised significantly higher when communicating to someone of higher status. In that same study, he also found that shoulder orientation was more direct to a person of higher status; in a study of seated encoders (Mehrabian and Friar, 1969), a composite measure was obtained from the mean angles of orientation for the head, shoulders and legs, which showed that orientation towards a disliked male of higher status was more direct than towards a female of lower status. In both studies, it was found that female encoders used more arm openness when communicating with people of higher status; in the study of standing encoders (Mehrabian, 1968a), it was also found that male encoders used more leg openness when communicating with people of higher status. In that same study, it was also found that more hand and leg relaxation was used in addressing someone of lower status; in a study of seated encoders (Mehrabian and Friar, 1969), it was found that sideways trunk lean was used more when addressing someone of lower status. Finally, in the study of standing encoders (Mehrabian, 1968a), it was found that the arms akimbo position was used more when addressing someone of lower status.

In a decoding study by Spiegel and Machotka (1974), ratings of dominance appeared to be markedly affected by arm position. A group of figures were presented in which one had his arm extended, another had his arms akimbo, a third had his arms folded, a fourth had his hands in his pockets, a fifth had one hand behind his back and a sixth had both hands behind his back (see Figure 20). The pictures were rated by a group of American male and female students, and in terms of the rating scales provided by Spiegel and Machotka, the figure with one arm outstretched was perceived as the most superordinate, action-initiating, expressive and important. The figure with his arms akimbo was seen as the most self-concerned and haughty, and second only to the figure with one arm outstretched as superordinate, action-initiating, expressive and important. The figure with one hand behind his back was seen as humble and insignificant; only the figure with both hands behind his back was seen as more humble and insignificant.

In summary, Mehrabian's work suggests that in communicating with a person of higher status, a more direct body orientation is employed with more open body positions and a more erect head position. In communicating with a person of lower status, greater bodily relaxation is shown, and greater use is made of the arms akimbo position. Spiegel and Machotka found that a figure using the arms akimbo position was also perceived as more dominant, suggesting that arms akimbo constitutes a means of non-verbally communicating dominance.

132

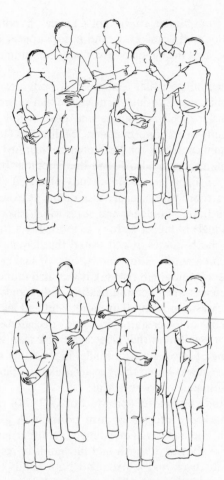

Figure 20. Body position and the perception of dominance. (Reprinted by permission of Macmillan Publishing Co. Inc. from J. P. Spiegel and P. Machotka (1974), *Messages of the Body*. New York: Free Press. Copyright © 1974 by the Free Press, a Division of Macmillan Publishing Co. Inc.)

In addition, Spiegel and Machotka found that a figure with one arm outstretched was perceived as highly dominant, whereas figures with one or both hands behind their backs were perceived as humble and insignificant. In the absence of other research on posture and status or dominance, it is difficult to know how to assess the generality of these findings. That this may be a serious problem is suggested by a field study carried out by Jorgensen (1975), in which he observed pairs of American male factory employees in conversation; they were either of equivalent or discrepant status (supervisors or nonsupervisors). Jorgensen's observations showed that pairs diverging in status conversed at a significantly more oblique angle than pairs of equivalent status, which directly contradicts Mehrabian's finding that people adopt a more direct orientation when conversing with someone of higher status.

In that same study, Jorgensen also took observations of the distance at which people conversed, but found no significant differences between pairs of equivalent or discrepant status. Similarly, in Mehrabian's studies of status (Mehrabian, 1968a; Mehrabian and Friar, 1969), no significant effects of status were found on interpersonal distance. Latta (1978) arranged for American male students to meet one of three people seated at the end of a table opposite the door (a college professor, a college student and a high school student). The students adopted a significantly greater distance from the college professor than from a fellow student. Dean, Willis and Hewitt (1975) observed interaction distances between United States' uniformed active duty naval personnel in the Navy exchange (a general-purpose shop for naval personnel), the cafeteria, the lobby of the station hospital and a station recreation centre. Interaction distance was recorded by using floor tiles, distances being measured to the nearest half-tile. Interactions initiated with a superior were characterized by significantly greater distance than with people of equal rank, and this distance increased significantly with discrepancy in rank. But when interactions were initiated by superiors with subordinates, interpersonal distance was found to be unrelated to discrepancy in rank. Dean, Willis and Hewitt argue that superiors feel free to approach subordinates at interpersonal distances which may indicate intimacy, whereas subordinates do not feel free to do so.

Results of group studies also show pronounced effects of status on interpersonal distance. Sommer (1961) organized visitors, volunteer workers and student nurses at an American psychiatric hospital in same-sex groups of between three and six people. They were asked to elect a leader for a brief discussion which took place at a rectangular table in the hospital café; typically the leader chose a seat at the head of the table. Subsequently, in a questionnaire study, Lott and Sommer (1967) asked American students how they would locate themselves in relation to a person of higher status (a professor), of equal status (a fellow student) and of lower status (a freshman whose academic performance was poor). To perform this task, the students were presented with drawings of rectangular tables, and their responses showed a clear tendency to accord the higher status figure the head of the table.

Roger and Reid (1978) found significant changes in interpersonal distance associated with changes in status. British Royal Marine recruits were divided into four-man discussion groups, and were asked to discuss a problem in which they were described as the four sole survivors of an air crash in the desert; the task of each group was to arrive at a mutually satisfactory strategy for survival. After 15 minutes' discussion, the recruits were instructed to choose a leader (who had contributed most to the discussion) and a non-leader (who had contributed least to the discussion); the results showed that ordinary members sat significantly closer to leaders than to non-leaders. Subsequently, Roger and

Reid (1982) carried out a similar study in which they investigated how interpersonal distance changes over time. Seating arrangements were recorded at four-minute intervals by marking the positions of the front legs of each chair on record sheets blocked off into $\frac{3}{4}$-inch squares which corresponded to the 12-inch-square floor tiles in the test area. Roger and Reid replicated the relationship between distance and status observed in the previous experiment, and in addition found that while the distances separating leaders and ordinary members remained more or less constant over time, the corresponding distances for the non-leaders showed a progressive increase. Thus it appears that it is the non-leaders who distance themselves from the other participants, rather than the ordinary members and leaders who draw closer to one another.

The evidence reviewed above suggest that certain bodily cues are related to dominance and status. But since researchers for the most part have tended to study either encoding or decoding, it is not clear to what extent bodily cues actually communicate information about dominance or status. If bodily cues do communicate such information, the question arises as to what role they play in the establishment and maintenance of dominance or status. Ethologists have in fact argued that the role of bodily cues is highly significant in the establishment of dominance. For example, Eibl-Eibesfeldt (1973b) notes that conflicts between members of the same species often take place within very specific rules, which have the adaptive advantage of reducing the risk of serious injury or death. Such conflicts take the form of threat displays, which presumably signal an individual's likelihood of attacking another individual, the conflict often being resolved when one contestant performs appeasement gestures as a sign of submission.

A number of studies have been carried out (mainly with young children) to test the relevance of these concepts to human relationships. Camras (1977) arranged for same-sex pairs of American children (aged between 49 and 78 months) to play with an object with which only one child could play at a time. Her results showed that each player who won conflict with an aggressive expression was more likely to defend the toy on the next attempt. Aggressive expressions were defined as lowered brows, stare, face thrust forward, lips pressed together with tightened mouth corners and nose wrinkle. The non-player would also wait significantly longer before making another attempt to obtain the toy if the player either showed an aggressive expression or the oblique eyebrows of sadness (with the inner corners of the eyebrows raised). Camras (1980) also carried out another study (discussed in Chapter 2, pp. 51–52) to investigate how a different group of American children (aged between 62 and 80 months) perceived the facial expressions which occurred during conflict. In one experiment, the children were told a story about two children fighting over a toy which one wanted to keep very much. They were shown six target expressions identified in the study described above (lowered brows, oblique brows, nose wrinkle, both lips thrust forward and two forms of lips pressed together), and ten non-target expressions which had also occurred in earlier studies of conflict. The children showed a significant tendency to choose the target expressions as indicating that the child wanted to keep the toy. In a second experiment, the children were told stories intended to evoke particular emotions, and were asked to choose an appropriate facial expression from a set of three including the target expressions. Camras's results showed that the children were able to choose appropriate expressions at a level significantly above chance. Her data thus suggest that particular bodily cues do have an influence on the outcome of conflicts, and that children can adequately decode the expressions. But the suggestion that such cues function as threat displays because they frequently precede an attack (e.g. Grant, 1969) was not supported; no physical attacks occurred even following a child's aggressive expressions and subsequent loss of the toy (Camras, 1977). Camras argues that bodily cues influence the outcome of conflicts, not as threat displays but simply because they communicate the child's anger or sadness at the prospect of losing the toy, which in turn influences the behaviour of the other protagonist.

With reference to the concept of appeasement gestures, Ginsburg, Pollman and Wauson (1977) took up Darwin's (1872) suggestion that 'making oneself smaller' appeases and inhibits human aggression. Ginsburg, Pollman and Wauson observed aggressive encounters between 8- to 12-year-old boys over a 6-week period (aggression was defined in terms of hitting, kicking, pushing, pulling or jumping on another child). They examined the behaviour of the child under attack just before the aggression ceased, and a highly significant proportion of the incidents observed were associated with a diminution of body stature just prior to the cessation of aggression. Examples of the behaviour observed included bowing of the head, slumping of the shoulders, lying motionless on the ground, kneeling, shoe tying and what was called 'waxy flexibility' (the child allows the aggressor to manipulate his body without offering muscular resistance). In another study, Ginsburg (1977) investigated fights which were terminated by the intervention of a third person. A significant proportion of those fights involved continued aggression by the antagonist while the child under attack exhibited some kind of appeasement display involving a diminution of body stature. Ginsburg also showed other children videotaped segments of fights which were terminated by the intervention of a third child and fights which ended of their own accord. He found that on the basis of seeing the fights alone (prior to an act of intervention) the children were able to predict an act of intervention at a level significantly above chance, although they were not able to identify the specific cues on which their judgements were based. Thus the work of Ginsburg, Pollman and Wauson certainly suggests that making oneself smaller functions as an appeasement gesture in human conflicts, which is also likely to provoke intervention by other people if the signals are ignored by the aggressor.

In ethological terms, the concepts of threat displays and appeasement gestures are essentially seen as ways of resolving dyadic conflicts which lead to the establishment of relatively stable dominance hierarchies which serve to regulate future conflict; bodily cues are also seen as a way of maintaining the dominance hierarchies so established. As has already been discussed, Chance (p. 129) has suggested an alternative definition whereby the structure of attention may be seen as providing important clues to the dominance hierarchy; this structure of attention need not be based on the outcomes of previous conflicts. Chance's observations also suggest not only a way in which dominance relationships within a group may be communicated, but also a way in which influence is actually exerted; if people look more at those who are dominant, then they are more easily able directly to influence the group. The relationship of interpersonal distance to dominance and status can be seen as related to gaze in similar ways. Howells and Becker (1962) found that American students when seated in groups of five (two opposite three) tended to choose the leader significantly more frequently from the two-seat side of the table, thus suggesting that greater visibility to the other participants facilitated the emergence of leadership. Similarly, the fact that leaders are often given the head of the table position (e.g. Sommer, 1961, Lott and Sommer, 1967, see p. 133) suggests that where a formal role structure exists, the leader may be given a position of greater visibility in order more easily to exert a position of influence.

Research on gaze, interpersonal distance, dominance and status suggests that while greater visibility in a group may facilitate leadership emergence, existing status differences may also be acknowledged by giving the person of higher status a position where he may more easily see and be seen, and hence more easily exert influence. Similarly, Ginsburg, Pollman and Wauson's (1977) finding that children inhibit aggression through making themselves smaller finds obvious parallels in formal status systems where an inferior greets a superior by bowing, kneeling or even by kowtowing, a custom in imperial China whereby the inferior touched the ground with his forehead in absolute submission. The obvious parallels in the bodily cues associated with dominance and status suggests the possibility that the way in which formal status systems prescribe behaviour may be based on the ways in which individuals achieve dominance, and hence serve to enhance the influence of the individuals of superior status. It would appear that not only do bodily cues communicate information about dominance and status, they also constitute part of the ways in which such relationships are established and maintained.

2. Role Relationships

(i) Mother–infant Relationships

Non-verbal communication is clearly of critical importance in mother–infant relationships, since it constitutes the only initial form of communication between infant and mother. It used to be argued according to the 'secondary drive hypothesis' that the infant's emotional dependence stems from his physical dependence on others to satisfy his basic needs of hunger, thirst, sex and bodily comfort; this view can be traced directly to Freud, and was subsequently elaborated in a learning theory framework by Dollard and Miller (1950). The secondary drive hypothesis has been criticized on a number of grounds; for example, Schaffer (1971) mentions animal studies which have shown that attachments are formed by the young in the absence of any physical gratification, while it has also been found that human infants frequently form strong attachments to such individuals as fathers, siblings and relatives who rarely or never participate in routine caretaking activities (Schaffer and Emerson, 1964). Dissatisfaction with the secondary drive hypothesis led Bowlby (1958) to suggest that the term 'dependence' with its particular theoretical connotations should be replaced by the more neutral term 'attachment'. Bowlby also proposed a new theory drawing particularly on ethology to account for the origins of attachments; he argued that an infant's attachment to his mother originates in a number of species-characteristic behaviour systems, which although relatively independent of one another at first, become organized towards the mother as the chief attachment figure. He identified five such behavioural systems as contributing to attachment: sucking, following and clinging, in which the child takes an active role in seeking and maintaining contact, and crying and smiling, which have a signalling function and bring the adult into proximity with the child. Bowlby (1969) proposed that attachment behaviour can be regarded as a 'control system', which comes into play whenever the infant's sense organs inform him that the distance between him and his mother has increased beyond a certain tolerable maximum; the attachment behaviours serve to restore an acceptable distance between him and his mother. The evolutionary function of such behaviours, Bowlby argues, is to protect the infant from danger, and especially from the danger of attack by predators. This view is certainly consistent with the hypothesis advanced in Chapter 2, that the facial expressions of happiness and sadness are innate signals which have evolved as a primary form of communication. It also suggests that non-verbal communication plays a principal role in establishing the bond between infant and mother.

Richards (1971) has criticized Bowlby's view that there are a specific number of infant behavioural systems which lead to proximity with the mother and hence to attachment between mother and child. He points out that if a new-born infant is in his cot, his crying will often bring his mother to his side, but so too will his choking, hiccupping, gross body movements and changes in breathing rhythm. Similarly, during feeding his sucking certainly patterns the mother's behaviour, but so too do his facial movements, sneezes, burps and so forth. Richards maintains that Bowlby's view gives little attention to what Richards regards as the central problem in the development of attachments: the timing and phasing of the participants' behaviours. From a frame-by-frame analysis of mother–infant interaction, Richards found that whereas the actions of some mothers are carefully phased with those of their infants, other mothers will expose their infants to a constant and unphased barrage of stimulation, allowing the infant no time in which to make a response.

More recent research on mother–infant relationships has in fact been focused on the sequential structure of mother–infant interaction. Typically, investigators have commented on how closely such interchanges resemble the structure of adult conversation. For example, Trevarthen (1977) has carried out slow-motion film analyses of mother–infant interaction, and has commented on how frequently mother and infant alternate in their non-verbal behaviour, taking turns in the same way in which adults take turns in speech. Trevarthen calls this process 'intersubjectivity' because it is devoid of reference to things in the external world, but nevertheless argues that it constitutes a form of communication because of the close patterning between the movements of mother and infant.

Jaffe, Stern and Peery (1973) carried out a statistical analysis of the patterning of gaze between pairs of infants and adults. They made observations of three pairs of twins (two male and one female pair) in the fourth month of life during free play with their mothers and with several experimenters. The gaze of both partners was coded at 0.6 second intervals into one of four states: neither looking, infant only looking, adult only looking and both looking. The probabilities of each state being followed by each other state were calculated from these observations, which showed that the sequential relationships between gaze were clearly not random. Jaffe, Stern and Peery found that adding information from the previous time interval (i.e. 1.2 seconds) in most cases did not significantly increase the accuracy of prediction of subsequent gaze, and so argued that most gaze patterns could be accommodated in what is known as a first-order Markov model, where information on the immediately preceding event is sufficient to predict the current event without requiring further information on earlier events. Previously they had carried out studies on adult conversation, classifying it at 0.3 second intervals into four states of neither speaking, person A speaking, person B speaking and both speaking, and again found that a first-order Markov model was sufficient to predict conversational events. Jaffe, Stern and Peery argue that this similarity between adult–infant interaction and adult–adult conversation (in that information concerning what happened less than one second previously is sufficient to predict the next event) suggests that there may be some universal property of dyadic communication which is apparent in gaze patterns long before the onset of speech.

Kaye and Fogel (1980) took observations of infants in free play, with their mothers at three different ages (6, 13 and 26 weeks of age). Seven modes of behaviour were coded (head orientation, eye quality and facial expression of the infant; head movement, facial expression, touching and changing baby's position by the mother). Kaye and Fogel's findings show how the interchange between mother and infant increasingly comes to resemble a kind of dialogue. In a previous study of one infant during his fifth to thirteenth week in interaction with his mother, Fogel (1977) had found that maternal behaviour could be seen as alternating between 'on' and 'off' phases of infant attention, where in the 'on' phases the mother used, for example, clusters of facial expression, head movement and vocalization to maintain the infant's attention. In this study, Kaye and Fogel (1980) found that the infants' vocalization, smiling and mouth opening clustered into 'runs' which at six weeks occurred only during the mother's 'on' phases, but which by 26 weeks alternated with the mothers' clusters of expressions in a kind of dialogue. Similarly, the infants' periods of attention towards the mother significantly overlapped with the mothers' facially expressive behaviour, and this became increasingly the case with age.

Kaye and Fogel's data support the hypothesis that non-verbal communication between mother and infant increasingly comes to resemble adult conversation in form, that is, with clusters of expressions being produced by each partner in turn. This resemblance in form to adult conversation lends support to Trevarthen's belief that such patterning of expressive behaviour does constitute a kind of communication, albeit devoid of reference to events in the external world. It also suggests that infant communication should not be seen as confined to smiling and crying (which Bowlby has argued are key features in the development of attachments), but can be extended to a much wider range of infant expressive behaviours.

(ii) Marital Relationships

A number of studies have suggested that poor marital adjustment may be indicated by non-verbal communication. For example, Beier and Sternberg (1977) videotaped conversations between recently married couples who had been asked to fill in the Beier–Sternberg Discord Questionnaire. The couples were divided into four groups according to whether both partners reported a high level of discord, whether the wife or husband reported a high level of discord or whether neither reported discord. Beier and Sternberg found that the couples who reported the least discord were rated highest on non-verbal behaviours indicative of closeness, such as gaze, touching the other person and using open-arm and open-leg positions. Similarly, Gottman, Markman and Notarius (1977) videotaped conversations from two groups of married couples who had responded to an advert asking for people who considered their marriage was either satisfactory or unsatisfactory; there were also some couples who had been referred by marital counselling agencies. Videotapes of the conversations of the satisfied and dissatisfied pairs were transcribed and coded both for speech content and non-verbal communication. The ratings of non-verbal communication were made simply in terms of positive, neutral or negative affect, and were based on the work of Mehrabian (1972). Results show that the satisfied and dissatisfied couples differed significantly both in terms of non-verbal communication and in the ratio of agreeing to disagreeing statements. Riskin and Faunce (1972) concluded that the ratio of agreement to disagreement was the most consistent discriminator across studies between distressed and non-distressed families. In this study, Gottman, Markman and Notarius found more sizeable differences associated with non-verbal communication, and argue accordingly that it may be a more powerful indicator of marital distress; alternatively, this might simply reflect differences in the scoring procedures used to measure non-verbal communication and the ratio of agreeing to disagreeing statements. Whatever the case, it certainly appears that non-verbal communication is a clear indicator of a poor marital relationship.

Noller (1980) has argued that a relative failure to appreciate non-verbal communication may be a cause of poor marital adjustment. She arranged for each member of a number of married couples to send a standard set of ambiguous messages to his or her spouse and to decode a similar set received from the spouse. The ambiguous messages were designed so that the verbal content could have a positive, neutral or negative meaning depending on the non-verbal communication which accompanied it. Each person was also asked to complete a questionnaire intended to measure degree of marital adjustment. Noller's results showed that couples with high marital adjustment communicated significantly better than those with low adjustment (an item was marked as correct when the decoder's response corresponded to the alternative the encoder was asked to send by the experimenter). Noller interprets the data as supporting the hypothesis that an insensitivity to non-verbal communication may be a possible cause of poor marital relationships; in fact her findings demonstrate only a correlation between poor marital adjustment and poor non-verbal communication, which does not of course establish the existence of a causal relationship.

SITUATIONS

The significance of bodily cues can also be examined within the context of particular situations; the number of situations which can be discussed is virtually limitless, but since research has been concentrated on six particular situations, namely, psychotherapy, education, interviews, helping, deception and the psychological experiment, these will each be discussed in turn.

1. Psychotherapy

The term 'psychotherapy' covers a number of different types of treatments, ranging from Freudian psychoanalysis, based on the analyst's interpretations of the patient's free associations and dreams, to Rogers' client-centred therapy, with its stress on the client discovering his own solutions to his problems through his relationship to the therapist. Nevertheless, therapists of widely differing theoretical persuasions have argued that non-verbal communication is of central importance in psychotherapy. This view can of course be traced to the work of Freud himself. 'He that has eyes to see and ears to hear may convince himself that no mortal can keep a secret. If his lips are silent, he chatters with his finger-tips; betrayal oozes out of him at every pore' (Ekman and Friesen, 1969b, p. 89). Deutsch (1947, 1949, 1952) set out to record all the postures of patients undergoing psychoanalysis, together with a record of what the patient actually said. He gave numerous examples of how different postures accompanied different free associations; for example, he described how one female patient held her hands under her neck when fearful of being punished for masturbation, lifted her right hand and held her left hand protectively over her head when she was angry with men, and lifted both arms when she was angry with both parents (Deutsch, 1947). Deutsch argued that an awareness of postural expression is of great value in psychoanalysis both for the analyst in providing him with clues to the patient's unconscious feelings and for the patient in helping him to become aware of his own repressed feelings through the analyst's interpretations of the particular postures adopted. Similarly, Jacobs (1973) argued that the analyst can learn a great deal about his own emotions from the bodily positions he adopts.

Other writers working outside the framework of psychoanalysis have also emphasized the significance of non-verbal communication in psychotherapy. Kiesler (1979), deriving his theoretical framework from the work of Sullivan (1953, 1954), argued that interpersonal relationships are the momentary and cumulative result of the reciprocal messages, primarily non-verbal, exchanged between the participants. Abnormal behaviour Kiesler defined as inappropriate or inadequate interpersonal behaviour, whereby a person rigidly and continuously evokes from others responses which he does not intend, which are aversive and for which he cannot account. Kiesler argued that the essential tasks of the psychotherapist are to identify the predominantly self-defeating style of the client, and to metacommunicate with him about that style; in doing so, an awareness of non-verbal communication is of central importance.

There has, however, been no real attempt to test this belief in the importance of non-verbal communication for psychotherapy. Research on psychotherapy has taken two main forms: studies of process and studies of outcome. Outcome studies were stimulated by Eysenck's (1952) contention that there is no good evidence for the effectiveness of psychotherapy, based on Eysenck's claim that there was no difference between the success rates reported by psychotherapists and the number of patients who recovered without treatment. Subsequently, many controlled outcome studies have been carried out, where a treatment group is typically compared with a control group who receive no treatment. Smith and Glass (1977) review a whole number of such studies using an approach which they call meta-analysis. Meta-analysis refers to the same technique which Hall (1978) used in her review of sex differences in decoding non-verbal cues, where effect sizes are calculated using a common statistical procedure for each individual study. The effect sizes in Smith and Glass's review were calculated by dividing the mean difference between the treated and control subjects by the standard deviation of the control group. Their review indicated that controlled studies of psychotherapy do show a consistent improvement in the treatment group when compared with an untreated control group, and that this success rate is comparable to that obtained from other types of psychological treatment (such as behaviour therapy).

Process studies in psychotherapy are typically concerned with studying the interaction which takes place in psychotherapy, and attempting to relate that to outcome. If non-verbal communication is central to the process of psychotherapy, then it should form the centre-piece of such studies, but in fact the most substantial body of research on process is notable primarily for its inattention to bodily cues, namely, research inspired by the client-centred therapy of Carl Rogers. Rogers (1957) argued that therapeutic change can only take place through a relationship, and that the therapist is successful only to the extent that he conveys three personality characteristics of congruence (genuineness), unconditional positive regard (warmth) and empathic under-standing. Rating scales were devised to measure these three dimensions in psychotherapy, but these ratings were made on the basis of transcripts and audiotapes alone. In fact studies performed using this approach have failed to provide convincing evidence for Rogers' arguments. For example, Truax, Carkhuff and Kodman (1965) investigated the effectiveness of group psychotherapy, with improvement measured by the MMPI. The psychothera-pists were rated for empathy, warmth and congruence, and although empathy showed significant positive correlations with a positive outcome, self-congruence actually showed significant negative correlations with positive outcome.

One obvious criticism of this approach is that it may not be possible to make adequate ratings of congruence, warmth and empathy in the absence of visible bodily cues. Haase and Tepper (1972) investigated the relative contributions of speech and bodily cues to the judged level of empathy by arranging for American counsellors to rate videotapes of a counsellor conversing with a client, where the counsellor's speech and bodily cues were systematically varied. The counsellor showed either eye contact or no eye contact, forward trunk lean or backward trunk lean, direct or rotated body orientation and two levels of distance (36 or 72 inches). The counsellor also used three levels of verbal empathy, the statements being selected from examples in Truax and Carkhuff (1967) and Carkhuff and Berenson (1967), and subsequently rated by another group of counsellors to establish high-, medium- and low-empathy statements. Speech and bodily cues were presented in all possible combinations to create 48 10-second sequences. The sequences were randomly presented to the counsellors, who rated them on Truax and Carkhuff's (1967) 5-point scale of empathy. Results showed significant main effects for eye contact, trunk lean, distance and verbal empathy, and that each of these factors contributed independently to higher levels of judged empathy. Bodily cues accounted for 45 per cent of the variance in judged empathy, speech for 22 per cent and interactions for the remaining 33 per cent. The optimum combinations for the communication of high empathy appeared to be eye contact, forward trunk lean, far distance and a medium-empathic message, or eye contact, forward trunk lean, close distance and high-empathy message. The least effective combination for communicating empathy was no eye contact, backward trunk lean, far distance and low-empathy message.

Subsequently, Tepper and Haase (1978) have carried out a similar but more elaborate study. In this experiment, facial expression and intonation were included as independent variables, as well as the trunk lean and gaze mani-pulations employed before. Two levels of facial expression and intonation were used, pre-rated to convey concern or indifference. The messages were rated on respect and genuineness, as well as on empathy by American male counsellors and clients. The results showed significant main effects for all the non-verbal cues on all three rating scales, with facial expression being the most influential factor. When the main effects alone were considered, non-verbal cues accounted for twice as much of the variance in judged empathy as speech content, five times as much of the variance in judged respect and 23 times as much of the variance in judged genuineness.

The overwhelming significance of non-verbal cues in judgements of genuineness is of particular interest, in that one might expect inconsistency between non-verbal cues and speech content to exert a strong influence on such judgements. This hypothesis is supported by a study carried out by Graves and Robinson (1976). They arranged for American male and female students to take part in simulated counselling interviews where a confederate of the experimenter (described as a counsellor in training) used either positive or negative speech content with either positive bodily cues (eye contact, direct body orientation, forward trunk lean with legs forward and parallel) or negative bodily cues (infrequent eye contact, rotated body orientation, backward trunk lean with legs crossed and to the side). Results showed that inconsistent messages resulted in the students rating the counsellor as significantly less genuine and adopting a significantly greater interpersonal distance, especially when the bodily cues were negative and the speech positive.

There seems to be strong evidence that not only are bodily cues important in judgements of empathy, warmth and genuineness, but that they are a great deal more important than speech. Failure satisfactorily to measure these aspects of communication may be one of the reasons why researchers have failed to demonstrate convincingly the therapeutic significance of empathy, warmth and genuineness. What the evidence does suggest is that the perception of the therapist is strongly influenced by bodily cues; what still remains open to question is the much more fundamental question of whether and in what ways therapeutic outcome is related to the therapist's skills in decoding and encoding bodily cues.

2. Education

Galloway (1968) has argued that non-verbal communication is of considerable significance in education, and that non-verbal cues are given considerable importance by pupils in assessing the genuineness of a teacher. Galloway also argues that non-verbal communication is important in facilitating or inhibiting communication between teacher and pupil. For example, he argues that non-verbal cues which convey either enthusiastic support, or a helpful attitude to the pupil, or receptiveness towards the pupil's talk will tend to facilitate communication; conversely, non-verbal cues which convey inattentiveness to the pupil, or disapproval, or a lack of responsiveness will tend to inhibit communication. Galloway's argument is that too many teachers are unaware of their own non-verbal behaviour which may in a number of ways inhibit communication between them and their pupils, and that through greater awareness of non-verbal communication teacher–pupil relationships could be enhanced.

Even more significance has been ascribed to the communication between teacher and pupil in the concept of the self-fulfilling prophecy. A self-fulfilling prophecy is a false definition of a situation which evokes a new behaviour which makes the originally false conception come true. Rosenthal and Jacobson (1968) carried out an experiment in which children were given an intelligence test, and 20 per cent of them were randomly assigned to an experimental condition in which the teachers were told that they would show unusually good academic development. At the end of the year the children completed another intelligence test, and the results showed a significant improvement for the experimental group, thus suggesting that the teachers' expectations (which were initially false) had in fact brought about an improvement in the performance of the children in the experimental group. Rosenthal and Jacobson's experiment aroused tremendous controversy, but has in fact been replicated on a number of occasions (Rosenthal, 1976). Chaikin, Sigler and Derlega (1974) investigated the possibility that teacher expectations are communicated non-verbally. They arranged for American male and female students to tutor one of two 12-year-old boys, who were described as being either bright (IQ of 130) or dull (IQ of 85); in a control condition, the students were given no information about their pupils' intelligence. The boys were actually confederates of the experimenter, instructed to behave in the same way to all the students, but they were unaware of the experimental hypothesis. The boys were taught by the students in a brief interview, which was videotaped. The videotapes were then scored for bodily cues which might indicate liking or approval, and results showed that tutors expecting an intelligent child showed a number of significant differences in their behaviour when compared with those who were expecting a dull child or those who were not given any prior expectations. Specifically, tutors expecting an intelligent child leaned forward more, leaned backward less, looked their pupils in the eye more, nodded their heads more and smiled more. Results from a questionnaire also indicated that tutors expecting a bright child did perceive him as significantly more intelligent than tutors expecting a dull child.

Chaikin, Sigler and Derlega's results do support the hypothesis that bodily cues may play an important role in the communication of teacher expectations. Nevertheless, it has not been established whether verbal statements of teacher expectations may be of greater significance, nor whether bodily cues associated with positive expectations are accurately decoded by the children. In fact the arguments that teacher non-verbal communication is important both because it conveys information about teacher expectations and because it may either facilitate or inhibit teacher–pupil communication depends ultimately on the decoding skills of the children. Although developmental data show that children are quite capable of recognizing emotional expressions at a level significantly above chance by the ages of six or seven (Ekman and Friesen, 1971; Camras, 1980), the work of Bugental, Kaswan and Love (1970) and Bugental *et al.*

(1970) suggest that young children are at a relative disadvantage when decoding information from visible bodily cues, and attribute less importance to them (see Chapter 4, pp. 101–102).

Woolfolk and Woolfolk and their associates (Woolfolk and Woolfolk, 1974, 1975; Woolfolk, Garlinsky and Nicolich, 1977; Woolfolk, Woolfolk and Garlinsky, 1977; Woolfolk, 1978) have carried out a number of studies to compare the relative importance of speech content and non-verbal cues in the perception of teachers by pupils. All the studies are based on the same procedure which takes the form of a vocabulary lesson. The teacher displays eight vocabulary words in turn, spelling each word and using it in two example sentences. After presenting the vocabulary word, the teacher instructs the pupils to write as many 'interesting and original sentences' as possible in two minutes using the word. During this two-minute period the teacher walks around the room ostensibly examining the children's work. Immediately after each two-minute session, the teacher gives a two-sentence evaluation of the children's work; this evaluation is either favourable or unfavourable, and is accompanied by either positive non-verbal cues (pleasant voice tone, head nod and smiling face) or negative non-verbal cues (angry voice tone, horizontal movement of the head and frowning face).

Using this procedure, the effects of teacher communication on a number of dependent measures have been investigated. In two studies (Woolfolk and Woolfolk, 1974; Woolfolk, Woolfolk and Garlinsky, 1977), the relative effects of speech content and non-verbal cues on the pupils' perception of the teacher were examined. Woolfolk and Woolfolk (1974), in a study with American fourth-grade schoolchildren (approximately 9 years of age), found significant main effects associated both with speech content and non-verbal cues, in that the pupils rated a female teacher more positively and were more attracted to her when either her verbal or non-verbal communication was positive; however, speech content accounted for far more of the variance than non-verbal cues. Woolfolk, Woolfolk and Garlinsky (1977) repeated the study with teachers and children of both sexes (the children were aged between 11 and 12). They again found significant main effects associated both with speech content and non-verbal cues, but from significant interactions between non-verbal cues and the sex of the teacher, it appeared that it was only female teachers who evoked greater attraction and a more positive response from pupils when they used positive non-verbal cues. As before, speech content accounted for far more of the variance in the pupils' ratings than non-verbal cues.

In another two studies, the dependent measure was pupils' willingness to disclose information about themselves. In one study with a female teacher and fourth-grade schoolboys and schoolgirls (approximately 9 years of age), Woolfolk and Woolfolk (1975) found a significant interaction between sex of pupil and teacher communication, in that the boys were significantly less willing to disclose information about themselves (according to a questionnaire measure of self-disclosure) in the condition in which the teacher gave both negative verbal and negative non-verbal feedback. In another study, Woolfolk, Garlinsky and Nicolich (1977) used teachers and children of both sexes (the children were in the sixth grade, approximately 11 years of age). The results showed a significant main effect of speech content on the questionnaire measure of self-disclosure, in that the pupils were more willing to self-disclose after a positive than after a negative evaluation. There was no significant main effect of non-verbal cues on self-disclosure, although a significant interaction did show that the effect of non-verbal cues on willingness to disclose was mediated by the individual teacher and the sex of the pupil. Again, speech content accounted for far more of the variance than non-verbal cues.

Finally, Woolfolk (1978) has investigated the relative importance of speech content and non-verbal cues on the number of sentences pupils are willing to write in this vocabulary lesson. Male and female teachers were used with sixth-grade schoolboys and schoolgirls (approximately 11 years of age). Results showed a significant main effect for non-verbal cues, such that pupils receiving negative non-verbal feedback wrote significantly more sentences. In addition, there was a significant interaction between speech content and individual teachers; for three of the teachers, positive verbal statements were associated with better performance by the pupils; for the fourth (a female teacher), the reverse was true. No information is reported in this study on the relative proportions of variance accounted for by speech content and non-verbal cues.

Studies carried out using this vocabulary lesson procedure have thus provided little support for Galloway's contention that non-verbal communication is of considerable significance in education. Galloway (1974) has criticized this procedure on a number of grounds; he maintains that non-verbal cues and speech content are not adequately matched, and that the teacher's expressive behaviour, which may be of central importance for the pupil, is not always under direct voluntary control in the way in which it is manipulated in these experiments. Nevertheless, the problem still remains that Galloway has yet to provide any hard evidence in support of his claims. It may in fact be the case that non-verbal communication is important in some educational contexts and not in others. Friedman (1978) asked American high school pupils (aged between 12 and 18, the exact ages are not reported) to make judgements from photographs of a teacher's facial expressions paired with written sentences; for example, a pupil might see an angry face with the written sentence, 'Listen, as far as I'm concerned you're the best student I've ever had.' Pupils saw four facial expressions (happiness, sadness, anger, surprise) paired in all possible ways with four sentences which were positive or negative and dominant or submissive. When asked to state how positive they considered the teacher was being, facial expression had a greater effect on the pupils' judgements than speech content; when asked what course grade the teacher would probably give the imagined pupil this term, speech content had a greater effect on the pupils' judgements than facial expression. This study would suggest that generalizations about the importance of non-verbal communication in education may be misleading, and that teacher non-verbal communication may have an important influence on some kinds of pupil judgements but not on others.

3. Interviews

If bodily cues communicate information about emotion, speech, individual differences and interpersonal relationships, then clearly one would expect them to be important in interviews. A number of studies of interviews have been carried out with reference both to the way the behaviour of the interviewee affects the judgements and decisions of the interviewer, and to the way the interviewer may affect the interviewee through his own behaviour.

Wexley, Fugita and Malone (1975) examined the effects of bodily cues on judgements by American male and female students of a candidate's suitability for a loan. Three hypothetical applicants varying in suitability for a loan (high, average or low) were created by different responses to a loan application form, and these were judged as differing significantly in suitability by students on the basis of the application forms alone. Six videotapes were then made of a male American graduate student who role played the loan applicant and gave the three different sets of answers to the loan application form in either an enthusiastic or non-enthusiastic manner (by varying the amount of hand gesturing, smiling and gaze). Results showed significant main effects on the students' judgements of the candidate's suitability for the loan from both the responses to the questionnaire and from his degree of non-verbal enthusiasm; there was no significant interaction between these factors.

Imada and Hakel (1977) arranged for American female students to rate the performance of a female job 'applicant' in a simulated interview; the applicant had been trained to vary her behaviour according to Mehrabian's concept of immediacy (e.g. Mehrabian, 1972) while keeping to the same prearranged script. In the immediate condition, she used eye contact, smiling, an attentive posture, gestures, smaller interpersonal distance and a direct body orientation; in the non-immediate condition, she used no eye contact, no smiling, a slouched posture, greater interpersonal distance and an indirect body orientation. The student raters either played the role of an interviewer, or attended the interview as an observer, or watched the interview from a television monitor; they evaluated the applicant on nine rating scales, as well as on her suitability for the job. The results showed that, in the immediate condition, the applicant was judged significantly more favourably on all nine rating scales, and that 86 per cent of the subjects in that condition recommended the person for the job; in the non-immediate condition, only 19 per cent made a such a recommendation. There were no significant effects according to the conditions under which the observers made their judgements.

Keenan and Wedderburn (1975) investigated in what ways the behaviour of the interviewee is influenced by the behaviour of the interviewer. They were particularly interested to test the hypothesis that the approval or disapproval of the interviewer might lead to significant differences in the amount the interviewee was prepared to say in the interview. Again a simulated interview was devised, with British male and female students role playing the part of the interviewer; the interviewees were also British students (mainly male). Each interviewer used a standardized interview protocol, designed to be appropriate for selecting young graduate trainees for general management. In the approval condition, candidates' utterances were acknowledged with smiles, positive head nods and eye contact; in the disapproval condition, the interviewer used frowns, head shakes and avoided eye contact. Each interviewer took part in both the approval and disapproval conditions. Keenan and Wedderburn did not find any significant effects of approval or disapproval on interviewee talking time, although they did find that approving interviewers were rated as significantly more likable, more friendly, less nervous and as making the candidate feel more at ease. In a subsequent experiment, Keenan (1976) showed videotapes of these interviews to another group of British male and female students. The observers saw a split-screen recording of the interview with the interviewer's half of the screen occluded, so that bodily cues from the interviewer could not affect their judgements. Candidates were perceived as significantly more comfortable and at ease in the approval interview, and were also judged to have created a significantly better impression; at the same time, their perceived competence was not significantly affected.

All these studies of simulated interviews do suggest that bodily cues influence the way the interviewee is perceived, and that the behaviour of the interviewer in turn can influence the behaviour of the interviewee. Nevertheless, the use of students in simulated interviews does raise serious questions about the relevance of these findings to non-simulated interviews. One problem is that the judgements of students may differ in certain respects from the judgements of professionals who actually have to make job decisions after an interview. Some evidence to support this view comes from a study by McGovern, Jones and Morris (1979) who compared the judgements of American students with those of professional personnel representatives. Both groups of judges saw videotape of an interview in which either an actor or an actress role played the part of an interviewee using a standard script, but varying non-verbal cues according to two conditions. In the 'high' non-verbal condition, the interviewee gazed steadily at the camera, gestured, smiled, expressed appropriate affect and responded to interviewer questions fluently with no speech disturbances; in the 'low' non-verbal condition, the interviewee averted gaze, displayed little or no affect or body movement and spoke in a broken, non-fluent manner. Both groups of judges rated the interviewee in one of the conditions on a number of 7-point scales describing various personality characteristics, and on the interviewee's suitability for a job as a general management trainee. Both groups of judges were influenced by the manipulation of non-verbal cues, giving more favourable descriptions of the interviewee in the 'high' non-verbal condition. But students tended to be more 'lenient' in their judgements, giving more favourable ratings than the personnel representatives of the interviewee in the 'low' non-verbal condition; 30 per cent were still prepared to hire the interviewee in this condition, whereas none of the personnel representatives were prepared to do so. (In the 'high' non-verbal condition, 87 per cent of the students would have hired the interviewee, and 89 per cent of the personnel representatives would have done so.)

A second problem arising from the use of simulated interviews is that the behaviours used in such simulations may not appropriately represent what normally happens in interviews. For example, in the study by Imada and Hakel (1977), a female job 'applicant' who used no eye contact, no smiling, a slouched posture, greater interpersonal distance and an indirect body orientation was considered by most judges as unsuitable for the job. Nevertheless, the question must arise as to how many actual job applicants do behave in this way; if the role-played behaviour is atypical of job interviews, then the study may overestimate the significance of bodily cues in interview judgements.

One study which did attempt to assess the role of bodily cues in non-simulated interviews was carried out by Forbes and Jackson (1980). They took observations of British school-leavers who were being interviewed by a four-man panel for places on an engineering apprentice training scheme; a decision was made after each interview to either accept or reject the candidate, or to place him on a reserve list. Their observations did show a number of significant relationships between interview outcome and the bodily cues used by the interviewee. Interviewees made significantly greater use of eye contact in acceptance interviews, significantly greater use of gaze avoidance in rejection interviews and significantly greater use of eye wandering in rejection and reserve list interviews. Interviewees smiled significantly more in acceptance interviews, and showed a neutral face significantly more in rejection and reserve list interviews. Finally, interviewees showed significantly more head shaking and head nodding in acceptance interviews; there were no significant differences for forward trunk lean. Forbes and Jackson's work clearly shows that bodily cues are related to the outcome of interviews, but do not enable us to say whether those cues are a cause or effect of that outcome.

Hollandsworth *et al.* (1979) set out to investigate the relative importance of non-verbal cues and speech content in the judgements of on-campus recruiters in an American university. The recruiters were asked to evaluate the students after an interview on seven 4-point scales intended to assess eye contact, loudness of voice, body posture, speech fluency, appropriateness of speech content, personal appearance and composure. Recruiters were also asked to indicate their likelihood of hiring the candidate on a fourfold classification corresponding to 'not a chance', 'probably not', 'probably' and 'definitely'. A multivariate comparison of these four groups was made through a direct discriminant function analysis with the seven rated interview behaviours being used simul-taneously. The results showed that each of the seven behaviours differentiated significantly between the four groups, but that appropriateness of speech content was the single most important variable followed by speech fluency and composure. Eye contact, body posture, loudness of voice and personal appearance also contributed to the decisions in that order, but much less strongly than the first three variables.

Hollandsworth *et al.*'s study is the only one in which an attempt has been made to evaluate the relative importance of non-verbal cues and speech content in interviews, and clearly shows that speech content had a greater effect on the judgements of recruiters. At the same time, Hollandsworth *et al.* did find that these judgements were also significantly affected by non-verbal behaviour, a finding which is supported by the studies of both simulated and non-simulated interviews reviewed above. In the light of the available evidence, it seems likely that non-verbal behaviour does affect the outcome of interviews, but is nevertheless less important than the content of what the interviewee actually says.

4. Helping

A number of studies have been carried out to investigate whether the bodily cues employed when a person makes a request for assistance in some way significantly affect compliance with that request. In particular, studies have been focused on the interpersonal distance at which the request is made, and whether the person seeking assistance makes eye contact with the person from whom he is seeking assistance.

Ernest and Cooper (1974) investigated the effects of interpersonal distance on obtaining change to use a telephone. Their experimenters (male and female American graduate students) each stood in a telephone booth with telephone in hand and asked passers-by for change either when they were level with the telephone booth or about 4 feet past it. Ernest and Cooper found that significantly more passers-by complied with a request made when they were level with the booth. Baron and Bell (1976) investigated the effects of interpersonal distance on requests to help in a psychology experiment. American students (of both sexes) seated alone at tables in cafeterias were approached by an experimenter (a male or female student) at either a close distance (12 to 18 inches) or a far distance (36 to 48 inches), and were asked if they would like to participate in a psychology experiment. The found that the students offered significantly more time for the experiment when the experimenter made the request at the closer interpersonal distance. The students were also asked to fill in a questionnaire about the experiment, which showed both that they perceived the experimenter as too close in the near condition, and that at that distance they perceived him as significantly more in need of assistance; their judgement of his friendliness was not affected by the distance at which he approached. Subsequently Baron (1978) repeated the experiment, but in one condition (the high-need condition) the experimenter told the students that the project counted for half a grade on his course; in the other condition (low-need condition), the experimenter said the project was just for fun. A significant interaction between interpersonal distance and the need of the experimenter showed that more time was offered for the high-need condition at the close than at the far distance, whereas in the low-need condition the reverse was true, with more time being offered at the far distance. The results of the questionnaire showed that the manipulation of the experimenter's perceived need had been successful. Overall the results of these studies do support the notion that interpersonal distance affects compliance with a request for assistance, but suggest too that distance cannot be considered independently of the perceived need of the person seeking assistance.

A number of other studies of helping have been carried out to investigate the effects of gaze upon acquiescence to a request. Ernest and Cooper (1974) repeated their experiment discussed above on obtaining change to use a telephone, but in this instance they varied gaze rather than interpersonal distance. All the requests were made at a distance of 4 feet, but in one condition the experimenter maintained eye contact, whereas in the other condition after initial eye contact the experimenter focused his attention on the coins in his hand. Significantly more passers-by acceded to the request in the condition in which the experimenter maintained eye contact. Kleinke (1977) arranged for American female students to approach people of both sexes in a middle-class shopping mall and to ask, 'Excuse me. Could you lend me a dime?' The students varied both whether they gazed at the passer-by and whether they touched them, and the results showed that significantly more passers-by complied in both the touch and gaze conditions. Snyder, Grether and Keller (1974) investigated the effects of gaze on attempting to hitch a lift from passing cars. Their experimenters were either a single man, a single woman or a man and a woman who attempted to hitch rides at four different traffic locations in and around Palo Alto, California. The hitch-hikers either stared or did not stare at the drivers of passing cars; the results showed that staring significantly increased the chance of obtaining a lift, irrespective of the sex of the hitch-hiker, a finding which was replicated by Morgan et al. (1975). Shutland and Johnson (1978) arranged for a male confederate to stage a fall as he approached college-age people walking alone on a university campus, either gazing or not gazing at each passer-by as he fell. The confederate received significantly more offers of help in the condition in which he gazed at the passer-by as he fell.

The results of these studies certainly suggest that eye contact significantly increases the chances of a person complying with a request for assistance. Nevertheless, there are other studies which have failed to show such an effect, or which have shown complex interactions with other variables. For example, Kleinke (1977) arranged for dimes to be placed on the shelves of phone booths in an American airport. Men leaving the phone booths who had found the dime were approached by an experimenter (a female student) who asked if they had found the dime left in the telephone booth. The experimenters varied both whether they gazed at the subject and whether they touched them, but found that only touching significantly affected whether subjects returned the dime. Valentine and Ehrlichman (1979) arranged for a male or female confederate with arm in a sling to approach people standing alone at a bus stop in various areas of Staten Island, New York. The confederate stood directly facing the subject at a distance of approximately 7 feet, and with obvious difficulty tried to take some coins out of a trouser pocket, dropping some of them on the pavement. The confederate then either looked at the subject for five seconds after having dropped the change, or looked at the ground. When both confederate and subject were female, significantly more subjects helped the experimenter retrieve the coins in the gaze condition; when they were both male, the reverse result was obtained. Valentine and Ehrlichman hypothesize that for women gaze may be seen as more affiliative, thereby facilitating assistance, whereas for men gaze may be seen as more dominant, thereby hindering assistance.

However, in a different situation Kleinke and Singer (1979) found that gaze only affected compliance to a request by men. Kleinke and Singer arranged for male and female experimenters to offer leaflets to passers-by in the Harvard Square area of Cambridge, Massachusetts; the experimenters varied both whether they gazed at the subject and the way in which they made the request. The request to take a leaflet was made either in a conciliatory tone ('Excuse me. Would you like one?') or a demanding one ('Take one!') or simply without saying anything. The results showed that passers-by did take more leaflets when gazed at by the experimenters, but from a significant interaction with the sex of the experimenter this effect appeared to be confined to male experimenters. However, since Kleinke and Singer also found that passers-by took more leaflets from females (80.2 per cent) than from males (71.2 per cent), this may simply reflect a ceiling effect influencing the results of the female experimenters.

In that same experiment, Kleinke and Singer also found that gaze interacted significantly with the way in which the request to take a leaflet was made, such that compliance was only affected by gaze when the experimenter offered the leaflet in a conciliatory fashion or offered it without saying anything. Subsequently Kleinke (1980) has investigated whether the effects of gaze on compliance interact with the perceived legitimacy of a request. Specifically, Kleinke hypothesized that gaze would increase compliance with a request perceived as legitimate (asking someone for a dime for a telephone call), but would decrease compliance with a request perceived as illegitimate (asking someone for a dime to buy some gum). Experimenters (American female students) approached subjects on the basis of the first adult they could find either sitting or standing alone in an airport. Results did in fact show that gaze significantly increased compliance with the legitimate request, but significantly decreased compliance with the illegitimate request. Thus it appears that as with studies of interpersonal distance, gaze does affect compliance with a request for assistance, but that it is also dependent both upon the sex of the person making the request and upon the perceived legitimacy of the request.

5. Deception

Another situation in which bodily cues have been regarded as of particular importance is that of deception. For example, Darwin's (1872) view that facial expressions actually constitute part of the emotional response would suggest a number of reasons why such cues might be useful guides to deception. If a person is attempting to conceal the fact that he is experiencing a particular emotion, he might not succeed in suppressing all the expressive movements associated with that particular emotion. Again, if a person wishes to convey an emotion he is not experiencing, he may fail to reproduce the appropriate response by omitting certain important features or by mismanaging the timing. The hypothesis that emotional expressions are drive-reducing suggests a further reason why they may be important in deception; if people are motivated to express themselves through bodily cues to release tension, they may in certain circumstances find it difficult to prevent themselves from doing so, thus 'giving away' their true feelings.

These kinds of assumptions are clearly implicit in Ekman and Friesen's concept of 'non-verbal leakage'. Ekman and Friesen (1969b) argued that the sending capacity of a particular part of the body can be measured in terms of three indices—average transmission time, number of discriminable patterns which can be produced and visibility. According to these criteria, the face is the best sender, the legs/feet the worst. Facial muscle changes are rapid, they allow for a wide variety of expressions and they are usually clearly visible; the feet and legs move much less quickly, they are capable of only a limited number of movements and they are often screened from view by articles of furniture. Ekman and Friesen went on to hypothesize that because of the greater sending capacity of the face, people are more careful to control their facial expressions; hence attempts at deception may be more often 'leaked' through movements of the legs and feet. To test this hypothesis, they showed films (without sound) of two psychiatric patients to two groups of observers. One group viewed the face of the speaker, while the other group viewed the body from the neck downwards. The observers rated what they considered to be the feelings and attitudes of the two patients on a list of adjectives. For the first patient, who was attempting to conceal that she was upset, a good many negative adjectives were ascribed to both the facial and bodily messages. For the second patient, who was withholding information about feeling confused and anxious, the results provided more support for the hypothesis, in that the facial messages were rated as generally positive, while the bodily messages were rated as negative.

In a more carefully controlled study, Ekman and Friesen (1974b) asked American female nursing students to view two films, one intended to be pleasant, the other intended to be stressful (showing amputations and the treatment of severe burns). The nurses were interviewed individually by a female interviewer after seeing the films, and were asked to be honest in describing their reactions to the pleasant film, but to attempt to conceal any negative feelings they might have felt when describing their response to the stress films. The nurses were asked what expressions they thought they should control or what they should avoid doing in order to escape detection; significantly more of the nurses mentioned the face than the body, a finding which supports Ekman and Friesen's hypothesis that people are more concerned to manage the face during deception. Videotapes of the interviews were shown to American male and female students who were asked to guess which interview they had just seen. In one condition, the observers first of all saw a tape of the nurse which was identified as non-deceptive; in the other condition, the observers were not given any such prior information. Ekman and Friesen found that the observers were significantly more accurate in judging the interview from the body than from the face, but only in the condition where they were given prior viewing of the non-deceptive behaviour. Ekman and Friesen also found that observers trained on the Facial Action Coding System were able to detect deception at a level significantly above chance from seeing just the faces of the nurses during these interviews.

In a subsequent study using the same videotapes, Ekman, Friesen and Scherer (1976) found that when honest and deceptive responses were rated by observers, facial expressions rated alone were judged as significantly more positive when seen in the deceptive than in the honest condition, whereas for judgements of the body alone the reverse was true. Littlepage and Pineault (1979) arranged for two male American students to answer two questions twice, once truthfully and once untruthfully; videotapes were made of their answers showing either the face or the body alone. In this study, the observers (American male and female students) viewed the videotapes with sound, and they all saw an initial shot of the encoder truthfully stating his name; the results showed again that the observers were significantly more accurate at detecting deception from seeing the body alone. Thus both the studies of Ekman and Friesen (1974b) and Littlepage and Pineault (1979) have supported the non-verbal leakage hypothesis when observers have had prior exposure to truthful responses. But Feldman (1976) found results which directly contradict the leakage hypothesis. Feldman arranged for American female students to teach a brief lesson in which they were instructed always to give positive evaluations of the pupil (another female student). The pupil was in fact a confederate of the experimenter, and performed either very well or very badly according to prearranged instructions. Videotapes of the lessons were judged by another group of female students (without sound) either from the face or the body alone, and the results showed that the observers were only able to guess with a significant degree of accuracy from videotapes of the face when the teacher was lying (by giving false praise when the pupil had in fact performed badly).

Other research has been focused on attempting to identify the cues which may reveal that deception is taking place; such studies have in fact shown that cues to deception are available from both the face and the body. For example, Feldman, Devin-Sheehan and Allen (1978) arranged for American boys and girls each to act as tutors to another younger child, and instructed the tutors to praise the pupil regardless of whether the pupil's answers were correct or incorrect. The pupils were in fact confederates of the experimenter instructed to answer most items correctly in one condition and most items incorrectly in the other condition. When giving false praise, tutors smiled significantly less, and showed significantly more mouth displeasure. Burns and Kintz (1976) found that American male and female students gazed significantly more at a confederate of the experimenter when attempting to deceive, but only when conversing in opposite-sex pairs; this contrasts with the common belief that people avert their gaze when attempting to deceive. Janisse and Bradley (1980) found some evidence to suggest that pupil size is related to deception. They arranged for Canadian male students to choose a numbered card from a set of five, and an experimenter asked them which number it was, going in turn one to five. The pupils of the students dilated when the experimenter mentioned the number of the card which they had chosen, but this was irrespective of whether or not they were attempting to deceive him.

Other studies have shown that cues from the body are also associated with deception. Ekman, Friesen and Scherer (1976), in the study referred to above, found that during deceptive interviews the nurses displayed significantly fewer hand illustrators than during the non-deceptive interviews. Schneider and Kintz (1977) found that American male and female students showed either significantly more or significantly fewer movements of the legs and feet when lying to a confederate of the experimenter than when not attempting to deceive him. McClintock and Hunt (1975) arranged for American male and female students to be interviewed individually by a female interviewer who asked them a number of questions on a variety of topics and on controversial issues. In response to certain key questions each student was instructed by the experimenter through an earphone to lie to the interviewer. Results showed significant positive correlations between the deception questions and the amount of time spent in self-manipulations (movements of arms/hands or legs/feet in contact with another part of the body) and in postural shifts (major movements of the trunk).

However, it is still open to question to what extent it is appropriate to search for specific cues indicative of deception. One problem is that the relevant cues may vary as a function of the situation and what information the encoder is attempting to conceal. For example, if a person is attempting to conceal from the experimenter which of a set of numbered cards he has chosen, the cues may be different from those which convey that he is feeling sad when he is attempting to look happy. Another difficulty stems from individual differences in deception. Mehrabian (1972) administered a measure of test anxiety to American male and female students, and arranged for a confederate to induce the students to cheat in an experiment which was supposed to be investigating extra-sensory perception. When interviewed afterwards by the experimenter, low-anxious students exhibited more facial pleasantness in the deceptive than in the honest condition, whereas high-anxious students showed the reverse pattern, with greater facial pleasantness in the honest condition. Nevertheless, what does seem clear from the studies reviewed above is that deception can be detected from bodily cues alone, even if the cues themselves may vary according to particular situations and particular individuals. There is also some evidence consistent with the hypothesis that the body 'leaks' more information about deception than the face, but at the same time there is evidence inconsistent with this hypothesis. It has, however, yet to be established how important bodily cues are in relation to other sources of information about deception such as vocal cues and speech content, since the relevant studies comparing these different sources of information have yet to be carried out.

6. The Psychological Experiment

The effects of non-verbal communication in the psychological experiment itself have been systematically investigated in a series of studies by Rosenthal, based on an experimental design which is purported to be a study of person perception. Rosenthal and Fode (1961) presented 57 photographs to American male and female students who were asked to judge whether the people in the photographs had experienced success or failure. From the original photographs, a number were selected which had all been rated on average as neither successful nor unsuccessful. Copies of these photographs were then given to 10 students (mainly males) who were asked to work as experimenters and to present the photographs to other male and female students, who would be asked to judge whether the people in the photographs had experienced success or failure. Half the experimenters were led to believe that typically the people in the photographs were rated as having just experienced success, the other half were led to believe that people were rated as having just experienced failure. The results obtained by the two groups of experimenters were in fact significantly different from one another, with experimenters led to expect success ratings obtaining higher ratings of success than those led to expect failure ratings. Rosenthal (1976) reviewed 114 studies using this procedure of which 27 per cent showed significant expectancy effects with an estimated mean effect size of 0.51 standard deviation units.

The question naturally arises as to how the experimenter communicates his expectations to the subject. To test the hypothesis that this is done non-verbally, Rosenthal and Fode (1963) again used the person perception task, but varied the way in which the experimenter presented it to the subjects. In one condition the experimenter gave the subject the instructions in writing, so there was no other communication between them. In a second condition, the experimenter and subject were shielded by a visual screen, so that although they could talk, they could not see one another. Finally, there was a face-to-face condition in which they could both see and talk to one another. The results showed that where written instructions alone were employed, there was no significant difference in the results obtained by experimenters led to expect success ratings as distinct from those led to expect failure ratings. When experimenter and subject could talk but not see one another, there was a significant difference in the results obtained consistent with the experimenters' expectations. Finally, in the face-to-face condition there was also a significant difference in line with the experimenters' expectations, which was significantly greater than the condition in which experimenter and subject could talk but not see one another. Rosenthal and Fode took these results to show that both vocal and visible bodily cues are important in transmitting experimenter expectancies to the subject.

Zuckerman *et al.* (1978) investigated whether individual differences in sensitivity to non-verbal cues may affect experimenter bias. To test encoding ability, the experimenters (American male and female students) watched four videotaped scenes designed to arouse different degrees of pleasantness. They also talked about their reactions to the scenes, and were asked to pose appropriate emotions for each scene. Judges were then asked to guess which scene the encoders were observing from videotapes of their facial expressions, and the experimenters were divided into good and poor encoders on the basis of how accurately the scenes could be judged on the basis of their facial expressions. The subjects of the experiment (another group of American male and female students) were administered Rosenthal *et al.*'s (1979) PONS test, and were divided into good and poor decoders on the basis of their response to the test. Experimenters then administered Rosenthal's person perception task, and the results showed no overall significant effect of experimenter expectations, but there was a significant interaction whereby experimenters who were good encoders influenced subjects who were good decoders in the direction of the experimenters' expectations. Hence it appears from Rosenthal's work that experimenters may bias the outcomes of psychological experiments by transmitting their expectations through non-verbal cues, but Zuckerman *et al.*'s findings suggest that this will only be a source of bias when the experimenter is a good encoder and the subjects are good decoders of non-verbal cues.

MEDIUM OF COMMUNICATION

The significance of bodily cues has been discussed within the context of particular interpersonal relationships and particular situations, but it is also the case that their significance is affected by the medium through which people communicate. With the development of non-verbal communication research, interest arose in the ways in which social interaction is affected by telecommunication systems such as the telephone. It was assumed that if non-verbal communication is as important as has been believed, then communication systems such as the telephone, where visual communication is presumed not to be possible, may affect communication in a number of significant ways. This assumption can be shown to be naïve, not least because people may accommodate their behaviour to the demands of a particular communication medium; so, for example, Wilson and Williams (1977) carried out an analysis of telephone and face-to-face conversations from the White House tapes involved in the Watergate scandal, and found that disagreements occurred significantly more frequently in the telephone conversations, arguing that in this respect the content of speech takes over from the non-verbal communication of disagreement. The assumption can also be shown to be naïve, in that Tartter (1980), in an experiment discussed in Chapter 2 (pp. 54–55), has shown that people are able to judge from the sound of a person's voice whether or not that person is smiling, so that strictly speaking it is not true to say that people are unable to obtain visual information from auditory communication alone; nevertheless, one can safely assume that aspects of facial expression which do not affect the vocal tract—and all other aspects of visible communication—are inaccessible to people communicating over the telephone. With these reservations in mind, the significance of bodily cues will be discussed with reference to the particular medium of communication through which interaction takes place.

Short, Williams and Christie (1976), in a major review of telecommunications research, have argued that there are three main areas where the effects of telecommunications have been demonstrated: attitude change, interpersonal relationships and bargaining. They review a number of studies concerned with attitude change, in which subjects complete an attitude questionnaire, discuss topics on which they disagree either face to face or over an audio or video system and them complete the questionnaire again; the results typically show there is more attitude change over the audio system. These findings seem extremely surprising in that one might expect bodily communication to affect attitude change, and hence that there would be more attitude change where visual communication is possible. Short, Williams and Christie mention one study in which Short investigated how the perception of the other person on a number of rating scales is affected by the medium of communication. The ratings were factor analysed, and of the five factors which emerged, a factor of 'trust' showed that people trusted their partners significantly more when discussing issues over audio than face to face.

This finding is particularly interesting in the light of a study by Andreoli and Worchel (1978), which was specifically intended to investigate the effects of communication medium and the perceived trustworthiness of the communicator. The particular issue in question was whether liquor by the drink should be legalized in a state in the USA (North Carolina); the effect of legalizing the sale of alcohol by the glass would be to make alcohol both more cheaply and more readily available. American students were exposed to persuasive communications either in favour or against this proposal; they received the communication either on videotape, or audiotape, or from a transcript. The communicator was introduced as either a political candidate, or as a member of the House of Representatives, or as a former member of the House, or as a newscaster; in fact the communicator was the same person in all cases, a 30-year-old male graduate student who played all the roles. The results showed significant main effects for communication medium and for the source of information, as well as a significant interaction. For the former representative and for the newscaster, video presentation resulted in greater attitude change, whereas the political candidate achieved significantly more attitude change on audio and through a written presentation. The retired representative and the newscaster were also perceived as significantly more trustworthy than the current member of the House of Representatives, while the political candidate was perceived as significantly less trustworthy than the current member of the House of Representatives. Andreoli and Worchel's results clearly suggest that the effects of communication medium on attitude change interact with the perceived trustworthiness of the communicator, such that a trusted communicator achieves greater attitude change using visual communication, whereas a distrusted communicator achieves less attitude change using visual communication. Thus, their findings suggest that it is not possible to make generalizations about the effects of communication medium on attitude change in the absence of information on the perceived trustworthiness of the communicator.

Studies of interpersonal relationships reviewed by Short, Williams and Christie (1976) suggest both that people's confidence in their judgements about others is affected by the medium of communication, and that group cohesion may also be affected. For example, they cite a study by Weston and Kristen (1973), who had groups of six students discuss their courses either face to face or over video or audio. The effects of communication medium showed on a number of scales intended to measure uncertainty, for example, to statements such as, 'I had quite a bit of trouble knowing how the people at the other end were reacting to the things I said.' In all cases, the video came out more favourably than the audio. Williams (1975) arranged for four-person groups (British middle-grade executives and administrators from the Civil Service and nationalized industries) to communicate either face to face, or over video or audio; for the telecommunications groups there were two subjects at each of the communication points. Each group had a 30-minute discussion to produce ideas for ameliorating the 'problems of travelling in Britain'. All ideas had to have proposers and seconders; dissenters from the ideas could also have their names noted, although they were encouraged not to argue. Results showed that ideas were generated significantly more often from the same end of the communication link or from the same side of the table (in the face-to-face condition), and that dissent came significantly more frequently from the opposite end of the audio link.

The most substantial body of research on the effects of telecommunications has been concerned with bargaining. One experiment was carried out by Short (1974), in which he set up a two-person bargaining game in which each pair of subjects (British civil servants drawn from government managerial training courses) were given a brief background to the game indicating that cuts were required in a hypothetical government corporation. Nine areas of potential cuts were listed (e.g. capital investment in new plant, recreational facilities for employees), and the joint task of both participants was to agree on a list of three. The civil servants privately ranked the options they favoured in order of preference, but whereas one person in each pair was instructed to argue in favour of his own personal preferences, the other person was instructed to argue for three options based on the first person's lowest three priorities, which of course bore no necessary relationship to his own opinions. The negotiations were conducted either face to face or over an audio link, and Short hypothesized that the party arguing for his own personal preferences would be more successful when negotiating face to face, since interpersonal considerations would be more salient; a significant interaction between communication medium and strength of conviction confirmed this hypothesis.

A whole series of studies on the effects of communication medium on bargaining have been carried out by Morley and Stephenson (1977). They argued that there are two main elements in bargaining, namely, that the negotiators must represent the demands of their own parties, but must also maintain some kind of personal relationship with their opposite number; the outcome will be influenced by the balance between these two processes. They also argue that communication systems can be seen as varying according to the number of social cues which one person can transmit to another. They refer to this dimension as one of the formality/informality, such that by definition the smaller the number of cues available, the more formal the system. Finally, they argued that the more formal the communication channel, the less important will be personal considerations, and the more important the considerations of the party they represent. Hence, they hypothesized that in bargaining, settlements in favour of the side with the stronger case will be positively associated with formality in the system of communication employed, since personal considerations will be less salient, the issues more so. It should be noted that whereas in Short's study the term 'strength' was used to refer to an individual's strength of convictions, in these studies this term is being used to refer to the relative merits of the case being argued; in Short's study one would expect strength of conviction to be associated with a better outcome face to face, whereas in Morley and Stephenson's studies one would expect strength of case to be associated with a better outcome over audio.

The first two studies carried out by Morley and Stephenson involved simulations of industrial negotiations; the participants were British male students. Pairs of students were given 15 minutes independently to read the background information to an industrial dispute, involving the introduction of a new wage agreement in a co-ownership plant. The students were randomly assigned to management or union sides, and the negotiations were conducted either face to face or over the telephone. Some specimen arguments for each side were provided, giving an initially stronger case to either the management or the union representative. Strength of case was varied in terms both of the quality and quantity of arguments used, and the students' perceptions of the case were always in line with the experimental induction. The outcome was assessed blind by the experimenters on a 7-point scale, which took into account the various sorts of outcome possible according to prearranged criteria. Besides testing the hypothesis that the side with the stronger case would do better over the telephone, a hypothesis was also tested that the side with the stronger case would do better under 'constrained' conditions, where constraint meant that no interruptions were allowed; this was a deliberate experimental manipulation of another aspect of formality. The results from both these studies confirmed both these hypotheses, and in addition showed that the side with the stronger case was most successful in the most formal condition (i.e. audio and constrained) and least successful in the least formal condition (i.e. face to face and unconstrained); the effects of communication medium were greater than those of constraint. Morley and Stephenson discuss a further four studies in which they investigated the effects of communication medium on outcome. Taking the six studies together, they found that in every case the side given the stronger case achieved a better outcome over audio; in four of these experiments the effect was statistically significant.

The results of Morley and Stephenson's studies clearly support their predictions concerning the effects of communication medium on bargaining outcome. The process which they hypothesize leads to this outcome is one where conversation during bargaining is more task-oriented and less personal over the telephone. Stephenson, Ayling and Rutter (1976) tested this hypothesis in another study of bargaining in which British male and female students met in same-sex pairs. Their conversations were coded using a technique called Conference Process Analysis; this allows communication to be scored according to how information is exchanged (mode), what source of information is being exchanged (resource) and who is being talked about (referent). Using this scoring system, Stephenson, Ayling and Rutter found that audio conversations were more depersonalized, in that there was significantly less praise for one's opponent and more references to 'party' than persons, and that the audio conversations were also more task-oriented, in that there were significantly more offers of information in this condition. In another study, Rutter and Stephenson (1977) looked at the effects of communication medium on speech style. In this study, British male and female students were given a questionnaire to complete, and were asked to discuss two items on which they had disagreed over audio and face to face in same-sex pairs. The results showed that duration and frequency of simultaneous speech were significantly greater in the face-to-face condition, and that the length of utterances were significantly longer over the audio link. Rutter and Stephenson argue that utterances are longer in the audio condition because of fewer interruptions. They also argue that interruptions can occur more easily face to face because signals can be communicated visually to maintain the conversation and prevent a breakdown of communication. Hence it can be argued that by reducing the number of interruptions, the social cues available to participants are reduced because of the reduced opportunities for feedback, and hence again that communication becomes more formal over an audio link.

All these studies support the argument that conversations over audio are more impersonal and more task-oriented, with a corresponding effect on outcome. Nevertheless, all the studies cited up to now have simply involved comparisons of face-to-face and audio conversations; hence visual communication is confounded with a second variable, namely that of physical presence, since in face-to-face conversations people are in the same room, whereas in audio conversations they are both visually and physically separated. Hence Rutter, Stephenson and Dewey (1981) introduced two new conditions, one using video so that a degree of visual communication was maintained although people were in different rooms, the other using a curtain drawn between the two conversationalists, so that although they were in the same room, visual communication was effectively precluded. Subjects were solicited from an advertisement in a local British newspaper (in Nottingham) and were asked to discuss in same-sex pairs issues from a questionnaire in one of the four conditions of communication medium (face to face, audio, curtain, video). The results showed that as before there were a number of significant differences between the face-to-face and audio conditions. In the audio condition, subjects showed more concern with procedures, reflecting a greater task orientation; simultaneous speech was more frequent face to face; the proportion of utterances which ended in a question was greater in the audio condition, as were the proportion of floor changes which occurred immediately after a question, thus suggesting a rather more formal way of exchanging information; and the number of acknowledgement and attention signals was greater face to face. What was more interesting was that in almost every case the results for the curtain and video conditions fell somewhere between the face-to-face and audio conditions, suggesting that it is neither visual communication nor physical presence which alone are the crucial variables, but some kind of combination of the two. Rutter, Stephenson and Dewey argue that the four conditions can be placed on a continuum of social information available which they call 'cuelessness'. In face-to-face conversation, information from both visual and physical presence is available; the curtain and video conditions allow information from one of these sources; neither source of information is available from an audio link. Rutter, Stephenson and Dewey conclude that it is not visual communication which is the important variable, but this dimension of cuelessness, which leads to task-oriented, impersonal conversations with a more formal exchange of information resulting in the effects described above on bargaining outcome. This concept of cuelessness is of course equivalent to the older concept of formality used by Morley and Stephenson (1977) in their original studies of bargaining.

An alternative explanation of communication medium effects has been put forward by Short, Williams and Christie (1976) in terms of what they call 'social presence'. This concept of social presence can be seen to differ from the concept of cuelessness, in that whereas cuelessness can be seen to be an objective quality of the communication medium (i.e. the number of social cues transmitted), social presence is regarded as a subjective quality of the medium, the extent to which one person feels another person is 'there'. Social presence will of course inevitably be affected by the number of social cues which can be transmitted through a particular communication medium, but according to Short, Williams and Christie it is not to be seen as synonymous with the number of social cues; social presence is typically measured by ratings on a questionnaire. Rutter, Stephenson and Dewey (1981) criticize the concept of social presence on two main grounds. Firstly, since the ratings of social presence are typically made after the encounter has taken place, the ratings are almost certainly influenced by whatever effect the communication medium may have had on the encounter. Any attempt subsequently to use the concept to explain effects on content, style, outcome or any other aspect of the encounter will inevitably be circular. The second difficulty is that Short, Williams and Christie are unable to say how the subject arrives at his impression of the social presence of a particular communication medium; their own suggestion is of course that it is based on the number of social cues available, and hence that the concept of social presence is in fact underpinned by the dimension of cuelessness. Conversely, Rutter,

Stephenson and Dewey can be criticized for not stating in sufficient detail what are the social cues which distinguish between different communication media; for example, it needs to be stated more precisely in what sense communicating over an audio link can be said to be less 'cueless' than communicating from behind a curtain.

Nevertheless, if with this reservation one accepts the concept of cuelessness as an explanation of communication medium effects on bargaining, the question naturally arises to what extent other findings can be accounted for in terms of this concept. Of the findings reviewed by Short, Williams and Christie (1976), the fact that people are less confident in their judgements of others in more cueless communication media is entirely consistent with the concept. Similarly, it would appear that coalition formation is also facilitated when more social cues are available. The findings on attitude change are less easy to explain, in that the availability of social cues seems to exacerbate the effects of the perceived trustworthiness of the communicator: if he is perceived as trustworthy, his influence will be greater the more social cues are available; if he is perceived as untrustworthy, his influence will diminish the more social cues are available.

The question also arises whether there are any other situations besides those reviewed by Short, Williams and Christie which can be explained in terms of cuelessness. Rutter and Robinson (1981) have investigated the effects of communication medium on teaching, with particular reference to the effects of telephone teaching in the British Open University. The Open University has a number of study centres throughout the country where tutorials can be held, but it is not always possible for students to attend these centres, either because of the distances involved, or due to personal circumstances such as shift-work or disablement; hence the Open University decided to experiment with telephone tutorials. The tutor and student each use their own domestic telephones, which are linked together by the operator so that everyone on the link can hear and speak to everybody else. What Rutter and Robinson decided to do was to investigate the effects of telephone teaching on content, style and outcome, extrapolating from the earlier work on bargaining. They studied five tutorial groups, arranging for them to meet once face to face, and then to have two telephone tutorials followed by two face-to-face tutorials or vice versa. They then compared the two conditions on a number of measures of content, style and outcome. They predicted that telephone tutorials would be more depersonalized, but in fact found no significant differences in content; however, the task orientation of all the tutorials was very high, accounting for 95 per cent of the speech acts. But there were significant differences in the way this task orientation was achieved, with tutors making more explicit efforts to elicit contributions over the telephone by asking questions and by calling on particular students by name. They also predicted that style would be less spontaneous over the telephone, and found that interruptions were significantly more frequent face to face, that filled pauses ('mmms' and 'ers', taken to be measure of verbal planning) occurred significantly more frequently over the telephone, and that the proportion of student utterances which were replies to questions was significantly greater over the telephone; hence the prediction of greater formality in style was confirmed. Finally, they found significant differences in outcome; participants rated telephone tutorials as more business-like, structured and formal, most students thought the material was covered 'more efficiently' in telephone tutorials, but face-to-face tutorials were preferred! Hershey (1977) compared face-to-face instruction with telephone teaching on a course for American schoolteachers, and found that on a questionnaire intended to measure knowledge and understanding of a course called 'The Creative Classroom', those taught by telephone did in fact perform significantly better.

The preference for face-to-face communication found in the Rutter and Robinson (1981) study is not in fact confined to tutorial teaching; Furnham (Argyle, Furnham and Graham, 1981) carried out an experiment in which subjects from the Oxford University subject panel were given a list of 16 messages, and asked to state whether they would prefer to deliver them by letter, by telephone or face to face. Over 80 per cent of the face-to-face/telephone and face-to-face/letter comparisons showed significant differences in preference for face-to-face communication; there was only one exception to this trend, that of refusing an unreasonable request for help, which people preferred to do by telephone. It appears then that for the most part people prefer face-to-face communication, and a likely explanation for this seems to be the greater number of social cues available. This also seems a plausible explanation for why people are more confident in making judgements of others face to face, why greater visual and physical contact has effects on coalition formation and why people with a weaker case do less well when bargaining through a communication medium which restricts the number of social cues available. Clearly, communication medium is another aspect of context which has to be considered when discussing the significance of bodily communication.

SUMMARY

In this chapter it has been argued that the significance of bodily cues can only be ultimately ascertained within particular contexts. It has been proposed that context can be examined in at least three main ways, namely, the relationship between the participants, the goals for which they meet in a given situation and the medium through which they communicate. It has been shown that the relationship between people in terms of age, acquaintanceship and sex can be discerned on the basis of bodily cues alone, even by quite young children; hence in addition to communicating information about emotion, language and individual differences, bodily cues also communicate information about interpersonal relationships to observers of the relationship. The role which bodily cues play for the participants within a particular relationship was discussed in terms of broad dimensions such as affiliation and dominance: it was argued that bodily cues both communicate information about affiliation and dominance, and constitute part of the ways in which such relationships are established and maintained. Bodily cues were also discussed in the context of specific role relationships. Studies of mother–infant interaction suggest that non-verbal communication between mother and infant increasingly comes to resemble adult conversation in form, that is, with clusters of expressions being produced by each partner in turn. Studies of marital relationships show that poor marital relationships are indicated by non-verbal communication, and also that poor marital adjustment is associated with insensitivity to non-verbal communication.

The significance of bodily cues can also be examined within the context of particular situations; research has been carried out on six particular situations, namely, psychotherapy, education, interviews, helping, deception and psychological experiments. Research on psychotherapy shows that the perception of the therapist is strongly influenced by bodily cues, although what is still very much at issue is the more fundamental question of whether and in what ways therapeutic outcome is related to the therapist's skills in decoding and encoding bodily cues. Research on education suggests that although pupils' perceptions of teachers are affected by non-verbal cues, they are more affected by the actual verbal content of how the teacher evaluates them. Similarly, studies of interviews show that although interviewers are affected by bodily cues in their assessment of an interviewee, they are more affected by the content of what an interviewee actually says. Studies of helping suggest that compliance to a request is affected by gaze and proximity, but that these cues also interact with other factors such as the perceived legitimacy of the request, the sex of the person making the request and their perceived need. It appears that deception can be detected on the basis of bodily cues alone, but the relative importance of different bodily cues in 'leaking' information about deception has yet to be firmly established, as has their relative importance in comparison to vocal cues and speech content. Finally, it has been demonstrated that psychologists through non-verbal cues may unwittingly transmit their expectations concerning the results of psychological experiments, and hence systematically bias the results they obtain in the direction of their own hypotheses.

The significance of bodily cues was also discussed within the context of the medium through which communication takes place. For the most part, people prefer face-to-face communication to communicating by letter or telephone, and a likely explanation for this seems to be the greater number of social cues available. This also seems a plausible explanation for why people are more confident in making judgements of others face to face, why greater visual and physical contact has effects on coalition formation and why people with a weaker case do less well when bargaining through a communication medium which restricts the number of social cues available.

Chapter 6

Body Movement and Social Skills Training

In the previous chapters, it has been argued that bodily cues are systematically related to emotion, speech, individual differences and interpersonal relationships, and that they also need to be understood in the context of interpersonal relationships, situations and the medium of communication employed. In short, bodily cues are of considerable social significance, and the question naturally arises whether it is possible through learning about bodily cues for people to enhance their interpersonal relationships and improve their social effectiveness.

In a highly influential paper, Argyle and Kendon (1967) argued that social interaction can be seen as a kind of motor skill, involving the same kinds of processes as, for example, driving a car or playing a game of tennis. The advantage of this approach, Argyle and Kendon maintained, is that we know a great deal about motor skill processes, and consequently can apply ideas and concepts developed in the study of skills to the study of social interaction.

Argyle and Kendon list six processes which they claim are common to motor skills and social performance: distinctive goals, selective perception of cues, central translation processes, motor responses, feedback and corrective action, and the timing of responses. Social performance can be seen as having distinctive goals; for example, an interviewer has the main goal of obtaining information from the interviewee, and sub-goals, such as establishing rapport. Selective perception of cues refers to the process whereby individuals pay particular attention to certain types of information which are relevant to achieving their particular objectives. Central translation processes prescribe what to do about any particular piece of information; people learn behavioural strategies with which to respond to certain types of perceptual information. Motor responses refer to the actual social behaviours themselves which are implemented as a consequence of the central translation processes. Feedback and corrective action refers to the ways in which an individual may modify his behaviour in the light of feedback from others; Argyle and Kendon argue that non-verbal cues are a particularly important source of feedback. Finally, the timing of responses is of importance, for example, choosing the right moment to make a point in a group discussion.

One major implication of the social skills model of social interaction, as it has become known, is that if social behaviour is seen as a skill, than it is possible for people to increase their social effectiveness through appropriate training procedures. Argyle has in fact argued that certain psychiatric difficulties can be seen as a consequence of lack of social skill leading to rejection and social isolation, resulting in turn in disturbed mental states, which can be alleviated through the use of appropriate social skills training. It is also argued that such procedures can be employed in non-psychiatric settings, for example, in the training of teachers or interviewers, since the procedure is regarded as a form of training in which new skills are taught, rather than as a therapy in which a 'cure' is provided for an illness.

An extensive literature has in fact developed on social skills training. No attempt is made here to provide a comprehensive review of this literature; nevertheless, a few studies are discussed below to illustrate the kinds of procedures which have been used. For example, Collett (1971) carried out a study of social skills training with people from different cultures. Collett arranged for a group of Englishmen to be instructed in Arab non-verbal behaviours to see whether this would improve their communication with Arabs. Specifically, the Englishmen were taught to shake hands on meeting, parting and just before parting; to allow the Arab through the door, first touching him on the shoulder as he passed through; to sit close enough to touch his chest with arm outstretched; to look and smile as much as possible; and in no circumstances to point to the soles of the feet of the Arab, since this is understood to indicate, 'You are worth as much as the dirt on the soles of my feet.' Conversations were arranged in pairs between Arabs and English male students, with each Arab conversing with one Englishman who had been trained and with one who had not been trained in Arab non-verbal behaviour. The students then filled in a questionnaire after the conversation, which showed that the Arabs had a significant preference for sharing a flat, being friends and trusting the Englishmen who had been trained in Arab non-verbal behaviour.

Most studies of social skills training, however, have been carried out in a psychiatric context. For example, Bryant et al. (1976) have provided detailed evidence of what is meant by a lack of social skill in a psychiatric setting. The study was concentrated on a group of out-patients who had been diagnosed as suffering from neuroses or personality disorders. A group of patients considered to be socially adequate were compared with a group judged to be lacking in social skill (as considered by agreement between two psychologists and two psychiatrists). Each patient took part in an eight-minute structured social situation test, involving conversation with a stranger; their behaviour was rated by two psychologists on 24 categories of behaviour. Most of the categories showed significant differences between the two groups, primarily in that the socially unskilled group tended to show 'too little' of most forms of behaviour. Hence they tended to show little variation in facial expression, adopted closed and inflexible postures and looked at their partner very little. They also tended to speak too softly, too indistinctly and too slowly, and in

168

a flat, monotonous tone of voice. Their speech tended to lack continuity and was punctuated with too many silences, while they failed to hand over or take up the conversation, leaving the other person to make all the conversational moves. They tended to choose stereotyped and dull topics of conversation, showing little interest in the other person. The only behaviour in which they exceeded the socially skilled group was in talking about themselves. As well as coding behaviour on 24 categories, the psychologists also rated the patients on a number of broad descriptive terms. In general, the socially unskilled group were rated as significantly more cold, non-assertive, socially anxious, sad, unrewarding and uncontrolling.

A detailed account of the procedures involved in social skills training is given by Trower, Bryant and Argyle (1978). Initially, a list is drawn up of the particular social difficulties experienced in particular social situations, and appropriate techniques identified for dealing with these situations. Then the specific skills themselves are taught through demonstrations, use of role play and feedback from a videotape-recorder. Trower, Bryant and Argyle give specific details of what they do in social skills training, and this can be subdivided into a number of different skills: skills in observation, listening, speaking, meshing and finally what they call non-verbal deficits. Observational skills involve, for example, recognizing emotions from non-verbal cues. People are trained both to recognize emotions from pictures of others, and asked to role play emotions themselves; videotape feedback gives them some idea of how well they succeed in this. An example of listening skills involves the use of appropriate listener responses such as head nods to indicate continued interest and attention in the other's conversation. Changing the topic of conversation can be seen as an example of a speaking skill; some people often change the topic of a conversation without warning in a highly disconcerting fashion. Trower, Bryant and Argyle suggest giving warning through some kind of non-verbal preparatory movement, or through phrases such as 'incidentally' or 'by the way'. Meshing skills refer to the way in which the participants regulate the conversation through, for example, turn-taking; Trower, Bryant and Argyle argue that participants can facilitate the flow of conversation through appropriate turn-taking and turn-yielding signals. Finally, training procedures are used to remedy what are called non-verbal deficits, characteristic mannerisms which are pointed out through videotape feedback; this stage is left to the end of the training procedure, since the experience of becoming aware of these deficits can be extremely demoralizing Ekman and Friesen (1975) list a number of facial styles which can be seen as examples of non-verbal deficits, for example, 'ever-ready expressors', who invariably show one emotional expression as a characteristic response to any event, or 'substitute expressors', who substitute one expression of emotion for another without being aware of it (e.g. looking surprised when they feel angry).

A number of studies have been carried out to investigate the value of social skills training. For example, Argyle, Bryant and Trower (1974) arranged for patients to be randomly allocated either to social skills training or to psychotherapy. The two groups were further subdivided into two groups each, where in one case there was a six-week delay followed by therapy, in the other case there was six weeks of therapy followed by six weeks of no treatment. Assessment took place at the outset of the study, and at the end of each six-week period. Self-ratings from both the social skills training and psychotherapy groups did show a significant decrease in reported feelings of social difficulty at the end of a treatment period when compared with a no-treatment period; however, there was no significant difference in effectiveness between the two forms of therapy.

In another study, Trower *et al.* (1978) compared the effects of social skills training with systematic desensitization. They compared 20 patients judged as socially unskilled with 20 patients diagnosed as social phobic; patients in each diagnostic group were randomly allocated to one or other treatment, so there were 10 in each group. Trower *et al.* hypothesized that the socially unskilled group would respond better to social skills training than to systematic desensitization, because here the social skills failure is seen to be the primary cause of their problem. Results from a self-report questionnaire did in fact show that the social skills training group reported significantly less social difficulty than the desensitization group after therapy. In the case of the social phobic group, it was hypothesized that lack of social skills would be simply a side-effect of the social phobia, so that systematic desensitization, which is supposed to treat the anxiety directly, should be a more effective form of treatment. There was in fact no evidence to support this hypothesis, although both groups did show significant improvement. Thus, although this study provided further evidence for the effectiveness of social skills training, the failure to confirm the predictions with the social phobic group does suggest that social skills training may work for rather different reasons than those postulated in the model of social interaction on which it is based. Specifically, Trower *et al.* argue that social skills training may have a dual therapeutic role, both through the training of explicit behaviours and through the reduction of general anxiety. Another study in which systematic desensitisation and social skills training were compared would appear to support this view. Hall and Goldberg (1977) arranged for patients suffering from social anxieties to be given either social skills training or systematic desensitization. Both groups showed a significant reduction in self-reported anxiety after treatment, thus supporting the view that social skills training does alleviate anxiety. The social skills training group also showed significant improvements with their particular social behaviour difficulties, while the systematic desensitization group showed a significant improvement in self-reported frequency of social participation.

Thus a number of studies do suggest that social skills training can alleviate both specific social problem behaviours and general social anxiety. Nevertheless, the failure in the Hall and Goldberg study to find improvements in social participation does raise some doubts about the generality of the effects of social skills training, in that while it may help people to deal with very specific problems, it does not necessarily increase their overall level of social competence. A more fundamental problem is the extent to which the social skills model adequately describes what is taking place in social skills training. It could be the case that although social skills training is effective, it is not necessarily effective for the reasons postulated in the theoretical model. In the case of social skills training with psychiatric groups, it could be that patients are reassured by the theoretical rationale and that this reassurance alleviates their social anxiety, the actual training procedures being largely irrelevant. It could also be the case that other features of social interaction not encompassed by the theoretical model, such as the relationship between the patient and the therapist, are responsible for improvements reported after social skills training. To attempt to answer such questions, the procedure needs to be evaluated not so much in terms of its overall social effectiveness but with respect to the particular processes which take place in social skills training, from both a conceptual and an empirical viewpoint. The empirical question is how effectively can social behaviours be taught: whether such behaviours are learned most effectively through video feedback, role play, practice or some other kind of procedure. The conceptual question arises as to what kinds of social behaviours can be taught as a skill, indeed, whether it is legitimate to regard such behaviours as a form of skill which can be learned and improved with practice. Since the focus of this review is on the encoding and decoding of body movement, the discussion of these conceptual and empirical questions will be addressed to the issue of whether the encoding and decoding of body movement can be taught as a skill.

The procedures employed in social skills training are derived from those which are believed to be important in perceptual and motor skills learning, summarized by Trower, Bryant and Argyle (1978) as practice, feedback, demonstration and guidance. Practice is necessary to the acquisition of skills, but is insufficient in itself. For practice to be effective, people need to have information about the consequences of their actions. For example, in throwing a ball at a target, increased accuracy will only improve if the individual knows the results of each attempt. Hence feedback is another important feature of skills acquisition, which can be either intrinsic, residing in the task itself (e.g. awareness of the muscular movements involved in throwing a ball) or extrinsic, supplied by factors external to the task (e.g. someone who tells the person how close each throw is to the target). Demonstration, Trower, Bryant and Argyle maintain, has three significant functions in skills acquisition: drawing attention to and magnifying important components of the task, setting a standard for future attempts and serving as a basis for imitation. Finally, guidance is important, especially in order to minimize errors in the initial stages of learning. Guidance may be important in order to learn a particular skill in an appropriate sequence, or in order not to acquire inappropriate habits at an early stage of learning.

Practice, feedback, demonstration and guidance are four variables which Trower, Bryant and Argyle argue have been shown to be important in perceptual and motor skills learning. The question naturally arises whether these same processes are important in the acquisition of social skills. There have been comparatively few studies of these processes in social skills training, but such studies as have been carried out do support the value of these procedures. One study on the role of feedback was carried out by Maguire *et al.* (1978). They arranged for medical students to take part in a study to assess the value of giving students some feedback about their interviewing skills. The students were divided into four groups, all of whom received the standard training from their clinical firms. In addition, three of the groups received different forms of feedback comprising either ratings of their performance, an audiotape replay of a practice interview or a videotape replay of a practice interview. All groups were rated on their performance in a subsequent practice interview, and all three feedback groups were rated as having improved in their ability to elicit accurate and relevant information. The audiotape and videotape groups were rated significantly more highly with regard to the techniques they used to elicit information, the videotape group being rated more highly than the audiotape group, but not significantly so.

Another study carried out by Edelstein and Eisler (1976) suggested that the combination of feedback, demonstration and guidance is more effective than demonstration alone. They were trying to improve the social skills of a man suffering from schizophrenia. The dependent measures were duration of eye contact, frequency of head and hand gestures, expression of affect and overall assertiveness. They found that modelling alone significantly increased the expression of affect, but did not influence the amount of gesturing or the duration of gaze. However, when modelling was combined with guidance and feedback, then significant increases were observed in the duration of gaze and frequency of gesturing.

Such data as are available do suggest that social behaviours (including bodily cues) can be modified through social skills training, and there is some suggestion that the effects of the different processes (practice, feedback, demonstration and guidance) are cumulative. Nevertheless, even if it can be empirically demonstrated that bodily cues can be changed through social skills training, recommendations on what behaviours to change depend very much on one's own conception of non-verbal behaviour, and hence should arise directly from a theoretical consideration of the significance of non-verbal behaviour. Hence, it is intended to consider the practical significance of research on body movement in the light both of the above discussion of social skills training and the theoretical position advanced in this book as a whole.

In the Chapter 1, the definition of communication of Wiener *et al.* (1972) was put forward that there must be both systematic encoding and decoding for a non-verbal behaviour to be regarded as communicative. It was argued that one important implication of this definition is that the social significance of bodily cues may not necessarily be communicative—there may be systematic encoding without decoding, and there may be decoding without systematic encoding. These distinctions also have important practical implications. If encoding takes place without decoding, then this would suggest that social skills training should be concentrated on decoding skills, making people aware of the information that is available from bodily cues of which they may not be making full use. If decoding takes place without encoding, then this would suggest an alternative prescription, that instruction should concentrate on teaching people not to arrive at inferences on the basis of bodily cues which are not in fact justified from our knowledge of encoding. Finally, if there is evidence for both encoding and decoding, then it may be that practical instruction needs to be focused on individual differences in decoding, in instructing people who for some reason fail to make adequate use of non-verbal communication. Hence, these different possibilities need to be discussed with reference to the different kinds of information which have been related to bodily cues.

In Chapter 2, evidence on emotion was discussed with particular reference to cross-cultural universals in the decoding of emotion. In the absence of satisfactory encoding studies it is not possible to make any definitive statements about the communicative significance of bodily cues associated with emotion, although if the evidence of cross-cultural universals in decoding is taken as evidence of universal encoding (regardless of whether the encoding of emotion is innate or learned), then there would be clear justification for regarding bodily cues as a means of non-verbally communicating emotion. But if the innate hypothesis of emotional expression is accepted as valid, then this clearly does have important practical implications, since if the expression themselves are innate, then in one sense there is no need to instruct people how to encode particular emotions. Nevertheless, if Ekman's neuro-cultural model of emotional expression is accepted, then this would suggest that instruction in encoding might need to be concentrated rather on learning appropriate display rules. This might, for example, be particularly important for communication between members of different cultures or classes, which may differ in how acceptable it is to express particular emotions; failure to learn appropriate norms governing emotional expression might result in considerable social difficulties.

In Chapter 3, research on bodily cues was discussed in relation to speech. Three main types of speech-related bodily cues were distinguished, namely, emblems, illustrators and regulators. Emblems refer to those non-verbal acts which have a direct verbal translation; their function is communicative and explicitly recognized as such. Within a given culture one would expect emblems to be common knowledge, but a lack of knowledge of the emblems of another culture could cause serious difficulties in inter-cultural communication, especially if the same physical movement has different meanings for different cultures. Illustrators are movements which are directly tied to speech, and there is some evidence to show that they facilitate the comprehension of discourse, although the precise way in which this is done is not yet clear. As yet, our knowledge of illustrators is too limited to permit specific practical recommendations on how their use may facilitate the impact of the spoken word, but increased knowledge should have quite significant practical applications, for example, in the instruction of public speakers or actors. Regulators are movements which guide and control the flow of conversation, and they have been studied with particular reference to turn-taking. Detailed instruction in the turn-taking system may be of value to those whose conversational skills in this respect are poor, since a failure to appreciate the significance of such cues may lead to conversations characterized by excessive interruptions, or by prolonged embarrassed silences.

In Chapter 4, studies of individual differences were reviewed. Personality does not show particularly strong relationships to either encoding or decoding, so that it has yet to be established either that there are particular personality traits associated with sensitivity to non-verbal cues, or that there are particular cues which reveal important information about personality. The latter finding with respect to encoding may be an important one, in that people often assume that a great deal can be learned about someone's personality from 'just looking at them'. The failure to find substantial relationships with encoding suggests that this assumption may be an example of a decoding error, and also suggests the practical recommendation that people be cautioned against making sweeping judgements of personality on the basis of bodily cues alone, in that such cues seem to be more closely linked to transitory emotional states than to enduring personality dispositions.

There are, however, clear sex differences in both the encoding and decoding of bodily cues. The systematic advantage for women found in decoding would suggest that it is men who are more in need of instruction with regard to the significance of bodily cues. There are also clear differences in the encoding of bodily cues, and it has been suggested that certain forms of body movement are sex-linked and can be seen as 'gender identification signals' (Birdwhistell, 1971). Rekers, Lovaas and Low (1974) state that deviant use of such signals in childhood has been reported to be predictive of later adult sexual abnormalities such as transvestism, transsexualism and some forms of homosexuality. They report a case study of an eight-year-old boy with pronounced feminine sex-typed behaviours who as a consequence experienced social isolation, ridicule and increasing unhappiness. The boy was treated according to a behavioural programme which included his mother administering a token economy intended to change the boy's effeminate body movement; tokens could be exchanged for certain candies and rewarding activities (e.g. TV time). The boy received credit tokens for participating in masculine play with his younger brother, and debit tokens for using feminine gestures. Follow-up data 12 months after treatment suggested that the boy's sex-typed behaviours had become relatively normal and that major improvements had occurred in his social relationships.

In this case study reported by Rekers, Lovaas and Low, changing the boy's effeminate body movement could be justified on the grounds of the social isolation and consequent unhappiness which it was clearly causing him. Nevertheless, the question arises whether it is in fact appropriate to institute such training procedures with other pathological groups. For example, in the case of the study by Edelstein and Eisler (1976) referred to earlier in this chapter (p. 171), the question arises whether it is actually desirable to increase the amount of gaze and gesturing shown by a person suffering from schizophrenia. Rutter (1978) (see pp. 89–90) has argued that people suffering from schizophrenia only avert their gaze when talking about personal matters which appear to embarrass them; teaching them to look at others is not necessarily going to make them feel less embarrassed, indeed it may have exactly the reverse effect. Trower, Bryant and Argyle (1978) make a distinction between pathological conditions where the social skills failure is the primary problem, and pathological conditions where disturbances in social behaviour can be seen as a kind of by-product of a deeper disturbance. So, for example, the kind of behaviours associated with depression (lack of eye contact, downward angling of the head, drooping mouth, lack of hand movement) can be seen as a way of communicating a desire to reduce social contact, which is not necessarily going to be alleviated by changing those particular behaviours. The distinction made by Trower, Bryant and Argyle would suggest that instruction in encoding for pathological groups would only be appropriate where the disturbance in social behaviour is the primary problem.

The consistent finding that psychiatric groups are inferior to normal groups in the decoding of non-verbal cues, and that they attribute less importance to such cues than normal groups would suggest that instruction in decoding may also be an appropriate form of therapy. But the picture is greatly complicated by the finding of LaRusso (1978) that paranoid schizophrenic patients were actually significantly better than a normal group in decoding spontaneous expressions. The possibility exists that the inferior performance of psychiatric groups on tests of posed expressions might represent an inability to take such posed expressions at face value, rather than a lack of decoding ability as such; the issue can only be satisfactorily resolved by devising tests of decoding which are not based on posed expressions. It is also possible that skill at decoding what a person intends to convey by a particular expression may not necessarily be the same as skill at identifying spontaneous or deceptive expressions, a possibility which is supported by Rosenthal and DePaulo's (1979) finding that the advantage of women in decoding non-verbal cues appears to be confined to those expressions which are more closely controlled by the sender (and hence are likely to be the intended expressions). In fact whether training in decoding skills enhances social effectiveness may depend very much on the situation: in some circumstances it may be helpful to take expressions at face value to avoid embarrassment, in other circumstances, for example, a police officer conducting an interrogation, this may be quite inappropriate, and skill at detecting deceptive expressions may be the required form of decoding abililty.

The significance of situations was in fact discussed in Chapter 5 along with medium of communication and interpersonal relationships as contextual factors which need to be considered in discussing the importance of bodily cues. Research on interpersonal relationships was discussed both in terms of broad dimensions, such as affiliation and dominance, and in terms of specific role relationships. It was argued that bodily cues both communicate information about affiliation and dominance, and constitute part of the ways in which such relationships are established and maintained. From the studies of Argyle *et al.* (1970) and Argyle, Alkema and Gilmour (1972) it certainly appears that decoders attribute a great deal of importance to non-verbal cues in making judgements about affiliation and dominance, so that it is important for encoders to be aware that if they are trying to communicate a friendly or an egalitarian attitude, decoders will pay more attention to the manner of their communication than to the actual speech content itself. With regard to specific role relationships, Noller (1980) has argued that insensitivity to non-verbal communication may be a cause of poor marital relationships. Her data show only a significant correlation between poor non-verbal communication and poor marital relationships, but clearly the point has important practical implications if it can be established that improving the partners' sensitivity to non-verbal communication can result in an improvement in the quality of their relationship.

The practical implications of the studies of communication medium and bargaining carried out by Morley and Stephenson (1977) would seem to be fairly clear: for the person with a stronger case, it is better to bargain over the telephone, whereas for the person with a weaker case, it is better to bargain face to face! More generally, the underlying notion of cuelessness would suggest that people should adopt a communication medium which permits a greater number of social cues when personal considerations are more salient, and a more restricted medium of communication when personal considerations are of less importance.

Research on six situations was discussed, namely, psychotherapy, education, interviews, helping, deception and psychological experiments. Research on psychotherapy suggests that bodily cues have a significant effect on the way the psychotherapist is perceived, and hence that therapists need to be aware of this channel of communication if, for example, they wish to communicate empathy, warmth and positive regard to their clients. Research on education and interviews has not substantiated the view that bodily cues are more important than speech content in the way either the interviewee or the teacher is perceived, but nevertheless does show that interviewers and pupils are affected by bodily cues in the judgements they make, and hence that teachers and interviewees should have some awareness of what they are encoding in these situations. Studies of helping suggest that compliance to a request is affected by gaze and proximity, but that these cues also interact with the perceived legitimacy of the request, such that if a request is perceived as legitimate, a person may be more likely to secure compliance by gazing or adopting a closer interpersonal distance, whereas if the request is perceived as illegitimate, these same factors may reduce the amount of compliance to the request. Studies of deception have shown that it is possible to identify deception on the basis of bodily cues alone, but it is questionable whether there are universal cues which will indicate that deception is taking place; cues to deception may vary between individuals and according to situational context, such that in the present state of knowledge, it is not possible to make practical recommendations about which cues may be used to identify deceptive communications. In dealing with experimenter bias in psychology experiments, Rosenthal (1976) has recommended at the very least the use of written instructions so that the experimenter does not unwittingly communicate his expectations to his subjects through non-verbal cues. The most stringent way of controlling for experimenter bias is the so-called 'double-blind procedure', where neither the experimental subject nor the person administering the experiment know to which experimental condition the subject has been assigned; this procedure has been used particularly in medical trials to evaluate the effectiveness of different drugs, where patients are given either a chemically active or a chemically inactive drug (placebo condition), in order to ensure that any improvement in the patient's condition is actually brought about by the drug, not by the patient's expectation of improvement.

The practical applications of research on bodily cues have thus been discussed in the context of the social skills model formulated by Argyle and Kendon (1967), and in the context of the theoretical structure outlined in this book, with particular regard to Wiener et al.'s (1972) distinction between encoding and decoding. On the basis of this discussion, it has been argued that the encoding and decoding of information through bodily cues can be changed through social skills training, and recommendations for appropriate training procedures have been proposed on the basis of the theoretical discussion of the social significance of body movement put forward in the preceding five chapters of this book.

Chapter 7

Conclusions

The main purpose of this review of the literature on body movement and interpersonal communication has been to consider the social significance of body movement in relation to the distinction drawn by Wiener *et al.* (1972) between encoding and decoding: to consider whether bodily cues encode information without appropriate decoding, or whether bodily cues are inappropriately decoded in the absence of systematic encoding, or whether bodily cues are both encoded and decoded appropriately. The main conclusions drawn from this review are summarized below.

With regard to emotion, it is not possible in the absence of satisfactory encoding studies to make any definitive statements about the communicative significance of bodily cues, but if the evidence of cross-cultural universals in decoding facial expressions of emotion is taken as evidence of universal encoding (regardless of whether the encoding of emotion is innate or learned), then we would clearly be justified in regarding facial cues as a means of non-verbally communicating emotion. If the hypothesis that the facial expressions of emotion are innate is accepted, then this gives those cues a special status in conveying information about emotion; not only are we justified in regarding such cues as a form of communication (since the innate hypothesis automatically implies systematic encoding), but this would suggest that such cues are a particularly important and reliable source of information about emotion.

Bodily cues are related to speech in terms of its syntactic, semantic and phonemic clause structure. Emblems refer to those non-verbal acts which have an explicit verbal meaning; their function is communicative and explicitly recognized as such. Illustrators are movements which are directly tied to speech; there is some evidence to show that they facilitate the comprehension of discourse, thus suggesting that they too function as a form of communication. However, the precise way in which this is done is not yet clear, since there has been little systmatic study of what is either encoded or decoded by illustrators. Regulators are movements which guide and control the flow of conversation, and it has been argued that bodily cues play a role in initiating and terminating interactions, and in turn-taking, thus again suggesting that they, too, function as a form of communication.

The hypothesis that bodily cues communicate significant information about individual differences cannot be said to be strongly supported by the evidence. Personality does not show particularly strong relationships to encoding, so that the belief that body movement communicates important information about personality may be an example of a decoding error. There are, however, systematic encoding differences between the sexes in the use of bodily cues, and it has been suggested that such cues can be regarded as 'gender identification signals', communicating information about a person's identification with a particular sex role. There are also encoding differences systematically related to psychopathology; it has been argued that depression and anxiety are communicated through bodily cues, since observers can ascertain self-reported degree of anxiety and identify depressed patients on the basis of bodily cues alone. Decoding studies of individual differences have shown that culture, age, sex, psychopathology and to a certain extent personality are all related to performance in decoding non-verbal cues; hence the extent to which non-verbal cues function as a communication system will vary substantially according to the decoding skills and cultural similarity of the communicators.

Interpersonal relationships, in terms of age, acquaintanceship and sex, can be discerned on the basis of one individual's visible behaviour even by quite young children; hence in addition to communicating information about emotion, speech and individual differences, bodily cues communicate information about interpersonal relationships to observers of the relationship. It was argued too that bodily cues communicate information about aspects of the relationship such as affiliation and dominance to participants within the relationship, and constitute part of the ways in which such relationships are established and maintained. Research was discussed on the significance of bodily cues in six situations, namely, psychotherapy, education, interviews, helping, deception and the psychological experiment. Research on medium of communication was also discussed. Comparisons of face-to-face and telephone communication have shown that people for the most part prefer face-to-face communication, are more confident in making judgements of others face to face and are more successful in arguing a weaker case face to face; a likely explanation for all these findings seems to be the greater number of social cues available. It was proposed that the precise social significance of bodily cues can only ultimately be ascertained within the specific context of the relationship between the participants, the medium through which they communicate and the situation in which they find themselves.

Finally, it was argued that the encoding and decoding of information through bodily cues can be changed through social skills training, and that recommendations on what behaviours to change should arise from a theoretical consideration of the social significance of body movement. The theoretical position advanced in this book has been based on Wiener et al.'s distinction between encoding and decoding. It has been argued that bodily cues communicate information about emotion, speech and interpersonal relationships; bodily cues also communicate information about individual differences (such as sex-role attitudes and psychopathology), but the failure to demonstrate substantial encoding relationships between body movement and personality suggests that the belief that body movement communicates important information about personality may well be an example of a decoding error. Individual differences in the decoding of non-verbal cues suggest that the extent to which non-verbal cues function as a communication system will vary substantially according to the decoding skills and cultural similarity of the communicators. Finally, it has been proposed that the significance of bodily cues can only ultimately be ascertained within the specific contexts of interpersonal relationships, situations and the medium of communication employed, and that the encoding and decoding of information through body movement can be taught through social skills training.

In the present state of knowledge, it is often difficult to make firm statements about the communicative significance of body movement. Researchers have tended to concentrate primarily on studies of decoding or encoding alone, so that what is still required is further research based on the joint implementation of both encoding and decoding designs. If the encoding/decoding distinction is accepted as of fundamental importance for understanding the social significance of body movement, then it is only through the systematic study of both encoding and decoding that the social significance of body movement can be fully appreciated; in this way a deeper understanding will be acquired of the precise role played by body movement in the wider context of interpersonal communication

References

Abramovitch, R. (1976) The relation of attention and proximity to rank in preschool children. In M. R. A. Chance and R. R. Larsen (eds.), *The Social Structure of Attention*, pp. 153–176. New York: Wiley.

Abramovitch, R. (1977) Children's recognition of situational aspects of facial expression. *Child Development*, **48**, 459–463.

Abramovitch, R. and Daly, E. M. (1979). Inferring attributes of a situation from the facial expressions of peers. *Child Development*, **50**, 586–589.

Aiello, J. R. (1972) A test of equilibrium theory: visual interaction in relation to orientation, distance and sex of interactants. *Psychonomic Science*, **27**, 335–336.

Aiello, J. R. (1977) Visual interaction at extended distances. *Personality and Social Psychology Bulletin*, **3**, 83–86.

Andreoli, V. and Worchel, S. (1978) Effects of media, communicator and message position on attitude change. *Public Opinion Quarterly*, **42**, 59–70.

Argyle, M. (1969) *Social Interaction*. Methuen.

Argyle, M. (1970) Eye contact and distance: a reply to Stephenson and Rutter. *British Journal of Psychology*, **61**, 395–396.

Argyle, M., Alkema, F. and Gilmour, R. (1972) The communication of friendly and hostile attitudes by verbal and non-verbal signals. *European Journal of Social Psychology*, **1**, 385–402.

Argyle, M., Bryant, B. and Trower, P. (1974) Social skills training and psychotherapy: a comparative study. *Psychological Medicine*, **4**, 435–443.

Argyle, M. and Cook, M. (1976) *Gaze and Mutual Gaze*. Cambridge: Cambridge University Press.

Argyle, M. and Dean, J. (1965) Eye contact, distance and affiliation. *Sociometry*, **28**, 289–304.

Argyle, M., Furnham, A. and Graham, J. A. (1981) *Social Situations*. Cambridge: Cambridge University Press.

Argyle, M. and Kendon, A. (1967) The experimental analysis of social performance. In L. Berkowitz (ed.), *Advances in Experimental Social Psychology*, Vol. 3, pp. 55–98. New York: Academic Press.

Argyle, M., Salter, V., Nicholson, H., Williams, M. and Burgess, P. (1970) The communication of inferior and superior attitudes by verbal and non-verbal signals. *British Journal of Social and Clinical Psychology*, **9**, 222–231.

Aronow, E., Reznikoff, M. and Tryon, W. W. (1975) The interpersonal distance of process and reactive schizophrenics. *Journal of Consulting and Clinical Psychology*, **43**, 94.

Baron, R. A. (1978) Invasions of personal space and helping: mediating effects of invader's apparent need. *Journal of Experimental Social Psychology*, **14**, 304–312.

Baron, R. A. and Bell, P. A. (1976) Physical distance and helping: Some unexpected benefits of "crowding" in on others. *Journal of Applied Social Psychology*, **6**, 95–104.

Baxter, J. C. (1970) Interpersonal spacing in natural settings. *Sociometry*, **33**, 444–456.

Beach, D. R. and Sokoloff, M. J. (1974) Spatially dominated non-verbal communication of children: a methodological study. *Perceptual and Motor Skills*, **38**, 1303–1310.

Beattie, G. W. (1978) Floor apportionment and gaze in conversational dyads. *British Journal of Social and Clinical Psychology*, **17**, 7–15.

Beattie, G. W. (1979) Contextual constraints on the floor-apportionment function of speaker-gaze in dyadic conversations. *British Journal of Social and Clinical Psychology*, **18**, 391–392.

Beattie, G. W. and Barnard, P. J. (1979) The temporal structure of natural telephone conversations (directory enquiry calls). *Linguistics*, **17**, 213–229.

Beck, S. J. and Ollendick, T. H. (1976) Personal space, sex of experimenter, and locus of control in normal and delinquent adolescents. *Psychological Reports*, **38**, 383–387.

Beier, E. G. and Sternberg, D. P. (1977) Marital communication: subtle cues between newlyweds. *Journal of Communication*, **27**, 92–97.

Bem, S. L. (1974) The measurement of psychological androgyny. *Journal of Consulting and Clinical Psychology*, **42**, 155–162.

Benjamin, G. R. and Creider, C. A. (1975) Social distinctions in non-verbal behaviour. *Semiotica*, **14**, 52–60.

Birch, H. G. and Belmont, L. (1965) Auditory–visual integration, intelligence, and reading ability in school children. *Perceptual and Motor Skills*, **20**, 295–305.

Birdwhistell, R. L. (1971) *Kinesics and Context*. London: Allen Lane, the Penguin Press.

Bleuler, E. (1950) *Dementia Praecox or the Group of Schizophrenias*. Trans. J. Tinkin. New York: International Universities Press.

Blurton Jones, N. G. (1971) Criteria for use in describing facial expressions in children. *Human Biology*, **41**, 365–413.

Bond, M. H. and Ho, H. Y. (1978) The effect of relative status and the sex composition of a dyad on cognitive responses and non-verbal behaviour of Japanese interviewees. *Psychologia*, **21**, 128–136.

Bond, M. H. and Shiraishi, D. (1974) The effect of body lean and status of an interviewer on the non-verbal behaviour of Japanese interviewees. *International Journal of Psychology*, **9**, 117–128.

Booraem, C. D., Flowers, J. V., Bodner, G. E. and Satterfield, D. A. (1977) Personal space variations as a function of criminal behaviour. *Psychological Reports*, **41**, 1115–1121.

Bowlby, J. (1958) The nature of the child's tie to his mother. *International Journal of Psychoanalysis*, **39**, 350–373.

Bowlby, J. (1969) *Attachment*. London: Hogarth Press.

Brunner, L. J. (1979) Smiles can be back channels. *Journal of Personality and Social Psychology*, **37**, 728–734.

Bryant, B., Trower, P. Yardley, K., Urbieta, H. and Letemendia, F. J. J. (1976) A survey of social inadequacy among psychiatric outpatients. *Psychological Medicine*, **6**, 101–112.

Buck, R. W. (1977) Non-verbal communication of affect in pre-school children: relationships with personality and skin conductance. *Journal of Personality and Social Psychology*, **35**, 225–236.

Buck, R. W., Savin, V. J., Miller, R. E. and Caul, W. F. (1972) Communication of affect through facial expressions in humans. *Journal of Personality and Social Psychology*, **23**, 362–371.

Bugental, D. E., Kaswan, J. W. and Love, L. R. (1970) Perception of contradictory meanings conveyed by verbal and non-verbal channels. *Journal of Personality and Social Psychology*, **16**, 647–655.

Bugental, D. E., Kaswan, J. W., Love, L. R. and Fox, M. N. (1970) Child versus adult perception of evaluative messages in verbal, vocal and visual channels. *Developmental Psychology*, **2**, 367–375.

Bugental, D. E., Love, L. R. and Gianetto, R. M. (1971) Perfidious feminine faces. *Journal of Personality and Social Psychology*, **17**, 314–318.

Bull, P. E. (1978a) The interpretation of posture through an alternative methodology to role play. *British Journal of Social and Clinical Psychology*, **17**, 1–6.

Bull, P. E. (1978b) The psychological significance of posture. Unpublished Ph.D. thesis, University of Exeter.

Bull, P. E. (1981) Body movement scoring system. In *The Social Functions of Speech-related Body Movement*, SSRC End-of-grant Report, HR 6404/2, pp. 1–16.

Bull, P. E. and Brown, R. (1977) The role of postural change in dyadic conversation. *British Journal of Social and Clinical Psychology*, **16**, 29–33.

Burns, J. A. and Kintz, B. L. (1976) Eye contact while lying during an interview. *Bulletin of the Psychonomic Society*, **7**, 87–89.

Campbell, A. and Rushton, J. P. (1978) Bodily communication and personality. *British Journal of Social and Clinical Psychology*, **17**, 31–36.

Camras, L. A. (1977) Facial expressions used by children in a conflict situation. *Child Development*, **48**, 1431–1435.

Camras, L. A. (1980) Children's understanding of facial expressions used during conflict encounters. *Child Development*, **51**, 879–885.

Cannon, W. B. (1927) The James–Lange theory of emotions: a critical examination and an alternative theory. *American Journal of Psychology*, **39**, 106–124.

Cappella, J. N. (1981) Mutual influence in expressive behaviour: adult–adult and infant–adult dyadic interaction. *Psychological Bulletin*, **89**, 101–132.

Caproni, V., Levine, D., O'Neal, E., McDonald, P. and Garwood, G. (1977) Seating position, instructor's eye-contact availablity, and student participation in a small seminar. *Journal of Social Psychology*, **103**, 315–316.

Carkhuff, R. R. and Berenson, B. G. (1967) *Beyond Counselling and Therapy*. New York: Holt, Rinehart & Winston.

Cary, M. S. (1978) The role of gaze in the initiation of conversation. *Social Psychology*, **41**, 269–271.

Chaikin, A. L., Sigler, E. and Derlega, V. J. (1974) Non-verbal mediators of teacher expectancy effects. *Journal of Personality and Social Psychology*, **30**, 144–149.

Chance, M. R. A. (1967) Attention structure as the basis of primate rank orders. *Man* (New Series), **2**, 503–518.

Chapman, A. J. (1975) Eye contact, physical proximity and laughter: a re-examination of the equilibrium model of social intimacy. *Social Behaviour and Personality*, **3**, 143–155.

Charlesworth, R. and Kreutzer, M. A. (1973) Facial expressions of infants and children. In P. Ekman (ed.), *Darwin and Facial Expression*, pp. 91–168. New York: Academic Press.

Charny, E. J. (1966) Psychosomatic manifestations of rapport in psychotherapy. *Psychosomatic Medicine*, **28**, 305–315.

Christie, R. and Geis, F. (1970) *Studies in Machiavellianism*. New York: Academic Press.

Clancy, H. and McBride, G. (1969) The autistic process and its treatment. *Journal of Child Psychology and Psychiatry*, **10**, 233–244.

Cohen, A. A. (1977) The communicative functions of hand illustrators. *Journal of Communication*, **27**, 54–63.

Cohen, A. A. and Harrison, R. P. (1973) Intentionality in the use of hand illustrators in face-to-face communication situations. *Journal of Personality and Social Psychology*, **28**, 276–279.

Cohen, J. (1977) *Statistical Power Analysis for the Behavioural Science* (rev. edn.). New York: Academic Press.

Collett, P. (1971) Training Englishmen in the non-verbal behaviour of Arabs. *International Journal of Psychology*, **6**, 209–215.

Condon, W. S. (1975) Multiple response to sound in dysfunctional children. *Journal of Autism and Childhood Schizophrenia*, **5**, 37–56.

Condon, W. S. and Ogston, W. D. (1966) Sound film analysis of normal and pathological behaviour patterns. *Journal of Nervous and Mental Disease*, **143**, 338–347.

Condon, W. S. and Ogston, W. D. (1971) Speech and body motion synchrony of the speaker-hearer. In D. L. Horton and J. J. Jenkins (eds.), *Perception of Language*, Columbus, Ohio: Charles E. Merrill.

Cook, M. and Smith, J. M. C. (1975) The role of gaze in impression formation. *British Journal of Social and Clinical Psychology*, **14**, 19–25.

Cronbach, L. J. and Meehl, P. E. (1955) Construct validity in psychological tests. *Psychological Bulletin*, **52**, 281–302.

Crowne, D. P. and Marlowe, D. (1964) *The Approval Motive*. New York: Wiley.

Curran, S. F. Blatchley, R. J. and Hanlon, T. E. (1978) The relationship between body-buffer zone and violence as assessed by subjective and objective techniques. *Criminal Justice and Behaviour*, **5**, 53–62.

Dabbs, J. M. (1969) Similarity of gestures and interpersonal influence. *Proceedings of the 77th Annual Convention of the American Psychological Association*, **4**, 337–338.

Darwin, C. (1872) *The Expression of the Emotions in Man and Animals*. London: Murray.

Dashiell, J. F. (1927) A new method of measuring reactions to facial expression of emotion. *Psychological Bulletin*, **24**, 174–175.

Dean, L. M., Willis, F. N. and Hewitt, J. (1975) Initial interaction distance among individuals equal and unequal in military rank. *Journal of Personality and Social Psychology*, **32**, 294–299.

DeBoer, M. (1974) Sex differences in infant smiling. In D. G. Freedman (1979) Human Sociobiology: A Holistic Approach, pp. 174–175. New York: Free Press.

Deutsch, F. (1947) Analysis of postural behaviour. *Psychoanalytic Quarterly*, **16**, 195–213.

Deutsch, F. (1949) Thus speaks the body—an analysis of postural behaviour. *Transactions of the New York Academy of Sciences*, Series II, **12**, 58–62.

Deutsch, F. (1952) Analytic posturology. *Psychoanalytic Quarterly*, **21**, 196–214.

Dittman, A. T. and Llewellyn, L. G. (1969) Body movement and speech rhythm in social conversation. *Journal of Personality and Social Psychology*, **11**, 98–106.

Dollard, J. and Miller, N. E. (1950) *Personality and Psychotherapy*. New York: McGraw-Hill.

Dougherty, F. E. Bartlett, E. S. and Izard, C. E. (1974) Responses of schizophrenics to expressions of the fundamental emotions. *Journal of Clinical Psychology*, **30**, 243–246.

Duke, M. P. and Fenhagen, E. (1975) Self-parental alienation and locus of control in delinquent girls. *Journal of Genetic Psychology*, **127**, 103–107.

Duke, M. P. and Nowicki, S. (1972) A new measure and social-learning model for interpersonal distance. *Journal of Experimental Research in Personality*, **6**, 119–132.

Duke, M. P. and Wilson, J. (1973) A note on the measurement of interpersonal distance in preschool children. *Journal of Genetic Psychology*, **123**, 361–362.

Duncan, S. (1969) Non-verbal communication. *Psychological Bulletin*, **72**, 118–137.

Duncan, S. (1972) Some signals and rules for taking speaking turns in conversations. *Journal of Personality and Social Psychology*, **23**, 283–292.

Duncan, S. and Fiske, D. W. (1977) *Face-to-face Interaction: Research, Methods and Theory*. Hillsdale, New Jersey: Lawrence Erlbaum.

Duncan, S. D. and Niederehe, G. (1974) On signalling that it's your turn to speak. *Journal of Experimental Social Psychology*, **10**, 234–247.

Edelmann, R. J. and Hampson, S. E. (1979) Changes in non-verbal behaviour during embarrassment. *British Journal of Social and Clinical Psychology*, **18**, 385–390.

Edelstein, B. A. and Eisler, R. M. (1976) Effects of modelling and modelling with instructions and feedback on the behavioural components of social skills. *Behaviour Therapy*, **7**, 382–389.

Efron, D. (1941) *Gesture and Environment*. New York: King's Crown Press. Current ed.: *Gesture, Race and Culture*, 1972. The Hague: Mouton.

Eibl-Eibesfeldt, I. (1972) Similarities and differences between cultures in expressive

184

movements. In R. A. Hinde (ed.), *Non-verbal Communication*, pp. 297–314. Cambridge: Cambridge University Press.

Eibl-Eibesfeldt, I. (1973a) The expressive behaviour of the deaf-and-blind born. In M. von Cranach and I. Vine (eds.), *Social Communication and Movement*, pp. 163–194. London: Academic Press.

Eibl-Eibesfeldt, I. (1973b) *Love and Hate*. London: Methuen.

Ekman, P. (1964) Body position, facial expression and verbal behaviour during interviews. *Journal of Abnormal and Social Psychology*, **68**, 295–301.

Ekman, P. (1965) Differential communication of affect by head and body cues. *Journal of Personality and Social Psychology*, **2**, 726 – 735.

Ekman, P. (1972) Universal and cultural differences in facial expression of emotion. In J. R. Cole (ed.), *Nebraska Symposium on Motivation 1971*, pp. 207–283. Lincoln, Nebraska: University of Nebraska Press.

Ekman, P. (1973) Cross-cultural studies of facial expression. In P. Ekman (ed.), *Darwin and Facial Expression*, pp. 169–223. Academic Press: New York.

Ekman, P. (1977) Biological and cultural contributions to body and facial movement. In J. Blacking (ed.), *The Anthropology of the Body*, pp. 39–84. London: Academic Press.

Ekman, P. (1979a) Methods of measuring facial behaviour. Lecture delivered to NATO Advanced Study Institute on methods of analysing non-verbal communication, 6 September.

Ekman, P. (1979b) About brows: emotional and conversational signals. In M. von Cranach, K. Foppa, W. Lepenies and D. Ploog (eds.), *Human Ethology*, pp. 169–202. Cambridge: Cambridge University Press.

Ekman, P. (1980) Asymmetry in facial expression. *Science*, **209**, 833–834.

Ekman, P. and Friesen, W. V. (1967) Head and body cues in the judgement of emotion: a reformulation. *Perceptual and Motor Skills*, **24**, 711–724.

Ekman, P. and Friesen, W. V. (1969a) The repertoire of non-verbal behaviour: categories, origins, usage and coding. *Semiotica*, **1**, 49–98.

Ekman, P. and Friesen, W. V. (1969b) Non-verbal leakage and clues to deception. *Psychiatry*, **32**, 88–106.

Ekman, P. and Friesen, W. V. (1971) Constants across culture in the face and emotion. *Journal of Personality and Social Psychology*, **17**, 124–129.

Ekman, P. and Friesen, W. V. (1974a) Non-verbal behaviour and psychopathology. In R. J. Friedman and M. M. Katz (eds.), *The Psychology of Depression: Contemporary Theory and Research*, pp. 203–232. New York: Wiley.

Ekman, P. and Friesen, W. V. (1974b) Detecting deception from the body or face. *Journal of Personality and Social Psychology*, **29**, 288–298.

Ekman, P. and Friesen, W. V. (1975) *Unmasking the Face: A Guide to Recognising Emotions from Facial Clues*. Englewood Cliffs, New Jersey: Prentice-Hall.

Ekman, P. and Friesen, W. V. (1978) *Facial Action Coding System*. Consulting Psychologists Press.

Ekman, P. and Friesen, W. V. (in preparation) *The Facial Atlas*.

Ekman, P., Friesen, W. V. and Ellsworth, P. C. (1972) *Emotion in the Human Face: Guidelines for Research and an Integration of Findings*. New York: Pergamon.

Ekman, P., Friesen, W. V. and Malmstrom, E. J. (1970) Facial behaviour and stress in two cultures. Unpublished manuscript, Langley Porter Neuropsychiatric Institute, San Francisco.

Ekman, P., Friesen, W. V. and Scherer, K. R. (1976) Body movement and voice pitch in deceptive interaction. *Semiotica*, **16**, 23–27.

Ekman, P., Hager, J. C. and Friesen, W. V. (1981) The symmetry of emotional and deliberate facial actions. *Psychophysiology*, **18**, 101–106.

Ekman, P. and Oster, H. (1979) Facial expressions of emotion. *Annual Review of Psychology*, **30**, 527–555.

Ellsworth, P. C. and Tourangeau, R. (1981) On our failure to disconfirm what nobody ever said. *Journal of Personality and Social Psychology*, **40**, 363–369.

English, P. W. (1972) Behavioural concomitants of dependent and subservient roles. Paper, Harvard University.

Ernest, R. C. and Cooper, R. E. (1974) 'Hey mister, do you have any change?' Two real world studies of proxemic effects on compliance with a mundane request. *Personality and Social Psychology Bulletin*, **1**, 158–159.

Exline, R. V. (1963) Explorations in the process of person perception: visual interaction in relation to competition, sex, and need for affiliation. *Journal of Personality*, **31**, 1–20.

Exline, R. V. (1972) Visual interaction: the glances of power and preference. *Nebraska Symposium on Motivation 1971*, pp. 163–206.

Exline, R. V., Gottheil, I., Parades, A. and Winkelmeier, D. (1968) Gaze direction as a factor in judgement of non-verbal expressions of affect. *Proceedings 76th Annual Convention of the American Psychological Association*, **3**, 415–416.

Exline, R. V., Gray, D. and Schuette, D. (1965) Visual behaviour in a dyad as affected by interview content and sex of respondent. *Journal of Personality and Social Psychology*, **1**, 201–209.

Exline, R. V. and Winters, L. C. (1965) Affective relations and mutual glances in dyads. In S. Tomkins and C. Izard (eds.), *Affect, Cognition and Personality*, pp. 319–350. New York: Springer.

Eysenck, H. J. (1952) The effects of psychotherapy: an evaluation. *Journal of Consulting Psychology*, **16**, 319–324.

Fantz, R. L. (1964) Visual experience in infants: decreased attention to familiar patterns relative to novel ones. *Science*, **146**, 668–670.

Feldman, R. S. (1976) Non-verbal disclosure of teacher deception and interpersonal affect. *Journal of Educational Psychology*, **68**, 807–816.

Feldman, R. S., Devin-Sheehan, L. and Allen, V. L. (1978) Non-verbal cues as indicators of verbal dissembling. *American Educational Research Journal*, **15**, 217–231.

Fiedler, F. E. (1967) *A Theory of Leadership Effectiveness*. New York: McGraw-Hill.

Fogel, A. (1977) Temporal organisation in mother–infant face-to-face interaction. In H. R. Schaffer (ed.), *Studies in Mother–Infant Interaction*, pp. 119–151. London: Academic Press.

Forbes, R. J. and Jackson, P. R. (1980) Non-verbal behaviour and the outcome of selection interviews. *Journal of Occupational Psychology*, **53**, 65–72.

Forston, R. F. and Larson, C. U. (1968) The dynamics of space: an experimental study in proxemic behaviour among Latin Americans and North Americans. *Journal of Communication*, **18**, 109–116.

Freedman, D. G. (1974) *Human Infancy: An evolutionary perspective*. Hillsdale, New Jersey: Lawrence Erlbaum.

Freedman, D. G. (1979) *Human Sociobiology: A Holistic Approach*. New York: Free Press.

Freedman, N. and Hoffman, S. P. (1967) Kinetic behaviour in altered clinical states: approach to objective analysis of motor behaviour during clinical interviews. *Perceptual and Motor Skills*, **24**, 527–539.

Freedman, N., O'Hanlon, J., Oltman, P. and Witkin, H. A. (1972) The impact of psychological differentiation on kinetic behaviour in varying communicative contexts. *Journal of Abnormal Psychology*, **79**, 239–258.

Freud, S. (1946/1921) Instincts and their vicissitudes In Collected Papers, Vol. 4. London: Hogarth Press, 1946. (Originally published, 1921).

Frey, S. and von Cranach, M. (1973) A method for the assessment of body movement variablity. In M. von Cranach and I. Vine (eds.), *Social Communication and Movement*, pp. 389–418. London: Academic Press.

Friedman, H. S. (1978) The relative strength of verbal versus non-verbal cues. *Personality and Social Psychology Bulletin*, **4**, 147–150.

Friedman, H. S. (1979) The interactive effects of facial expressions of emotion and verbal messages on perceptions of affective meaning. *Journal of Experimental Social Psychology*, **15**, 453–469.

Friesen, W. V., Ekman, P. and Wallblatt, H. (1980) Measuring hand movements. *Journal of Nonverbal Behaviour*, **4**, 97–113.

Frieze, I. H. and Ramsey, S. J. (1976) Non-verbal maintenance of traditional sex roles. *Journal of Social Issues*, **32**, 133–141.

Fromme, D. K. and Schmidt, C. K. (1972) Affective role enactment and expressive behaviour. *Journal of Personality and Social Psychology*, **24**, 413–419.

Galloway, C. M. (1968) Non-verbal communication in teaching. In R. T. Hyman (ed.), *Teaching: Vantage Points for Study*, pp. 70–77. J. P. Lippincott.

Galloway, C. M. (1974) Non-verbal teacher behaviours: a critique. *American Educational Research Journal*, **11**, 305–306.

Gates, G. S. (1923) An experimental study of the growth of social perception. *Journal of Educational Psychology*, **14**, 447–462.

Gelhorn, E. (1964) Motion and emotion: the role of proprioception in the physiology and pathology of the emotions. *Psychological Review*, **71**, 457–472.

Giesen, M. and McClaren, H. A. (1976) Discussion, distance and sex: changes in impressions and attraction during small group interaction. *Sociometry*, **39**, 60–70.

Ginsburg, H. J. (1977) Altruism in children: the significance of non-verbal behaviour. *Journal of Communication*, **27**, 82–88.

Ginsburg, H. J., Pollman, V. A. and Wauson, M. S. (1977) An ethological analysis of non-verbal inhibitors of aggressive behaviours in male elementary school children. *Developmental Psychology*, **13**, 417–418.

Goffman, E. (1956) *The Presentation of Self in Everyday Life*. Edinburgh University Press.

Goffman, E. (1963) *Behaviour in Public Places*. New York: Free Press.

Goffman, E. (1972) *Relations in Public*. New York: Harper Colophon Books.

Goffman, E. (1975) *Frame Analysis: An Essay on the Organisation of Experience*. Harmondsworth: Penguin.

Gottman, J., Markman, H. and Notarius C. (1977) The topography of marital conflict: a sequential analysis of verbal and non-verbal behaviour. *Journal of Marriage and the Family*, **39**, 461–477.

Gough, H. G. (1957) *Manual for the California Psychological Inventory*. Palo Alto, California: Consulting Psychologists Press.

Gough, H. G. and Heilbrun, A. B. (1965) *The Adjective Check List Manual*. Palo Alto, California: Consulting Psychologists Press.

Graham, J. A. and Argyle, M. (1975a) The effects of different patterns of gaze combined with different facial expressions on impression formation. *Journal of Human Movement Studies*, **1**, 178–182.

Graham, J. A. and Argyle, M. (1975b) A cross-cultural study of the communication of extra-verbal meaning by gestures. *International Journal of Psychology*, **10**, 57–69.

Graham, J. A., Bitti, P. R. and Argyle, M. (1975) A cross-cultural study of the communication of emotion by facial and gestural cues. *Journal of Human Movement Studies*, **1**, 68–77.

Graham, J. A. and Heywood, S. (1975) The effects of elimination of hand gestures and of verbal codability on speech performance. *European Journal of Social Psychology*, **5**, 189–195.

Grant, E. C. (1969) Human facial expression. *Man*, **4**, 525–536.

Graves, J. R. and Robinson, J. D. (1976) Proxemic behaviour as a function of inconsistent verbal and non-verbal messages. *Journal of Counselling Psychology*, **23**, 333–338.

Greene, L. R. (1976) Effects of field dependence on affective reactions and compliance in dyadic interactions. *Journal of Personality and Social Psychology*, **34**, 569–577.

Haase, R. F. and Tepper, D. T. (1972) Non-verbal empathic communication. *Journal of Counselling Psychology*, **19**, 417–424.

Hager, J. C. and Ekman, P. (1981) Methodological problems in Tourangeau and

Ellsworth's study of facial expression and experience of emotion. *Journal of Personality and Social Psychology*, **40**, 358–362.

Haines, J. (1974) An ultrasonic system for measuring anxiety. *Medical and Biological Engineering*, **12**, 378–381.

Hall, E. T. (1959) *The Silent Language*. New York: Doubleday.

Hall, E. T. (1966) *The Hidden Dimension*. New York: Doubleday.

Hall, J. A. (1978) Gender effects in decoding non-verbal cues. *Psychological Bulletin*, **85**, 845–857.

Hall, J. A. (1979) Gender, gender roles and non-verbal communication skills. In R. Rosenthal (ed.), *Skill in Non-verbal Communication: Individual Differences*, pp. 32–67. Cambridge, Massachusetts: Oelgeschlager, Gunn and Hain.

Hall, R. and Goldberg, D. (1977) The role of social anxiety in social interaction difficulties. *British Journal of Psychiatry*, **131**, 610–615.

Hare, A. P. and Bales, R. F. (1963) Seating position and small group interaction. *Sociometry*, **26**, 480–486.

Hare, R. D. (1970) *Psychopathy: Theory and Research*. New York: Wiley.

Harris, H. (1949) *The Group Approach to Leadership Testing*. London: Routledge and Kegan Paul.

Hass, H. (1970) *The Human Animal*. New York: Putnam's Sons.

Hearn, G. (1957) Leadership and the spatial factor in small groups. *Journal of Abnormal and Social Psychology*, **54**, 269–272.

Hedge, B. J., Everitt, B. S. and Frith, C. D. (1978) The role of gaze in dialogue. *Acta Psychologica*, **42**, 453–475.

Henke, R. and Globerson, T. (1979) The measurement of pupillary dilation: a facilitative apparatus. *Behaviour Research Methods and Instrumentation*, **11**, 334–338.

Hershey, M. (1977) Telephone instruction: an alternative educational delivery system for teacher in-service. *Gifted Child Quarterly*, **21**, 213–217.

Hess, E. H. (1965) Attitude and pupil size. *Scientific American*, **212**, 46–54.

Hess, E. H. (1975a) The role of pupil size in communication. *Scientific American*, **233**, 110–119.

Hess, E. H. (1975b) *The Tell-tale Eye*. New York: Van Nostrand Reinhold.

Hess, E. H. and Polt, J. M. (1960) Pupil size as related to interest value of visual stimuli. *Science*, **132**, 349–350.

Hewes, G. W. (1955) World distribution of certain postural habits. *American Anthropologist*, **57**, 231–244.

Hewes, G. W. (1957) The anthoropology of posture. *Scientific American*, **196**, 123–132.

Hildreth, A. M., Derogatis, L. R. and McCusker, K. (1971) Body-buffer zone and violence: a reassessment and confirmation. *American Journal of Psychiatry*, **127**, 1641–1645.

Hill, D. (1974) Non-verbal behaviour in mental illness. *British Journal of Psychiatry*, **124**, 221–230.

Hinchcliffe, M. K., Lancashire, M. and Roberts, F. J. (1971) A study of eye-contact changes in depressed and recovered psychiatric patients. *British Journal of Psychiatry*, **119**, 213–215.

Hittelman, J. H. and Dickes, R. (1979) Sex differences in neonatal eye-contact time. *Merrill-Palmer Quartery*, **25**, 171–184.

Hjortsjö, C. H. (1970) *Man's Face and Mimic Language*. Malmo, Sweden: Nordens Boktryckeri.

Hobson, G. N., Strongman, K. T., Bull, D. and Craig, G. (1973) Anxiety and gaze aversion in dyadic encounters. *British Journal of Social and Clinical Psychology*, **12**, 122–129.

Hoffman, M. L. (1977) Sex differences in empathy and related behaviours. *Psychological Bulletin*, **84**, 712–722.

188

Hogan, R. T. (1969) Development of an empathy scale. *Journal of Consulting and Clinical Psychology*, **33**, 307–316.

Hollandsworth, J. G. Kazelskis, R., Stevens, J. and Dressel, M. E. (1979) Relative contributions of verbal, articulative, and non-verbal communication to employment decisions in the job-interview setting. *Personnel Psychology*, **32**, 359–367.

Horowitz, M., Duff, D. and Stratton, L. (1964) Body-buffer zone: exploration of personal space. *Archives of General Psychiatry*, **11**, 651–656.

Howells, L. T. and Becker, S. W. (1962) Seating arrangements and leadership emergence. *Journal of Abnormal and Social Psychology*, **64**, 148–150.

Huber, E. (1931) *Evolution of Facial Musculature and Facial Expression*. Baltimore: the Johns Hopkins Press.

Hutt, C. and Ounsted, C. (1970) Gaze aversion and its significance in childhood autism. In S. J. Hutt and C. Hutt (eds.), *Behaviour Studies in Psychiatry*, pp. 103–120. Exeter: Pergamon.

Imada, A. S. and Hakel, M. D. (1977) Influence of non-verbal communication and rater proximity on impressions and decisions in simulated employment interviews. *Journal of Applied Psychology*, **62**, 295–300.

Izard, C. E. (1971) *The Face of Emotion*. New York: Appleton-Century-Crofts.

Izard, C. E. (1977) *Human Emotions*. New York: Plenum Press.

Izard, C. E. (1981) Differential emotions theory and the facial feedback hypothesis of emotion activation: comments on Tourangeau and Ellsworth's 'The role of facial response in the experience of emotion'. *Journal of Personality and Social Psychology*, **40**, 350–354.

Izard, C. E. and Tomkins, S. S. (1966) Affect and behaviour: anxiety as a negative affect. In C. D. Spielberger (ed.), *Anxiety and Behaviour*, pp. 81–125. New York: Academic Press.

Jackson, D. N. (1967) *Manual for the Personality Research Form*. Research Bulletin 43. University of Western Ontario: London, Canada.

Jackson, D. N. (1976) *Jackson Personality Inventory*. Goshen, New York: Research Psychologists Press.

Jacobs, T. J. (1973) Posture, gesture and movement in the analyst: clues to interpretation and countertransferance. *Journal of American Psychoanalytical Association*, **21**, 77–92.

Jaffe, J., Stern, D. N. and Peery, J. C. (1973) 'Conversational' coupling of gaze behaviour in pre-linguistic human development. *Journal of Psycholinguistic Research*, **2**, 321–329.

James, W. (1890) *The Principles of Psychology*. New York: Holt.

Janisse, M. P. (1977) *Pupillometry: The Psychology of the Pupillary Response*. New York: Wiley.

Janisse, M. P. and Bradley, M. T. (1980) Detection, information and the pupillary response. *Perceptual and Motor Skills*, **50**, 748–750.

Janisse, M. P. and Peavler, W. S. (1974) Pupillary research today: emotion in the eye. *Psychology Today*, **7**, 60–63.

Jenni, D. A. and Jenni, M. A. (1976) Carrying behaviour in humans: analyses of sex differences. *Science*, **194**, 859–860.

Jones, H. E. (1960) The longitudinal method in the study of personality. In I. Iscoe and H. W. Stevenson (eds.), *Personality Development in Children*, pp. 3–27. Chicago: University of Chicago Press.

Jones, S. E. and Aiello, J. R. (1979) A test of the validity of projective and quasi-projective measures of interpersonal distance. *Western Journal of Speech Communication*, **43**, 143–152.

Jorgensen, D. O. (1975) Field study of the relationship between status discrepancy and proxemic behaviour. *Journal of Social Psychology*, **97**, 173–179.

Kaye, K. and Fogel, A. (1980) The temporal structure of face-to-face communication between mothers and infants. *Developmental Psychology*, **16**, 454–464.

Keenan, A. (1976) Effects of the non-verbal behaviour of interviewers on candidates' performance. *Journal of Occupational Psychology*, **49**, 171–176.

Keenan, A. and Wedderburn, A. A. I. (1975) Effect of the non-verbal behaviour of interviewers on candidates' impressions. *Journal of Occupational Psychology*, **48**, 129–132.

Kendon, A. (1967) Some functions of gaze direction in social interaction. *Acta Psychologica*, **26**, 22–63.

Kendon, A. (1972) Some relationships between body motion and speech. In A. W. Siegman and B. Pope (eds.), *Studies in Dyadic Communication*, pp. 177–210. New York: Pergamon.

Kendon, A. (1978) Some theoretical and methodological aspects of the use of film in the study of social interaction. In G. P. Ginsburg (ed.), *Emerging Strategies in Social Psychological Research*, pp. 67–91. New York: Wiley.

Kendon, A. and Cook, M. (1969) The consistency of gaze patterns in social interaction. *British Journal of Psychology*, **60**, 481–494.

Kendon, A. and Ferber, A. (1973) A description of some human greetings. In R. P. Michael and J. H. Crook (eds.), *Comparative Ecology and Behaviour of Primates*, pp. 591–668. London and New York: Academic Press.

Kenny, D. A. (1975) Cross-lagged panel correlation: a test for spuriousness. *Psychological Bulletin*, **82**, 887–903.

Kiesler, D. J. (1979) An interpersonal communication analysis of relationship in psychotherapy. *Psychiatry*, **42**, 299–311.

Kimble, C. E. and Olszewski, D. A. (1980) Gaze and emotional expression: the effects of message positivity–negativity and emotional intensity. *Journal of Research in Personality*, **14**, 60–69.

Kinzel, A. F. (1970) Body-buffer zone in violent prisoners. *American Journal of Psychiatry*, **127**, 59–64.

Kinzel, A. F. (1972) Abnormalities of personal space in violent prisoners. In J. H. Cullen (ed.), *Experimental behaviour: A Basis for the Study of Mental Disturbance*, pp. 224–229. Dublin: Irish University Press.

Kiritz, S. A. (1971) Hand movements and clinical ratings at admission and discharge for hospitalised psychiatric patients: Unpublished doctoral dissertation, University of California, San Francisco.

Kirkland, J. and Smith, J. (1978) Preferences for infant pictures with modified eye-pupils. *Journal of Biological Psychology*, **20**, 33–34.

Kleinke, C. L. (1977) Compliance to requests made by gazing and touching experimenters in field settings. *Journal of Experimental Social Psychology*, **13**, 218–223.

Kleinke, C. L. (1980) Interaction between gaze and legitimacy of request on compliance in a field setting. *Journal of Nonverbal Behaviour*, **5**, 3–12.

Kleinke, C. L., Desautels, M. S. and Knapp, B. E. (1977) Adult gaze and affective and visual responses of pre-school children. *Journal of Genetic Psychology*, **131**, 321–322.

Kleinke, C. L. and Singer, D. A. (1979) Influence of gaze on compliance with demanding and conciliatory requests in a field setting. *Personality and Social Psychology Bulletin*, **5**, 386–390.

Knapp, M. L., Hart, R. P., Friedrich, G. W. and Shulman, G. M. (1973) The rhetoric of goodbye: verbal and non-verbal correlates of human leave-taking. *Speech Monographs*, **40**, 182–198.

Kogan, N. and Wallach, M. A. (1964) *Risk Taking: A Study in Cognition and Personality*. New York: Holt Rinehart and Winston.

LaFrance, M. (1974) Non-verbal cues to conversational turn-taking between Black speakers. *Personality and Social Psychology Bulletin*, **1**, 240–242.

LaFrance, M. (1979) Non-verbal synchrony and rapport: analysis by the cross-lag panel technique. *Social Psychology Quartery*, **42**, 66–70.

LaFrance, M. and Broadbent, M. (1976) Group rapport: posture sharing as a non-verbal indicator. *Group and Organisation Studies*, **1**, 328–333.

LaFrance, M. and Carmen, B. (1980) The non-verbal display of psychological androgyny. *Journal of Personality and Social Psychology*, **38**, 36–49.

190

LaFrance, M. and Ickes, W. (1981) Posture mirroring and interactional involvement: sex and sex-typing effects. *Journal of Nonverbal Behaviour*, **5**, 139–154.

LaFrance, M. and Mayo, C. (1976) Racial differences in gaze behaviour during conversations: two systematic observational studies. *Journal of Personality and Social Psychology*, **33**, 547–552.

Laird, J. D. (1974) Self-attribution of emotion: the effects of expressive behaviour on the quality of emotional experience. *Journal of Personality and Social Psychology*, **29**, 475–486.

Lange, C. (1885) *The Emotions.* (Original reference unavailable. Trans. H. Kurella, Leipzig: Theodor Thomas, 1887. Retrans. Istar A. Haupt for K. Dunlap (ed.), *The Emotions*, 1922. Baltimore: Williams and Wilkins).

Lanzetta; J. T. and Kleck, R. E. (1970) Encoding and decoding of non-verbal affect in humans. *Journal of Personality and Social Psychology*, **16**, 12–19.

LaRusso, L. (1978) Sensitivity of paranoid patients to non-verbal cues. *Journal of Abnormal Psychology*, **87**, 463–471.

Latta, R. M. (1978) Relation of status incongruence to personal space. *Personality and Social Psychology Bulletin*, **4**, 143–146.

Laver, J. and Hutcheson, S. (eds.) (1972) *Communication in Face-to-face Interaction.* Harmondsworth, Middlesex: Penguin.

Lindenfeld, J. (1971) Verbal and non-verbal elements in discourse. *Semiotica*, **3**, 223–233.

Lippa, R. (1978) The naïve perception of masculinity–femininity on the basis of expressive cues. *Journal of Research in Personality*, **12**, 1–14.

Littlepage, G. E. and Pineault, M. A. (1979) Detection of deceptive factual statements from the body and the face. *Personality and Social Psychology Bulletin*, **5**, 325–328.

Lockard, J. S., Allen, D. J., Schiele, B. J. and Wiemer, M. J. (1978) Human postural signals: stance, weight-shifts and social distance as intention movements to depart. *Animal Behaviour*, **26**, 219–224.

Loewenfeld, I. E. (1966) Comment on Hess' findings. *Survey of Ophthalmology*, **11**, 291–294.

Lomranz, J. (1976) Cultural variations in personal space. *Journal of Social Psychology*, **99**, 21–27.

Lott, D. F. and Sommer, R. (1967) Seating arrangements and status. *Journal of Personality and Social Psychology*, **7**, 90–95.

McClintock, C. C. and Hunt, R. G. (1975) Non-verbal indicators of affect and deception in an interview setting. *Journal of Applied Social Psychology*, **5**, 54–67.

McDowall, J. J. (1978) Interactional synchrony: a reappraisal. *Journal of Personality and Social Psychology*, **36**, 963–975.

McGovern, T. V. Jones, B. W. and Morris, S. E. (1979) Comparison of professional versus student ratings of job interviewee behaviour. *Journal of Counselling Psychology*, **26**, 176–179.

Maguire, P., Roe, P., Goldberg, D., Jones, S., Hyde, C. and O'Dowd, T. (1978) The value of feedback in teaching interviewing skills to medical students. *Psychological Medicine*, **8**, 695–704.

Matarazzo, J. D. Saslow, G., Wiens, A. M., Weitman, M. and Allen, B. V. (1964) Interviewer head nodding and interviewee speech duration. *Psychotherapy, Theory, Research and Practice*, **1**, 54–63.

Mazur, A. (1977) Interpersonal spacing on public benches in 'contact' versus 'non-contact' cultures. *Journal of Social Psychology*, **101**, 53–58.

Mehrabian, A. (1967) Orientation behaviours and non-verbal attitude communication. *Journal of Communication*, **17**, 324–332.

Mehrabian, A. (1968a) Inference of attitude from the posture, orientation and distance of a communicator. *Journal of Consulting and Clinical Psychology*, **32**, 296–308.

Mehrabian, A. (1968b) Relationship of attitude to seated posture, orientation and distance. *Journal of Personality and Social Psychology*, **10**, 26–30.

191

Mehrabian, A. (1969) Significance of posture and position in the communication of attitude and status relationships. *Psychological Bulletin*, 71, 359–372.

Mehrabian, A. (1972) *Non-verbal Communication*. New York: Aldine Atherton.

Mehrabian, A. and Friar, J. T. (1969) Encoding of attitude by a seated communicator via posture and position cues. *Journal of Consulting and Clinical Psychology*, 33, 330–336.

Mehrabian, A. and Ksionsky, S. (1974) *A Theory of Affiliation*. Lexington, Massachusetts: D. C. Heath & Co.

Mehrabian, A. and Williams, N. (1969) Non-verbal concomitants of perceived and intended persuasiveness. *Journal of Personality and Social Psychology*, 13, 37–58.

Meltzoff, A. N. and Moore, M. K. (1977) Imitation of facial and manual gestures by human neonates. *Science*, 198, 75–78.

Michelini, R. L., Passalacqua, R. and Cusimano, J. (1976) Effects of seating arrangement on group participation. *Journal of Social Psychology*, 99, 179–186.

Morgan, C. J. Lockard, L. S., Fahrenbruch, C. E. and Smith, J. L. (1975) Hitchhiking: social signals at a distance. *Bulletin of the Psychonomic Society*, 5, 459–461.

Morley, I. E. and Stephenson, G. M. (1977) *The Social Psychology of Bargaining*. London: George Allen and Unwin.

Morris, D., Collett, P., Marsh, P. and O'Shaughnessy, M. (1979) *Gestures: Their Origins and Distribution*. London: Jonathan Cape.

Muzekari, L. H. and Bates, M. E. (1977) Judgement of emotion among chronic schizophrenics. *Journal of Clinical Psychology*, 33, 662–666.

Myers, I. B. (1962) *Myers–Briggs Type Indicator*. Princeton, New Jersey: Educational Testing Service.

Newman, R. C. and Pollack, D. (1973) Proxemics in deviant adolescents. *Journal of Consulting and Clinical Psychology*, 40, 6–8.

Noller, P. (1980) Misunderstandings in marital communication: a study of couples' non-verbal communication. *Journal of Personality and Social Psychology*, 39, 1135–1148.

Notarius, C. I. and Levenson, R. W. (1979) Expressive tendencies and physiological response to stress. *Journal of Personality and Social Psychology*, 37, 1204–1210.

O'Neal, E. C., Brunault, M. A., Carifio, M. S., Troutwine, R. and Epstein, J. (1980) Effect of insult upon personal space preferences. *Journal of Nonverbal Behaviour*, 5, 56–62.

O'Neal, E. C., Brunault, M. A., Marquis, J. F. and Carifio, M. (1979) Anger and the body-buffer zone. *Journal of Social Psychology*, 108, 135–136.

Oster, H. and Ekman, P. (1977) Facial behaviour in child development. In A. Collins (ed.) *Minnesota Symposia on Child Psychology*, Vol. 11, 231–276.

Patterson, M. L. (1975) Personal space—time to burst the bubble? *Man-environment Systems*, 5, 67.

Patterson, M. L. (1976) An arousal model of interpersonal intimacy. *Psychological Review*, 83, 235–245.

Patterson, M. L., Mullens, S. and Romano, J. (1971) Compensatory reactions to spatial intrusion. *Sociometry*, 34, 114–121.

Pedersen, D. M. (1973a) Development of a personal space measure. *Psychological Reports*, 27, 287–290.

Pedersen, D. M. (1973b) Prediction of behavioural personal space from simulated personal space. *Perceptual and Motor Skills*, 37, 803–813.

Pedersen, D. M. (1973c) Correlates of behavioural personal space. *Psychological Reports*, 32, 828–830.

Pittenger, R. E., Hockett, C. F. and Danehy, J. J. (1960) *The First Five Minutes: A Sample of Microscopic Interview Analysis*. Ithaca, New York: Martineau.

Plutchik, R. (1962) *The Emotions*. New York: Random House.

Rawls, J. R., Trego, R. E. and McGaffey, C. N. (1968) *A Comparison of Personal Space Measures*. Report of NASA Grant NGR-44-009-008, Institute of Behavioural Research, Texas Christian University, Fort Worth.

Reilly, S. S. and Muzekari, L. H. (1979) Responses of normal and disturbed adults and children to mixed messages. *Journal of Abnormal Psychology*, 88, 203–208.

Rekers, G. A. (1977) Assessment and treatment of childhood gender problems. In B. B. Lahey and A. E. Kazdin (eds.), *Advances in Child Clinical Psychology*, Vol. 1, pp. 267–306. New York: Plenum Press.

Rekers, G. A., Amaro-Plotkin, H. D. and Low, B. P. (1977) Sex-typed mannerisms in normal boys and girls as a function of sex and age. *Child Development*, **48**, 275–278.

Rekers, G. A., Lovaas, O. I. and Low, B. (1974) The behavioural treatment of a 'transsexual' pre-adolescent boy. *Journal of Abnormal Child Psychology*, **2**, 99–116.

Rekers, G. A. and Rudy, J. P. (1978) Differentiation of childhood body gestures. *Perceptual and Motor Skills*, **46**, 839–845.

Richards, M. P. M. (1971) Social interaction in the first weeks of life. *Psychiatria, Neurologia, Neurochirurgia*, **74**, 35–42.

Richer, J. M. and Coss, R. G. (1976) Gaze aversion in autistic and normal children. *Acta Psychiatrica Scandinavica*, **53**, 193–210.

Rimé, B., Bouvy, H., Leborgne, B. and Rouillon, F. (1978) Psychopathy and non-verbal behaviour in an interpersonal situation. *Journal of Abnormal Psychology*, **87**, 636–643.

Rimé, B. and McCusker, L. (1976) Visual behaviour in social interaction: the validity of eye-contact assessments under different conditions of observation. *British Journal of Psychology*, **67**, 507–514.

Riskin, J. and Faunce, E. E. (1972) An evaluative review of family interaction research. *Family Process*, **11**, 365–455.

Roger, D. B. and Reid, R. L. (1978) Small group ecology revisited: personal space and role differentiation. *British Journal of Social and Clinical Psychology*, **17**, 43–46.

Roger, D. B. and Reid, R. L. (1982) Role differentiation and seating arrangements: a further study. *British Journal of Social Psychology*, **21**, 23–29.

Roger, D. B. and Schalekamp, E. E. (1976) Body-buffer zone and violence: a cross-cultural study. *Journal of Social Psychology*, **98**, 153–158.

Rogers, C. R. (1957) The necessary and sufficient conditions of therapeutic personality change. *Journal of Consulting Psychology*, **21**, 95–103.

Rogers, W. T. (1978) The contribution of kinesic illustrators toward the comprehension of verbal behaviour within utterances. *Human Communication Research*, **5**, 54–62.

Rokeach, M. (1960) *The Open and Closed Mind*. New York: Basic Books.

Rosenthal, R. (1976) *Experimenter Effects in Behavioural Research*, New York: Irvington.

Rosenthal, R. and DePaulo, B. M. (1979) Sex differences in accommodation in non-verbal communication. In R. Rosenthal (ed.), *Skill in Non-verbal Communication*, pp. 68–103. Cambridge, Massachusetts: Oelgeschlager, Gunn & Hain.

Rosenthal, R. and Fode, K. L. (1961) The problem of experimenter outcome-bias. In D. P. Ray (ed.) *Series Research in Social Psychology*. Symposia studies series, No. 8, Washington, DC: National Institute of Social and Behavioural Science.

Rosenthal, R. and Fode, K. L. (1963) Three experiments in experimenter bias *Psychological Reports*, **12**, 491–511.

Rosenthal, R., Hall, J. A., DiMatteo, M. R., Rogers, P. L. and Archer, D. (1979) *Sensitivity to Non-verbal Communication: The PONS Test*. Baltimore: John Hopkins University Press.

Rosenthal, R. and Jacobson, L. (1968) *Pygmalion in the classroom: teacher expectation and pupils' intellectual development*. New York: Holt, Rinchart and Winston.

Ruble, D. N. and Nakamura, C. Y. (1972) Task orientation versus social orientation in young children and their attention to relevant social cues. *Child Development*, **43**, 471–480.

Rutter, D. R. (1976) Visual interaction in recently admitted and chronic long-stay schizophrenic patients. *British Journal of Social and Clinical Psychology*, **15**, 295–303.

Rutter, D. R. (1977a) Speech patterning in recently admitted and chronic long-stay schizophrenic patients. *British Journal of Social and Clinical Psychology*, **16**, 45–55.

Rutter, D. R. (1977b) Visual interaction and speech patterning in remitted and acute schizophrenic patients. *British Journal of Social and Clinical Psychology*, **16**, 357–362.

Rutter, D. R. (1978) Visual interaction in schizophrenic patients: the timing of Looks. *British Journal of Social and Clinical Psychology*, **17**, 281–282.

Rutter, D. R. Morley, I. E. and Graham, J. C. (1972) Visual interaction in a group of introverts and extraverts. *European Journal of Social Psychology*, **2**, 371–384.

Rutter, D. R. and Robinson, B. (1981) An experimental analysis of teaching by telephone: theoretical and practical implications for social psychology. In G. M. Stephenson and J. H. Davis (eds.), *Progress in Applied Social Psychology*, Vol. 1, pp. 345–374. Chichester: Wiley.

Rutter, D. R. and Stephenson, G. M. (1972a) Visual interaction in a group of schizophrenic and depressive patients. *British Journal of Social and Clinical Psychology*, **11**, 57–65.

Rutter, D. R. and Stephenson, G. M. (1972b) Visual interaction in a group of schizophrenic and depressive patients: a follow-up study. *British Journal of Social and Clinical Psychology* **11**, 410–411.

Rutter, D. R. and Stephenson, G. M. (1977) The role of visual communication in synchronising conversation. *European Journal of Social Psychology*, **7**, 29–37.

Rutter, D. R. and Stephenson, G. M. (1979) The functions of looking: effects of friendship in gaze. *British Journal of Social and Clinical Psychology*, **18**, 203–205.

Rutter, D. R., Stephenson, G. M., Ayling, K. and White, P. A. (1978) The timing of looks in dyadic conversations. *British Journal of Social and Clinical Psychology*, **17**, 17–21.

Rutter, D. R., Stephenson, G. M. and Dewey, M. E. (1981) Visual communication and the content and style of conversation. *British Journal of Social Psychology*, **20**, 41–52.

Sackeim, H. A. and Gur, R. C. (1978) Lateral asymmetry in intensity of emotional expression. *Neuropsychologia*, **16**, 473–481.

Sackeim, H. A. and Gur, R. C. (1980) Asymmetry in facial expression. *Science*, **209**, 833–834.

Sackeim, H. A., Gur, R. C. and Saucy, M. C. (1978) Emotions are expressed more intensely on the left side of the face. *Science*, **202**, 434–436.

Sainsbury, P. and Woods, E. (1977) Measuring gesture: its cultural and clinical correlates. *Psychological Medicine*, **7**, 63–72.

Schaffer, H. R. (1971) *The Growth of Sociability*. Harmondsworth: Penguin.

Schaffer, H. R. and Emerson, P. E. (1964) *The Development of Social Attachments in Infancy*. Monograph of the Society for Research in Child Development, No. 29 (whole no. 94).

Scheflen, A. E. (1964) The significance of posture in communication systems. *Psychiatry*, **27**, 316–331.

Scheflen, A. E. (1966) Natural history method in psychotherapy: communicational research. In L. A. Gottschalk and A. H. Auerbach (eds.), *Methods of Research in Psychotherapy*, pp. 263–289. New York: Appleton-Century Crofts.

Scheflen, A. E. (1968) Human communication: behavioural programmes and their integration in interaction. *Behavioural Science*, **13**, 44–55.

Scheflen, A. E. (1973) *Communicational Structure: Analysis of a Psychotherapy Transaction*. Bloomington: Indiana University Press.

Scherer, K. R. (1971) Randomised-splicing: a note on a simple technique for masking speech content. *Journal of Experimental Research in Personality*, **5**, 155–159.

Scherer, K. R. (1974) Acoustic concomitants of emotional dimensions: judging affect from synthesised tune sequences. In S. Weitz (ed.), *Non-verbal Communication: Readings with Commentary*, pp. 105–111. New York: Oxford University Press.

Schlosberg, H. (1954) Three dimensions of emotion. *Psychological Review*, **61**, 81–88.

Schneider, F. W., Coutts, L. M. and Garrett, W. A. (1977) Interpersonal gaze in a triad as a function of sex. *Perceptual and Motor Skills*, **44**, 184.

Schneider, S. M. and Kintz, B. L. (1977) The effect of lying upon foot and leg movement. *Bulletin of the Psychonomic Society*, **10**, 451–453.

194

Schutz, W. C. (1958) *FIRO: A three-dimensional theory of interpersonal behaviour*. New York: Holt, Rinehart Winston.

Schwartz, G. E., Fair, P. L., Greenberg, P. S., Friedman, M. J. and Klerman, G. L. (1973) Facial electromyography in the assessment of emotion. *Psychophysiology*, **11**, 237.

Schwartz, G. E., Fair, P. L., Salt, P., Mandel, M. R. and Klerman, G. L. (1976a) Facial expression and imagery in depression: an electromyographic study. *Psychosomatic Medicine*, **38**, 337–347.

Schwartz, G. E., Fair, P. L. Salt, P., Mandei, M. R. and Klerman, G. L. (1976b) Facial muscle patterning to affective imagery in depressed and non-depressed subjects. *Science*, **192**, 489–491.

Shennum, W. A. (1976) Field dependence and facial expressions. *Perceptual and Motor Skills*, **43**, 179–184.

Shimoda, K., Argyle, M. and Bitti, P. R. (1978) The intercultural recognition of emotional expressions by three national recial groups: English, Italian and Japanese. *European Journal of Social Psychology*, **8**, 169–179.

Shor, R. E. (1978) The production and judgement of smile magnitude. *Journal of General Psychology*, **98**, 79–96.

Short, J. A. (1974) Effects of medium of communication on experimental negotiation. *Human Relations*, **27**, 225–234.

Short, J. A., Williams, E. and Christie, B. (1976) *The Social Psychology of Telecommunications*. London: Wiley.

Shuter, R. (1976) Proxemics and tactility in Latin America. *Journal of Communication*, **26**, 46–52.

Shuter, R. (1977) A field study of non-verbal communication in Germany, Italy and the United States. *Communication Monographs*, **44**, 298–305.

Shutland, R. L. and Johnson, M. P. (1978) Bystander behaviour and kinesics: the interaction between the helper and the victim. *Environmental Psychology and Nonverbal Behaviour*, **2**, 181–190.

Silverstein, C. H. and Stang, D. J. (1976) Seating position and interaction in triads: a field study. *Sociometry*, **39**, 166–170.

Smith, M. L. and Glass, G. V. (1977) Meta-analysis of psychotherapy outcome studies. *American Psychologist*, **32**, 752–760.

Snyder, M. (1974) Self-monitoring of expressive behaviour. *Journal of Personality and Social Psychology*, **30**, 526–537.

Snyder, M., Grether, J. and Keller, K. (1974) Staring and compliance: a field experiment on hitchhiking. *Journal of Applied Social Psychology*, **4**, 165–170.

Snyder, R. A. and Sutker, L. W. (1977) The measurement of the construct of dominance and its relationship to non-verbal behaviour. *Journal of Psychology*, **97**, 227–230.

Sommer, R. (1959) Studies in personal space. *Sociometry*, **22**, 247–260.

Sommer, R. (1961) Leadership and group geography. *Sociometry*, **24**, 99–110.

Sommer, R. (1967) Small group ecology. *Psychological Bulletin*, **67**, 145–152.

Sommer, R. (1969) *Personal Space*. Englewood Cliffs, New Jersey Prentice-Hall.

Sousa-Poza, J. F. and Rohberg, R. (1977) Body movement in relation to type of information (person and non-person oriented) and cognitive style (field dependence). *Human Communication Research*, **4**, 19–29.

Spiegel, J. and Machotka, P. (1974) *Messages of the Body*. New York: Free Press.

Sroufe, L. A. and Waters, E. (1976) The ontogenesis of smiling and laughter: a perspective on the organization of development in infancy. *Psychological Review*, **83**, 173–189.

Starkweather, J. A. (1956) The communication value of content-free speech. *American Journal of Psychology*, **69**, 121–123.

Steiner, J. E. (1974) Innate, discriminative human facial expressions to taste and smell stimulation. *Annals of the New York Academy of Sciences* **237**, 229–233.

Steinzor, B. (1950) The spatial factor in face-to-face discussion groups. *Journal of Abnormal and Social Psychology*, **45**, 552–555.

Stephenson, G. M. Ayling, K. and Rutter, D. R. (1976) The role of visual communication in social exchange. *British Journal of Social and Clinical Psychology*, **15**, 113–120.

Stephenson, G. M. and Rutter, D. R. (1970) Eye contact, distance and affiliation: a re-evaluation. *British Journal of Psychology*, **61**, 385–393.

Stephenson, G. M., Rutter, D. R. and Dore, S. R. (1973) Visual interaction and distance. *British Journal of Psychology*, **64**, 251–257.

Strongman, K. T. and Champness, B. G. (1968) Dominance hierarchies and conflicts in eye contact. *Acta Psychologica*, **28**, 376–386.

Sullivan, H. S. (1953) *The Interpersonal Theory of Psychiatry*. New York: Norton.

Sullivan, H. S. (1954) *The Psychiatric Interview*. New York: Norton.

Tartter, V. C. (1980) Happy talk: perceptual and acoustic effects of smiling on speech. *Perception and Psychophysics*, **27**, 24–27.

Tepper, D. T. and Haase, R. F. (1978) Verbal and non-verbal communication of facilitative conditions. *Journal of Counselling Psychology*, **25**, 35–44.

Thomas, A. P. and Bull, P. E. (1981) The role of pre-speech posture change in dyadic interaction. *British Journal of Social Psychology*, **20**, 105–111.

Thorndike, R. L. (1966) *Thorndike Dimensions of Temperament Manual*. New York: Psychological Corporation.

Tomkins, S. S. (1962) *Affects, Imagery, Consciousness*. Vol. 1, *The Positive Affects*. New York: Springer.

Tomkins, S. S. (1963) *Affect, Imagery, Consciousness*. Vol. 11, *The Negative Affects*. New York: Springer.

Tomkins, S. S. (1981) The role of facial response in the experience of emotion: a reply to Tourangeau and Ellsworth. *Journal of Personality and Social Psychology*, **40**, 355–357.

Tourangeau, R. and Ellsworth, P. C. (1979) The role of facial response in the experience of emotion. *Journal of Personality and Social Psychology* **37**, 1519–1531.

Trager, G. L. and Smith, H. L., Jr. (1951) *An Outline of English Structure* (Studies in Linguistics: Occasional Papers, 3). Norman, Okla: Battenberg Press (republished: New York: American Council of Learned Societies, 1965).

Trevarthen, C. (1977) Descriptive analyses of infant communicative behaviour. In H. R. Schaffer (ed.), *Studies in Mother–Infant Interaction*, pp. 227–270. London: Academic Press.

Trout, D. L. and Rosenfeld, H. M. (1980) The effect of postural lean and body congruence on the judgement of psychotherapeutic rapport. *Journal of Nonverbal Behaviour*, **4**, 176–190.

Trower, P., Bryant, B. and Argyle, M. (1978) *Social Skills and Mental Health*. London: Methuen.

Trower, P., Yardley, K., Bryant, B. and Shaw, P. (1978) The treatment of social failure: a comparison of anxiety-reduction and skills-acquisition procedures on two social problems. Behaviour Modification, **2**, 41–60.

Truax, C. B. and Carkhuff, R. R. (1967) *Toward Effective Counselling and Psychotherapy*. Chicago: Aldine.

Truax, C. B., Carkhuff, R. R. and Kodman, F. (1965) Relationships between therapist-offered conditions and patient change in group psychotherapy. *Journal of Clinical Psychology*, **21**, 327–329.

Valentine, M. E. and Ehrlichman, H. (1979) Interpersonal gaze and helping behaviour. *Journal of Social Psychology*, **107**, 193–198.

Van De Sande, J. P. (1980) Cue utilisation in the perception of dominance. *British Journal of Social and Clinical Psychology*, **19**, 311–316.

Van Hooff. J. A. R. A. M. (1972) A comparative approach to the phylogeny of laughter and smiling. In R. A. Hinde (ed.), *Non-verbal communication*, pp. 209–238. Cambridge: Cambridge University Press.

196

Veitch, R., Getsinger, A. and Arkkelin, D. (1976) A note on the reliability and validity of the Comfortable Interpersonal Distance Scale. *Journal of Psychology*, **94**, 163–165.

Von Cranach, M. and Vine, I. (eds.) (1973) *Social Communication and Movement*. London: Academic Press.

Waldron, J. (1975) Judgement of like–dislike from facial expression and body posture. *Perceptual and Motor Skills*, **41**, 799–804.

Walkey, F. H. and Gilmour, D. R. (1979) Comparative evaluation of a videotaped measure of interpersonal distance. *Journal of Consulting and Clinical Psychology*, **47**, 575–580.

Watson, O. M. (1970) *Proxemic Behaviour: A Cross-cultural Study*. The Hague: Mouton.

Watson, O. M. and Graves, T. D. (1966) Quantitative research in proxemic behaviour. *American Anthropologist*, **68**, 971–985.

Watson, S. G. (1972) Judgement of emotion from facial and contextual cue combinations. *Journal of Personality and Social Psychology*, **24**, 334–342.

Waxer, P. H. (1974) Non-verbal cues for depression. *Journal of Abnormal Psychology*, **88**, 319–322.

Waxer, P. H. (1976) Non-verbal cues for depth of depression: set versus no set. *Journal of Consulting and Clinical Psychology*, **44**, 493.

Waxer, P. H. (1977) Non-verbal cues for anxiety: an examination of emotional leakage. *Journal of Abnormal Psychology*, **86**, 306–314.

Weitz, S. (ed.) (1974) *Non-verbal Communication: Readings with Commentary*. New York: Oxford University Press.

Weston, J. R. and Kristen, C. (1973) *Teleconferencing: A Comparison of Attitudes, Uncertainty and Interpersonal Atmospheres in Mediated and Face-to-face Group Interaction*. Department of Communications, Canada.

Wexley, K. N., Fugita, S. S. and Malone, M. P. (1975) An applicant's non-verbal behaviour and student-evaluators' judgements in a structured interview setting. *Psychological Reports*, **36**, 391–394.

White, G. L. and Maltzman, I. (1978) Pupillary activity while listening to verbal passages. *Journal of Research in Personality*, **12**, 361–369.

Wiener, M., Devoe, S., Robinson, S. and Geller, J. (1972) Non-verbal behaviour and non-verbal communication. *Psychological Review*, **79**, 185–214.

Wilds, C. E. (1973) Evaluation of a method of predicting violence in offenders. *Criminology: An Interdisciplinary Journal*, **11**, 427–435.

Williams, E. (1975) Coalition formation over telecommunications media. *European Journal of Social Psychology*, **5**, 503–507.

Williams, J. L. (1971) Personal space and its relation to extraversion–introversion. *Canadian Journal of Behavioural Science*, **3**, 156–160.

Wilson, C. and Williams, E. (1977) Watergate words: a naturalistic study of media and communication. *Communication Research*, **4**, 169–178.

Winkelmayer, R., Exline, R. V., Gottheil, E. and Paredes, A. (1978) The relative accuracy of U. S., British and 'Mexican raters in judging the emotional displays of schizophrenic and normal U. S. women, *Journal of Clinical Psychology*, **34**, 600–608.

Witkin, H. A., Dyk, R. B., Faterson, H. F., Goodenough, D. R. and Karp, S. A. (1962/1974) *Psychological Differentiation: Studies of Development*. New York: Wiley.

Woodmansee, J. J. (1970) The pupil response as a measure of social attitudes. In G. Summers (ed.), *Attitude Measurement*, pp. 514–533. New York: Rand McNally.

Woolfolk, A. E. (1978) Student learning and performance under varying conditions of teacher verbal and non-verbal evaluative communication. *Journal of Educational Psychology*, **70**, 87–94.

Woolfolk, A. E., Garlinsky, K. S. and Nicolich, M. J. (1977) The impact of teacher behaviour, teacher sex and student sex upon student self-disclosure. *Contemporary Educational Psychology*, **2**, 124–132.

Woolfolk, A. E. and Wookfolk, R. L. (1975) Student self-disclosure in response to teacher verbal and non-verbal behaviour. *Journal of Experimental Education*, **44**, 36–40.

Woolfolk, R. L. and Woolfolk, A. E. (1974) Effects of teacher verbal and non-verbal behaviours on student perceptions and attitudes. *American Educational Research Journal* **11**, 297–303.

Woolfolk, R. L., Woolfolk, A. E. and Garlinsky, S. (1977) Non-verbal behaviour of teachers: some empirical findings. *Environmental Psychology and Nonverbal Behaviour*, **2**, 45–61.

Yngve, V. H. (1970) *On Getting a Word in Edgewise*. Papers from the sixth regional meeting of the Chicago Linguistic Society. Chicago: Chicago Linguistic Society.

Young-Browne, G., Rosenfeld, H. M. and Horowitz, F. D. (1977) Infant discrimination of facial expressions. *Child Development*, **48**, 555–562.

Zuckerman, M., DeFrank, R. S., Hall, J. A. and Rosenthal, R. (1978) Accuracy of non-verbal communication as determinant of interpersonal expectancy effects. *Environmental Psychology and Nonverbal Behaviour*, **2**, 206–214.

Zuckerman, M., Hall, J. A., DeFrank, R. S. and Rosenthal, R. (1976) Encoding and decoding of spontaneous and posed facial expressions. *Journal of Personality and Social Psychology*, **34**, 966–977.

Author Index

Abramovitch, R., 119, 129–130
Aiello, J. R., 22, 126–127
Alkema, F., 120–121, 175
Allen, V. L., 154
Amaro-Plotkin, H. D., 97–98
Andreoli, V., 158–159
Argyle, M., 17–18, 28, 45–47, 65, 82, 106,
    120–121, 124–128, 164, 166–170,
    174–176
Arkkelin, D., 22
Aronow, E., 90–91
Ayling, K., 161

Bales, R. F., 74
Barnard, P. J., 72
Baron, R. A., 150–151
Bartlett, E. S., 105–106
Bates, M. E., 106
Bateson, G., 11
Baxter, J. C., 99
Beach, D. R., 99
Beattie, G. W., 72
Beck, S. J., 93
Becker, S. W., 136
Beier, E. G., 139
Bell, P. A., 150
Belmont, L., 102
Bem, S. L., 97, 109
Benjamin, G. R., 119
Berenson, B. G., 142
Birch, H. G., 102
Birdwhistell, R. L., 11, 20, 24–25, 27, 59,
    96–99, 114, 173
Bitti, P. R., 28, 47
Blatchley, R. J., 92
Bleuler, E., 91
Blurton-Jones, N. G., 11, 16
Bond, M. H., 96, 123
Booraem, C. D., 92
Bowlby, J., 37, 137, 139
Bradley, M. T., 154–155
Broadbent, M., 117–118

Brown, R., 60
Brunner, L. J., 70
Bryant, B., 167–168, 170, 174
Buck, R. W., 38, 86
Bugental, D. E., 101–102, 110, 144–145
Bull, P. E., 14, 20–21, 48, 50, 60, 73
Burns, J. A., 154

Campbell, A., 83
Camras, L. A., 51–52, 134–135, 144
Cannon, W. B., 38–39
Cappella, J. N., 126
Caproni, V., 74
Carkhuff, R. R., 142
Carmen, B., 110
Cary, M. S., 69
Chaikin, A. L., 144
Champness, B. G., 85
Chance, M. R. A., 129, 131, 135–136
Chapman, A. J., 127
Charlesworth, R., 101
Charny, E. J., 117
Christie, B., 158–159, 162–163
Christie, R., 104
Clancy, H., 92
Cohen, A. A., 64, 67
Cohen, J., 95
Collett, P., 167
Condon, W. S., 58, 115
Cook, M., 17, 44–45, 82–83
Cooper, R. E., 150–151
Coss, R. G., 91
Coutts, L. M., 96
Cranach, M. von, 11, 20
Creider, C. A., 119
Cronbach, L. J., 100
Crowne, D. P., 104
Curran, S. F., 92
Cusimano, J., 74

Dabbs, J. M., 117
Daly, E. M., 119
Danehy, J. J., 59, 65

Darwin, C., 24–25, 28, 36–37, 43–45, 47, 50–53, 152
Dashiell, J. F., 51
DeBoer, M., 96
DePaulo, B. M., 111–113, 174
Dean, L. M., 23, 133
Derlega, V. J., 144
Derogatis, L. R., 92
Desautels, M. S., 95
Deutsch, F., 9, 140–141
Devin-Sheehan, L., 154
Dewey, M. E., 161–163
Dickes, R., 96
Dittman, A. T., 59, 65, 67
Dollard, J., 136
Dore, S. R., 17, 126–127
Dougherty, F. E., 105–106
Duff, D., 90–91
Duke, M. P., 21, 92–93
Duncan, S., 11–13, 69–75 *passim*, 77, 79–82, 84–85, 96

Edelmann, R. J., 14
Edelstein, B. A., 171, 173–174
Efron, D., 60, 65–66
Ehrlichman, H., 151–152
Eibl-Eibesfeldt, I., 11, 25–26, 61, 68, 134
Eisler, R. M., 171, 173–174
Ekman, P., 16, 19, 21, 25–52 *passim*, 55, 60, 62, 66, 88, 103, 112, 140, 144, 153–155, 168, 172
Ellsworth, P. C., 25, 27, 29, 55
Emerson, P. E., 137
English, P. W., 110
Ernest, R. C., 150–151
Everitt, B. S., 72
Exline, R. V., 14, 44, 95–96, 121
Eysenck, H. J., 141

Fantz, R. L., 52
Faunce, E. E., 139
Feldman, R. S., 154
Fenhagen, E., 92
Ferber, A., 68–69
Fiedler, F. E., 104
Fiske, D. W., 11–13, 69–71, 79–80, 82, 84–85, 96
Fode, K. L., 156
Fogel, A., 138–139
Forbes, R. J., 149
Forston, R. F., 78
Freedman, D. G., 96
Freedman, N., 58, 84
Freud, S., 38, 136, 140

Frey, S., 20
Friar, J. T., 121–122, 129, 131, 133
Friedman, H. S., 54, 146
Friesen, W. V., 16, 21, 25–37, 43, 45–48, 51–52, 55, 60, 62, 66, 88, 103, 112, 140, 144, 153–155, 168
Frieze, I. H., 110
Frith, C. D., 72
Fromme, D. K., 44, 50
Fugita, S. S., 147
Furnham, A., 164

Galloway, C. M., 143, 146
Garlinsky, K. S., 145
Garrett, W. A., 96
Gates, G. S., 51
Geis, F., 104
Gelhorn, E., 38
Getsinger, A., 22
Gianetto, R. M., 102, 110
Giesen, M., 99
Gilmour, D. R., 21–22
Ginsburg, H. J., 135
Glass, G. V., 141
Globerson, T., 18–19
Goffman, E., 12, 68–69
Goldberg, D., 169
Gottman, J., 139
Gough, H. G., 80, 103
Graham, J. A., 45–47, 65, 67–68, 128–129, 164
Graham, J. C., 17
Grant, E. C., 11, 16, 135
Graves, J. R., 143
Graves, T. D., 78–79
Gray, D., 95
Greene, L. R., 84
Grether, J., 151
Gur, R. C., 34–36

Haase, R. F., 142
Hager, J. C., 34, 39
Haines, J., 15
Hakel, M. D., 147, 149
Hall, E. T., 78–79
Hall, J. A., 94–95, 108–113, 141
Hall, R., 169
Hampson, S. E., 14
Hanlon, T. E., 92
Hare, A. P., 74
Hare, R. D., 93
Harris, H., 74
Harrison, R. P., 64, 67
Hass, H., 43, 45

200

Hearn, G., 74
Hedge, B. J., 72
Heilbrun, A. B., 80
Henke, R., 18–19
Hershey, M., 164
Hess, E. H., 2–9
Hewes, G. W., 50
Hewitt, J., 23, 133
Heywood, S., 67–68
Hildreth, A. M., 92
Hill, D., 87
Hinchcliffe, M. K., 89
Hittelman, J. H., 96
Hjortsö, C. H., 29
Ho, H. Y., 96
Hobson, G. N., 44–45
Hockett, C. F., 59, 65
Hoffman, M. L., 109
Hoffman, S. P., 58
Hogan, R. T., 109
Hollandsworth, J. G., 149–150
Horowitz, F. D., 52
Horowitz, M., 90–91
Howells, L. T., 136
Huber, E., 28
Hunt, R. G., 155
Hutcheson, S., 1
Hutt, C., 91–92

Ickes, W., 118
Imada, A. S., 147, 149
Izard, C. E., 38–43, 45, 47–48, 52,
    105–106

Jackson, P. R., 149
Jackson, D. N., 103–104, 109
Jacobs, T. J., 141
Jacobson, L., 144
Jaffe, J., 138
James, W., 38
Janisse, M. P., 5–6, 18–19, 154–155
Jenni, D. A. and M. A., 97–98
Johnson, M. P., 151
Jones, B. W., 148
Jones, H. E., 80, 86–87
Jones, S. E., 22
Jorgensen, D. O., 132–133

Kaswan, J. W., 101, 144–145
Kaye, K., 138–139
Keenan, A., 147–148
Keller, K., 151
Kendon, A., 15, 60, 68–69, 71, 75, 83,
    166, 176

Kenny, D. A., 118
Kiesler, D. J., 120, 128, 141
Kimble, C. E., 45
Kintz, B. L., 154–155
Kinzel, A. F., 92–93
Kiritz, S. A., 66, 88
Kirkland, J., 7
Kleck, R. E., 38, 86
Kleinke, C. L., 95–96, 151–152
Knapp, B. E., 95–96
Knapp, M. L., 75–76
Kodman, F., 142
Kogan, N., 90
Kreutzer, M. A., 101
Kristen, C., 159
Ksionsky, S., 84–85, 124–125, 128

LaFrance, M., 75, 110, 116–118
Laird, J. D., 39
Lancashire, M., 89
Lange, C., 38
Lanzetta, J. T., 38, 86
Larson, C. U., 78
LaRusso, L., 107–108, 174
Latta, R. M., 133
Laver, J., 1
Levenson, R. W., 38, 86
Lindenfeld, J., 58–59, 66
Lippa, R., 97
Littlepage, G. E., 154
Llewellyn, L. G., 59, 65, 67
Lockard, J. S., 75
Loewenfeld, I. E., 6
Lomranz, J., 78
Lott, D. F., 133, 136
Lovaas, O. I., 173
Love, L. R., 101–102, 110, 144–145
Low, B. P., 97–98, 173

McBride, G., 92
McClaren, H. A., 99
McClintock, C. C., 155
McCusker, K., 92
McCusker, L., 17–18
McDowall, J. J., 115–116
McGaffey, C. N., 21–22
McGovern, T. V., 148
Machiavelli, N., 104
Machotka, P., 130–132
Maguire, P., 171
Malmstrom, E. J., 27, 29
Malone, M. P., 147
Maltzman, I., 6
Markman, H., 139

Marlowe, D., 104
Matarazzo, J. D., 70–71
Mayo, C., 75
Mazur, A., 79
Meehl, P. E., 100
Mehrabian, A., 14, 20, 66, 84–85, 109,
    121–125, 128–129, 131, 133, 139,
    147, 155
Meltzoff, A. N., 53
Miller, N. E., 136
Moore, M. K., 53
Morley, I. E., 17, 159–162, 175
Morris, D., 61–64
Morris, S. E., 148
Mullens, S., 127
Muzekari, L. H., 106
Myers, I. B., 104

Nakamura, C. Y., 83
Newman, R. C., 93
Nicolich, M. J., 145–146
Niederehe, G., 69–70
Noller, P., 140, 175
Notarius, C. I., 38, 86, 139
Nowicki, S., 21

O'Neal, E. C., 50
Ogston, W. D., 58, 115
Ollendick, T. H., 93
Olszewski, D. A., 45
Oster, H., 26–27, 42–43
Ounsted, C., 91–92

Passalacqua, R., 74
Patterson, M. L., 22, 127–128
Peavler, W. S., 5
Pedersen, D. M., 21–23, 83
Peery, J. C., 138
Pineault, M. A., 154
Pittenger, R. E., 59, 65
Plutchik, R., 28
Pollack, D., 93
Pollman, V. A., 135
Polt, J. M., 2

Ramsey, S. J., 110
Rawls, J. R., 21–22
Reid, R. L., 133–134
Reilly, S. S., 106
Rekers, G. A., 97–98, 173
Reznikoff, M. 90–91
Richards, M. P. M., 137
Richer, J. M., 91
Rimé, B., 17–18, 94

Riskin, J., 139
Roberts, F. J., 89
Robinson B., 163–164
Robinson, J. D., 143
Roger, D. B., 92–93, 133–134, 140
Rogers, C. R., 142
Rogers, W. T., 64–66
Rohberg, R., 84
Rokeach, M., 104
Romano, J., 127
Rosenfeld, H. M., 52, 117
Rosenthal, R., 100–105, 108, 111–113,
    144, 156–157, 174, 176
Ruble, D. N., 83
Rudy, J. P., 98
Rushton, J. P., 83
Rutter, D. R., 17–18, 71–73, 89–90,
    124–127, 161–162, 174

Sackheim, H. A., 34–36
Sainsbury, P., 15
Saucy, M. C., 34–36
Schaffer, H. R., 137
Schalekamp, E. E., 92–93
Scheflen, A. E., 11–12, 59–60, 66,
    116–118, 120
Scherer, K. R., 54, 100, 154–155
Schlosberg, H., 46
Schmidt, C. K., 44, 50
Schneider, F. W., 96
Schneider, S. M., 155
Schuette, D., 95
Schutz, W. C., 80
Schwartz, G. E., 15, 40
Shennum, W. A., 84
Shimoda, K., 28
Shiraishi, D., 123
Shor, R. E., 54
Short, J. A., 158–159, 162–163
Shrout, P., 8–9
Shuter, R., 79
Shutland, R. L., 151
Sigler, E., 144
Silverstein, C. H., 74
Singer, D. A., 152
Smith, H. L., Jr., 59
Smith, J., 7
Smith, J. M. C., 44–45
Smith, M. L., 141
Snyder, M., 80, 86–87
Snyder, R. A., 85
Sokoloff, M. J., 99
Sommer, R., 21, 93, 99, 133, 136
Sousa-Poza, J. F., 84

Spiegel, J., 130–132
Sroufe, L. A., 26
Stang, D. J., 74
Starkweather, J. A., 100
Steiner, J. E., 27
Steinzor, B., 74
Stephenson, G. M., 17–18, 72–73, 89–90,
    124–127, 159–163, 175
Stern, D. N., 138
Sternberg, D. P., 139
Stratton, L., 90–91
Strongman, K. T., 85
Sullivan, H. S., 141
Sutker, L. W., 85

Tartter, V. C., 54–55, 157
Tepper, D. T., 142
Thomas, A. P., 73
Thorndike, R. L., 80
Tomkins, S. S., 28, 38–41
Tourangeau, R., 38–40
Trager, G. L., 59
Trego, R. E., 21–22
Trevarthen, C., 138–139
Trout, D. L., 117
Trower, P., 168–170, 174
Truax, C. B., 142
Tryon, W. W., 90–91

Valentine, M. E., 151–152
Van Hoof, J. A. R. A. M., 37
Van de Sande, J. P., 129
Veitch, R., 22
Von Cranach, M., 11, 20

Waldron, J., 123
Walkey, F. H., 21–22
Wallach, M. A., 90
Wallblatt, H., 19
Waters, E., 26
Watson, O. M., 78–79
Watson, S. G., 55–56
Wauson, M. S., 135
Waxer, P. H., 87–89
Wedderburn, A. A. I., 147–148
Weitz, S., 110
Weston, J. R., 159
Wexley, K. N., 147
White, G. L., 6
Wiener, M., xi, 2, 4, 9, 171, 176–178
Wilds, C. E., 92–93
Williams, E., 157–159, 162–163
Williams, J. L., 83
Williams, N., 66
Willis, F. N., 23, 133
Wilson, C., 157
Wilson, J., 21
Winkelmayer, R., 91
Winters, L. C., 14, 121
Witkin, H. A., 83–84
Woodmansee, J. J., 5–6
Woods, E., 15
Woolfolk, A. E., and R. L., 145–146
Worchel, S., 158

Yngve, V. H., 70
Young-Browne, G., 52

Zuckerman, M., 95, 156–157

Subject Index

accommodation, as explanation of sex differences, 111–113
adaptive responses, emotional expressions as, 36–37
Adjective Check List, 80
adolescents, delinquent, 92–93
affiliation, 14, 84–85, 120–128, 174–175
  see also attraction
age differences in decoding, 101–102
aggression, 39, 45, 129, 134–136
amplification of emotional expression, 27
anger, and facial expressions, 25–26, 28–29, 31, 33, 37, 40–41, 54–55
  and gaze, 44
  illustrations of, 32
  interpersonal distance and, 50
  posture and, 47
  speech and, 54
anxiety, and deception, 155
  and encoding studies, 87–88
  and facial expressions, 28
  and gaze, 44–45
  and hand movements, 113
  and social skills training, 169–170
appeasement gestures, 135–136
approval, 147–148
arm movements, 58–59, 84, 98, 131–132
  see also hand movements arousal, 86
  and autism, 91–92
  and facial expressions, 29, 38
  and pupil size, 6, 8, 43
asymmetrical facial expressions, 34, 36
  illustration of, 35
attachment, mother-infant, 37, 137
attention, structure of, 129–131, 136
attenuation of emotional expression, 27
attitudes, 28, 66, 106, 128, 158
attraction, 2–9
  see also affiliation
autism, 91–92
awareness and definition of non-verbal communication, 2, 4

back channel in speech, 70–71
bargaining in telecommunications, 158–161, 163, 175
Beier–Sternberg Discord Questionnaire, 139
Bernreuter Personality Inventory, 85
blocking responses, 127
blushing, 43
body lean, see lean, body
body movement, defined, 2
  measurement of, 14–23
body movement and interpersonal communication, emotion, 24–57
  individual differences, 77–114
  research concepts and methods, 1–23
  social skills training, 166–176
  specific contexts, 115–165
  speech, 58–76
body size and appeasement, 135–136
body-touching, 80–82, 84, 139, 151
boredom, 48, 50, 54, 66
  illustrations of, 49
buffing, 76

California Psychological Inventory, 85, 103–104
central translation processes, 166
cheek-screw, 62
  illustration of, 61
children, as decoders, 51–53, 101–102, 106, 113
  education, 143–146
  facial expressions of emotion, 26–27
  handicapped, 26
  personality and, 83, 86
  relationships and, 119–120, 127, 129–130, 134–139
  sex differences, 95–99
Choice Dilemmas Questionnaire, 90
closed/open body positions, 121–122, 124, 131, 139

203

Comfortable Interpersonal Distance Scale, 21–22, 92
communication, defined, 2
    see also body movement and interpersonal communication
composite faces, 34, 36
    illustrations of, 35
comprehension of speech, 62–66
concealment of emotional expression, 27
concepts of non-verbal communication, 1–10
conflicts, 135–136
congruence, 142–143
contact cultures, 78–79
contempt, 41–42, 47–48, 106
control of speech, 68–76
control system, attachment as, 137
conversation, see speech
corrective action in social skills model, 166
cross-cultural studies, decoding, 102–103, 105
    emotions and, 27–29, 41–43, 50
    encoding, 77–79, 91, 96–97
    speech and body movements, 61–62, 65, 68, 71, 75
    social skills training, 167
crying, 37, 44
cuelessness, 162–163

deception, 112, 152–155, 175
decoding, 9–10, 13, 172–175
    emotion, 25, 28–29, 38, 43–47, 51–53, 55, 172
    in relationships, 122–123, 140
    speech, 54
    studies of individual differences, 100–108
delinquents, 92–93
demonstration in motor and social skills, 170–171
dependence, field, 83–84
dependence in relationships, 137
depression, 28, 66, 88–89, 174
desensitization, 169
deviance, sexual, 92, 173
differences, individual, 77–114, 173
    decoding, 100–108
    encoding, 77–99
    see also age differences in decoding; cross-cultural studies; personality; psychopathology; sex differences
dimensions of interpersonal relationships, 120–136

affiliation, 120–128
dominance, 128–136
disapproval, 147–148
disgust, and facial expressions, 25, 27–29, 31, 36, 41–42, 52, 106
    and gaze, 44
    and illustration, 31
    and posture, 47
    and speech, 54
disliking, see affiliation
distance, see interpersonal distance
Dogmatism Scale, 104
dominance, 85, 174–175
    and gaze, 45
    in relationships, 128–136
    in situations, 146
    in speech, 54
double-blind procedure, 176
Duncan and Fiske personality study, 80–82

education, 143–146, 175
elation, 39, 54
embarrassment, 14, 95
emblems, 19, 60–63, 78, 172
    illustrations of, 61–64
emotion, 24–57
    and facial expressions, 8, 24–57 passim, 78, 84, 105–106, 152–153
    functions of emotional expression, 36–40
    generality of innate hypothesis, 40–53
    innate hypothesis of, 24–36
    recognition of, 51–53, 168, 172
    speech and, 54–55, 66
empathy, 109, 113, 142–143
encoding, emotion, 9–10, 28–29, 39–40, 44–45, 47, 50, 86, 88
    individual differences, 77–99, 173–174
    psychological approach, 13–14
    relationships and, 119, 121–122, 125, 140
    situations and, 140–157 passim
    speech and, 67
enjoyment, 106
equality, 106, 128
equilibrium level for intimacy, 125–127
ethological approach, 11, 24, 53, 134
ever-ready expressors, 168
excitement, 41
externalizers, 86–87
extraversion, 82–83, 104
eyes, movements of, 59, 71–72, 75–76, 88–89

pupil size, 2–10, 18–19, 43, 154–155
see also gaze
eyebrow flash, 61, 68
Eysenck Personality Inventory, 82

Facial Action Coding System, 16, 21, 36
facial atlas, 28–29
facial expression, asymmetrical, 34–36
    emotion and, 8, 24–57 passim, 78, 84,
        105–106, 152–153
    illustrations of, 30–35, 42
    measurement of, 16
    psychopathology and, 88–89
    relationships and, 119, 123, 125, 129,
        134–135, 138–139
    sex differences in, 94, 96
    situations and, 142–143, 146, 152–153,
        155
    social skills training and, 168
FACS, see Facial Action Coding System
fear, facial expressions and, 25, 28–29, 31,
        36, 39–41, 47
    and gaze, 44–45
    and illustration of, 30
    and interpersonal distance, 50
    and posture, 47
    and speech, 54
feedback, 44–45
    in social skills training, 166, 170–171
field dependence/independence, 83–84
foot movements, and deception, 155
    and personality, 80, 82
    and speech, 58, 76
    see also leg movements
formality, 160, 162
free expression of emotion, 37–38
friendliness, see affiliation
frowning, 26, 31–33, 39
functions of emotional expression, 36–40

galvanic skin response, 86
gaze, and emotion, 43–46
    and measurements, 16–18
    and personality, 80–83, 85
    and psychopathology, 89–93
    and relationships 121, 124–131, 136,
        138–139
    and sex differences, 95–96, 108, 110
    and situations, 142–144, 147–154
    and speech, 71–72, 75
    to collect information, 124
    see also eyes
gender identification signal, 96–99, 173
    see also sex differences

generality of innate hypothesis of
        emotional expression, 40–53
    decoding, 51–53
    number of innate facial expressions,
        41–43
    other bodily cues, 43–51
genuineness, 142–143
gesture, see posture and gesture
global personality differences, 85–87
goals in social skills training, 166
goodness, emblem of, 62
Gough 60 Point Dominance Scale, 85
greetings, 68–69
group cohesion in telecommunications, 159
guidance in social skills training, 170–171
guilt, 41–42, 45

hand movements, and anxiety, 87–88, 113
    and personality, 81–82, 85
    and psychopathology, 88–89, 93
    relationships and, 125, 127
    sex differences, 98
    situations and, 148, 155
    speech and, 58–59, 61–64, 70, 73
    see also arm movements
handicapped children, 26
happiness, and facial expressions, 25–26,
        28–29, 33–34, 37, 40–41, 47, 52,
        54–55
    and gaze, 44
    and illustration, 33
    and posture, 47
    and speech, 54
head movements, and facial expressions,
        43, 47
    and personality, 80
    and psychopathology, 88
    and relationships, 130–131, 138
    and speech, 59, 70–71, 73, 76
helping situations, 150–152, 175
homosexual anxiety, 92
homosexuality, 173
hostility, 28
    see also affiliation
humiliation, 41, 106

ideographic gestures, 66
illustrations, composite faces, 35
    facial expressions of emotion, 30–35, 42
    gestures, 61–63
    postures, 48–49
    pupil size, 3, 7
illustrators, 19, 60, 63–68, 78, 89, 172
immediacy, 124

inattention, civil, 69
independence, field, 83–84
individual differences, *see* differences, individual
infants, as decoders, 52–53
    facial expressions of, 26–27
    mother–infant interaction, 13, 136–139
    personality and, 86
    sex differences, 96
    see also children
inferiority, 106, 110–111, 128, 135–136
inheritance, *see* innate
innate hypothesis of emotional expression, 24–36
    generality of, 40–53
institutionalization, 93
insults, 62–63
intelligence, 95
intentionality and definition of non-verbal communication, 2, 4
interactional synchrony, 58, 115–116
interactionist model of non-verbal cues, 27–28, 102–103, 114
interest, 41–45, 47–48, 50, 54, 66
    illustrations of, 42, 48
internalizers, 86–87
interpersonal communication, *see* body movement and
interpersonal distance, culture and, 78–79
    and emotions, 50–51
    and measurement of, 21–23
    and personality, 83
    and psychopathology, 90–94
    and relationships, 124–127, 133–134, 136
    and sex differences in, 99, 108
interviews, 147–150, 175
intimacy, equilibrium level for, 125–128
intonation, 54–55, 142–143
    see also speech
introversion, 82–83, 104

James–Lange theory of emotion, 38
joy, 106

Kuethe technique, 91

laughter, 37, 44, 51
leadership, 74–75, 104
    see also dominance
lean, body, 48, 121–125, 142–144
learning of emotional expressions, 24, 26–27
Least Preferred Coworker Scale, 104

left-side composite faces, 34, 36
    illustration of, 35
leg movements, 48, 58, 76, 131, 143, 155
    see also foot movements
liking, *see* affiliation
locution cluster, 60
love, *see* affiliation

Machiavelli Scale, 104
manipulators, 19
    see also self-adaptors
marital relationships, 139–140, 175
Markov process, 72, 138
Marlowe–Crowne Social Desirability Scale, 104
Maudsley Personality Inventory, 83, 106
measurement, of bodily cues, 14–23
    context of, 11–14
medium of communication, 157–164
mental illness, 87
    see also psychiatric patients; psychopathology; psychotherapy
meta analysis, *see* standard deviation units
methodology of non-verbal communications research, 10–23
Minnesota Multiphasic Personality Inventory, 88, 142
MMPI, *see* Minnesota Multiphasic Personality Inventory
mockery, 62
mother–infant relationships, 13, 136–139
motor responses in social skills training, 166
Myers–Briggs Type Indicator, 104

negative, cues 145–146
    reinforcement, 84, 124–125, 127
neuro-cultural model of emotional expression, 27, 172
neuroticism scale, 106
non-contact cultures, 78–79
non-verbal communication, defined 1–2
    research concepts, 1–10
    research methodology, 10–23
    see also body movement and interpersonal communication
non-verbal leakage, 153–154
nose-thumb, 62

observers, women as, 111
occupational groups, encoding of non-verbal cues, 86
    decoding of non-verbal cues, 100–101

open/closed body positions, 121–122, 124, 131, 139
outcome studies of psychotherapy, 141

pain, 51
paralinguistic overloudness, 70
partings, 75–76
peace, emblem of, 62
Pedersen Personal Space Measure, 22
person perception task, 156–157
personality, 12–13, 173
    Duncan and Fiske study, 80–82
    decoding studies, 103–105
    encoding studies, 79–87
    global differences, 85–86
    single-trait approaches, 82–87
phonemic clause structure of speech, 58–60, 65
physiographic gestures, 65
pictures, see illustrations
pleasantness, judgements of, 46
point in speech, 60
PONS, see Profile of Nonverbal Sensitivity
position in speech, 60
positive, cues, 145–146
    regard, 142–143
    reinforcement, 84, 124–125, 127
    speech, 54
posture and gesture, and emotions, 46–50, 52–53
    and illustrations of, 48–49, 61–64, 98, 116, 130, 132
    and measurement of, 19–21
    and personality, 80–82, 84–85
    and psychopathology, 87, 93
    and relationships, 116–119, 121–125, 130–133, 139
    and sex differences, 96–98, 109
    and situations, 140–144, 147, 149, 155
    and speech, 75–76
power differences, 110–111, 113
practice, effects 111, 113
    in social skills training, 170–171
praise, emblem of, 62
presentation in speech, 60
process studies in psychotherapy, 141–142
Profile of Nonverbal Sensitivity, 100–105, 108–109, 111, 157
psychiatric patients, 58, 66, 140–143, 167–169, 174–175
psychodynamics, 9
psychological, approach, 12–14, 24, 53
    experiment, 156–157, 175–176

psychopathology, decoding studies, 105–108
    encoding studies, 87–94
psychotherapy, 58, 140–143, 168–169, 175
pupil size, 43, 154–155
    illustrations of, 3, 7
    measurement of, 18–19
    research, 2–10

reciprocity in affiliation, 124–125
regulation of emotion, 37–38
regulators, 60, 68–76, 172–173
rejection, sensitivity to, 84–85, 124–125
relationships, dimensions of interpersonal, 120–136, 174–175
    role, 136–140, 174–175
    telecommunications and, 158–159
respect, 142–143
right-side composite faces, 34, 36
    illustration of, 35
ring emblem, 62
    illustration of, 63
role expectations, see role relationships; sex roles
role-playing, 14, 97, 168
role relationships, 136–140, 174–175

sadness, and facial expressions, 25, 28–29, 33–34, 37, 39–41, 52, 54–55
    and gaze, 44
    illustration of, 34
    interpersonal distance and, 50
    posture and, 48, 50
    speech and, 54
salutations, 68–69
schizophrenia, 44, 89–91, 105, 107, 174
    see also psychopathology
Schutz's FIRO scales, 80
scorn, 41–42, 51
secondary drive hypothesis, 136–137
self-adaptors, 80–81, 84
    see also manipulators
self-disclosure, 145–146
self-fulfilling prophecy, 144
self-monitoring, 86–87, 104–105
self-ratings, 101, 169
self-synchrony, 58
semantic structure of speech, 58, 66
sex differences, 94–99, 108–113
    decoding, 108, 173–174
    encoding, 94–99, 173–174
    explanations of non-verbal cue differences, 108–111

sex differences (*continued*)
  relationships and, 121–122, 124, 131
  situations and, 145–146, 152
sex roles, 96–99, 109–113
sexual, deviance, 92, 173
  insults, 62
shame, 41–43, 45, 48, 106
  illustration of, 42
simultaneous speech, 72–73
single-trait approach to personality study,
  82–87
situations, 140–157, 174–176
  deception, 152–155
  education, 143–146
  helping, 150–152
  interviews, 147–150
  judgements of emotion, 55–56
  psychological experiment, 156–157
skills, social, 166–176
sleep/tension ratings, 46
smiling, and emotional expression, 24–27,
  34–37, 39
  and personality, 80–81, 84
  and psychopathology, 88, 92
  relationships and, 138
  sex differences in, 96, 108, 110
  situations and, 144, 147–149
  speech and, 54–55, 70
Snyder's Self-Monitoring Scale, 86–87,
  104–105
social desirability, 104
social presence, 162–163
social roles, *see* role relationships; sex roles
social skills training, 166–176
sociological approach, 12, 24, 53
sorrow, *see* sadness
specific contexts, 115–165
  communication medium, 157–164
  relationships, 115–140
  situations, 140–157
speech, and body movement, 19, 58–76,
  78, 89, 172
  and content, 54
  and electronically-filtered devices 100
  and relationships, 120, 125, 129
  and situations, 142–143, 148–149
  and social skills training, 168, 172–173
  and telecommunications, 161–162
  and turn-taking, 69–75, 168, 173
Spielberger State-trait Anxiety Inventory,
  87–88
Standard deviation units, 95, 141
statistical analysis of non-verbal behaviour,
  11–12

status, and relationships, 128–136
  speech and, 74–75
stress points in speech, 59–60, 65–66
structural approach, 11–12, 24, 53
submission, 135–136, 146
  see also dominance
substitute-expressors, 168
substitution of emotional expression, 27,
  168
superiority, 106, 128
  see also dominance
suppression of emotional expression,
  37–38
surgency, 39
surprise, and facial expressions, 25, 28–29,
  31, 36, 41, 47, 51–52, 54
  and gaze 44
  and illustration, 30
  and posture, 47
  and speech, 54
synchrony, 58
  see also interactional synchrony
syntactic structure of speech, 58–59, 66

Taylor Manifest Anxiety Scale, 45
teacher expectations, 144
telecommunications, 157–164, 175
telephone conversations, 64, 72, 157–164
  passim, 175
telephone teaching, 163–164
tension, 85, 87
Thorndike Dimensions of Temperament,
  80
touch, 80–81, 84, 139, 151
  see also manipulators
Truax and Carkhuff 5-point scale of
  empathy, 142
trustworthiness, 158–159
turn-taking in speech, 69–75, 168, 173

universals of emotional expression, 25
unpleasantness, judgements of, 46

V sign, 62
  illustration of, 64
verbal communication, 1, 54–56, *see also*
  speech
victory, emblem of, 62
vocal cues, 1–2, 54–55, 100, 156, 165

warmth, 142–143
Wechsler Intelligence Scale, 95

weight-shifting, 75–76
  see also posture
women, as decoders, 108–113, 173–174
  as encoders, 94–99, 109
  women's facial expressions, children's
    reactions to, 102

word adoption and dominance, 129
worthlessness, emblem of, 62
  illustration of, 63